REFORMING
OUR
UNIVERSITIES

REFORMING
OUR
UNIVERSITIES

THE CAMPAIGN FOR
AN ACADEMIC BILL OF RIGHTS

DAVID HOROWITZ

Since 1947
REGNERY
PUBLISHING, INC.
An Eagle Publishing Company • Washington, DC

Cataloging-in-Publication data on file with the Library of Congress

ISBN 978-1-59698-637-4

Published in the United States by
Regnery Publishing, Inc.
One Massachusetts Avenue, NW
Washington, DC 20001

www.regnery.com

Manufactured in the United States of America

10 9 8 7 6 5 4 3 2 1

Books are available in quantity for promotional or premium use. Write to Director of Special Sales, Regnery Publishing, Inc., One Massachusetts Avenue NW, Washington, DC 20001, for information on discounts and terms or call (202) 216-0600.

Distributed to the trade by:
Perseus Distribution
387 Park Avenue South
New York, NY 10016

In memoriam:
Jeannie Rutenberg (1950–2009)
Tree Scholar and Courageous Woman

Contents

INTRODUCTION

THIS BOOK TELLS THE STORY OF A CAMPAIGN I BEGAN IN SEPTEMBER 2003 with the goal of restoring academic standards to liberal arts programs in America's universities. The idea was to persuade universities to adopt an "Academic Bill of Rights" for students, which was based on academic traditions that had been allowed to atrophy and fall into disuse. It was designed to ensure that instructors 1) provide students with materials reflecting both sides of controversial issues; 2) do not present opinions as facts; and 3) allow students to think for themselves. These are not only educational rights; they are rights basic to a republic created by dissenters, whose political system is founded on respect for the pluralism of ideas.

In terms of resources available, our campaign was relatively modest. I never employed more than three full-time staff people to assist me, and for several years there was only one, my National Campus Director, Sara Dogan.[1] By contrast, our opposition—mainly teachers unions and academic guilds—constituted an immensely powerful political lobby. They were able to draw on hundred million dollar treasuries and rely on operatives based in every college and located in every congressional district.[2] In addition, they could count on the support of the Democratic Party, the education media, and the local press in every university locale.

Despite the odds, my assistants and I were able to recruit hundreds of student volunteers and organize them in chapters on 135 college campuses. Together we managed in a relatively short time to achieve tangible results, bringing our issues to the attention of the public and effecting actual institutional reforms. An early assessment of our efforts by Professor Stephen Aby, a member of the American Association of University Professors and an unfriendly critic, provides a reasonable summary of our accomplishments. His account appeared in the preface to a 2007 book devoted to our campaign and titled *The Academic Bill of Rights Debate.* "In just three short years," he wrote, "the debate over the Academic Bill of Rights has become one of the most controversial issues in America's colleges and universities. By November of 2006, it had already generated over 74 articles in major newspapers, at least 143 articles in all newspapers nationwide, 54 television and radio broadcasts, 47 news wire articles, 20 articles in the *Chronicle of Higher Education,* 73 articles in Inside-HigherEd.com, dozens of articles in major magazines, and some 150,000 hits in the obligatory Google search."[3]

There were other accomplishments as well. Within the first five years of its creation, the Academic Bill of Rights or some version of its principles were 1) written into the federal "authorization act" for higher education and passed through the House of Representatives; 2) unanimously endorsed by both houses of the Colorado legislature; and 3) incorporated in a formal statement by the American Council on Education, an organization that represents more than 1,800 colleges and universities. Pressured by our legislative efforts in Ohio, all of that state's public universities, acting through the "Inter-University Council," agreed to implement the Council's statement and to provide students with formal grievance procedures to protect their academic freedom rights. This included seventeen universities, including Ohio and Ohio State. In 2005, the Academic Bill of Rights inspired legislation in the Pennsylvania House leading to formal academic freedom hearings—the first such on record. These hearings resulted in the adoption of academic freedom provisions for students at Penn State and Temple universities. Along with the Ohio schools, these are the only universities in the United States today with academic freedom rights for students.

The campaign we launched can only be understood in the context of previous developments in higher education. The modern research university was created in the second half of the nineteenth century during the era of America's great industrial expansion. Its curriculum was shaped by two innovations: the adoption of scientific method as the professional standard for knowledge, and the extension of educational opportunity to a democratic public. Before these developments, America's institutions of higher learning were primarily religious and moral schools of instruction. In the words of James Duderstadt, president of the University of Michigan, "Colleges trained the ministers of each generation, passing on 'high culture' to a very small elite."[4] The explicit mission of these early collegiate institutions was to instill the doctrines of a particular religious denomination. The teaching of non-religious liberal arts subjects was not designed to foster the analytic skepticism associated with modern science but to pass on the literary and philosophical culture that supported a specific faith.

By contrast, "the core mission of the research university," as recently summarized by one of its leaders, "is … expanding and deepening what we know." In pursuit of this goal, "the research university relies on various attributes, the most important of which are the processes of rigorous inquiry and reasoned skepticism, which in turn are based on articulated norms that are not fixed and given, but are themselves subject to re-examination and revision. In the best of our universities faculty characteristically subject their own claims and the norms that govern their research to this process of critical reflection."[5] This open-minded approach has been the credo of American higher education throughout the modern era and is still the norm in the physical and biological sciences and most professional schools throughout the contemporary university.

Liberal arts colleges are the divisions of the university through which all undergraduates pass, and have been traditionally viewed as corner-stones of a democratic society, where students are taught *how* to think rather than told *what* to think. The curricula of liberal arts colleges within the modern research university supported these objectives. They were designed to inculcate pragmatic respect for the pluralism of ideas and the test of empirical evidence, and thus support a society dependent on an informed citizenry.

All this began to change when a radical generation of university instructors were hired onto liberal arts faculties in the 1970s and began altering curricula by creating new inter-disciplinary fields whose inspira-tions were ideological and closely linked to political activism. Women's Studies was one of the earliest of the new disciplines and remains the most influential, providing an academic model emulated by others.[6] The cur-ricula of Women's Studies programs are not governed by the principles of disinterested inquiry about a subject but rather by a political mission: to teach students to be radical feminists. The formal Constitution of the Women's Studies Association makes this political agenda clear:

Women's Studies owes its existence to the movement for the lib-eration of women; the feminist movement exists because women are oppressed. Women's studies, diverse as its components are, has at its best shared a vision of a world free not only from sexism but also from racism, class-bias, ageism, heterosexual bias— from all the ideologies and institutions that have consciously or unconsciously oppressed and exploited some for the advantage of others.... Women's Studies, then, is equipping women not only to enter the society as whole, as productive human beings, but to transform the world to one that will be free of all oppression.[7]

As a result of the political pressures from feminists, ethnic nationalists, and "anti-war" activists, and the curricular innovations they were able to institute, the academic landscape was transformed. In 2006, state legislators in Pennsylvania gathered at Philadelphia's Temple University to hold hearings on academic freedom. Among the witnesses to appear before them was Stephen Zelnick, a former Vice Provost for Undergraduate Studies and a member of the Temple faculty for thirty-six years. Zelnick told the legislators of his concern that Temple faculty had grown increasingly monolithic and politically partisan in the years he had been there. "The one-sidedness of the faculty," he said, "in their ideological commitments and a growing intolerance of competing views [has] resulted in abuse of students, occasionally overt and reported, but most often hidden and normalized, and the degrading of the strong traditions of intellectual inquiry and free expression."[8]

Zelnick then spelled out what this meant in terms of the instruction he had personally reviewed. "As director of two undergraduate programs, I have had many opportunities to sit in and watch instructors. I have sat in on more than a hundred different teachers' classes and seen excellent, indifferent, and miserable teaching.... In these visits, I have rarely heard a kind word for the United States, for the riches of our marketplace, for the vast economic and creative opportunities made available for energetic and creative people (that is, for our students); for family life, for marriage, for love, or for religion."[9]

Zelnick's experience reflected a shift in the academic practices of liberal arts schools that was national in scope and a transformation as dramatic as the changes that took place at the end of the nineteenth century.[10] If those changes have been rightly perceived as an educational revolution, the current academic turn represents a counter-revolution—the resurrection of a curriculum that is doctrinal rather than analytic, and the return to a method of instruction in which knowledge proceeds from authority and is designed to instill sectarian truths rather than pursue skeptical inquiries into the facts.

While the new academic orthodoxies are secular, they are no less intolerant of opposing views than their religious predecessors. Their faculty adherents also assign texts to reinforce orthodoxies, while treating dissenters as unbelievers and dismissing their views as not requiring serious consideration. The new academic orthodoxies teach that America is an oppressive society governed by hierarchies that are "racist," "sexist," and "classist." Far from being academic in the dictionary sense of "theoretical" and "not leading to a decision or practice," the new curriculum is designed to provide cultural support for doctrines that are sectarian and political and that have immediate practical implications. Engagement in political activism is often incorporated directly into the lesson plan.

For example, a course description at the University of California Santa Cruz explains, "The goal of this seminar is to learn how to organize a revolution." The character of the revolution is then specified as "anti-capitalist" and "anti-racist,"[11] and the only texts provided are those that articulate and support these specific revolutionary agendas. No skeptical examination of revolution or of the critics of capitalism or of the left-wing perspectives on racism presented in the course is incorporated into its syllabus.

Similarly, a sociology course in "Collective Behavior and Social Movements" at the University of Arizona offers students credit for political activity and provides them with a menu of left-wing organizations to serve. In the words of the official syllabus, "Here it is, activism for credit. Give four hours to a social movement organization and I'll give you 200 points."[12] The instructor elaborates,

> Tucson has a bunch of great organizations that could use your help. For example, Wingspan has loads of things you can do for lesbians, gay men, transgendered and bisexual people right here in the Old Pueblo. Maybe you're more interested in endangered species and ecosystem protection—check out the Center for Biological Diversity, an important and influential organization that just happens to be based in Tucson. Consider the Brewster Center, Society of Friends (Quakers), Women's International League for Peace and Freedom, Border Action Network, Humane Borders, or Food Not Bombs.

The political corruption of the academic enterprise is hardly confined to a single university, or to one academic field. Three articles in a recent issue of *PMLA*, the official journal of the Modern Languages Association, give an indication of the scope of the problem. With forty thousand members, the Modern Languages Association is the largest academic professional organization and is ostensibly concerned with literary scholarship. One of the articles in this issue, however, is titled "Get Up, Stand Up: Teaching Civil Disobedience in the Literature Classroom." A second is titled, "Using the Civil Rights Movement to Practice Activism in the Classroom." The third, a dissent from these two, is by Gerald Graff, the outgoing president of the Association. Graff notes mournfully that "it is no longer controversial that a goal of teaching should be to 'challenge oppressions and advance social justice.' The only pertinent questions now are technical ones about how to achieve this goal."[13] In short, according to the testimony of the president of the largest organization of literary scholars, classroom indoctrination in left-wing political ideologies by professors of literature is now an accepted educational practice.

Graff is himself a political progressive but is distinguished by his professional dissent from progressive orthodoxy, in particular his view that teachers should not preach one side of the ideological argument in the classroom but "teach the conflicts," allowing students to draw their own conclusions. This was the norm in the recent academic past, so it is not surprising that someone like Graff, who belongs to an older academic generation, should defend it. I myself am a contemporary of Graff, and it was my own collegiate experience that prompted me to begin the academic freedom campaign, the goal of which is to provide institutional support for a student's right to receive a modern scientific education and not be indoctrinated in any orthodoxy, whether it reflects the political prejudices of the Right or the Left.

Because the campaign I organized was about process, it was viewpoint neutral. Consequently, I began it under the assumption that I would be joined by others, liberals such as Gerald Graff among them, and not just conservatives. But for reasons that will become clear in the ensuing narrative, I received almost no support from those quarters, and Graff himself never endorsed my campaign, but only suggested that the concerns it raised were important and deserved consideration.

I was disappointed by this response, but not surprised. What I was not prepared for was the reluctance of many conservatives to support our campaign. While conservatives had long been precise and insightful in recognizing the problematic developments in the university culture, they remained determinedly passive in their response to it.

More than fifty years earlier, William F. Buckley had published *God and Man at Yale*, a jeremiad lamenting the transformation of Yale from a college whose founders intended it to instill Christian values into a modern research university, the attitudes of which were secular and increasingly liberal. Buckley's book was the first in a series of critiques of the university that conservatives were to write. These eventually included Alan Bloom's *The Closing of the American Mind*, Dinesh D'Souza's *Illiberal Education*, Richard Bernstein's *Dictatorship of Virtue*, Neil Hamilton's *Zealotry and Academic Freedom*, Roger Kimball's *Tenured Radicals*, and Daphne Patai and Noretta Koertge's *Professing Feminism: Education and Indoctrination in Women's Studies*, which was an analysis of Women's Studies as an ideological rather than an academic discipline.

But among these knowledgeable and perceptive texts, there were none that formed the basis for an effort towards institutional reform. Conservatives were content to argue against the educational *status quo* in the hope that others would be persuaded to do something about it—or not. Perhaps this reflected a fatalism inherent in the conservative outlook, leaving many of its adherents content to describe and then regret a cultural fall, but not to support a movement to correct it. Conservatives ably made their case, but little action seemed to follow.

Three years after the appearance of *God and Man at Yale*, Buckley became the first president of the Intercollegiate Studies Institute, an organization founded by Frank Chodorov. The Institute was designed to teach the curriculum that Yale and schools like it were in the process of abandoning.[14] Its target audience consisted of conservative students whom it intended to reach during after-school hours. It was a plan of action typical of the conservative campus organizations that followed—the Young America's Foundation, the Leadership Institute, Accuracy in Academia, the Eagle Forum Collegians, the Clare Booth Luce Institute, College

Republicans, and various conservative Christian groups. All of these sponsored conservative speakers on campus and recruited on-site representatives to distribute conservative literature. But with exception of the College Republicans, whose principal focus is electoral politics, they did not create student activist organizations or conduct efforts to alter campus structures.[15] Their intent was to develop alternative institutions, not reform existing ones; to foster a traditional culture among conservative college students and develop future conservative leaders. The agenda was to educate individuals, not change the existing educational system.

This was also true of the adult organizations involved in higher education. The National Association of Scholars focused on legitimizing dissenting voices in the academy rather than altering the structures of university governance, although this attitude began to change under the impact of our campaign. The American Council of Trustees and Alumni was organized to uphold academic standards and support a quality education, but did not promote system-wide reform, although it too began to propose institutional changes under the influence of our efforts.

While I was influenced by Buckley's work, my concern in organizing our campaign was different. Since Yale was a private institution which had been specifically created to transmit a Christian heritage, I was sympathetic to Buckley's distress over its transformation into a secular university at odds with the values of its founders. Moreover, Buckley was justified in his claim that Yale had severed its religious ties without a formal divorce. But unlike Buckley's efforts, the campaign I organized was not at odds with the research university itself, nor with its secular foundations or intellectual pluralism. The research university was now an established institution. More than 85 percent of American college students attended publicly funded schools which, unlike Yale, had been created as secular institutions. These schools were not dedicated to the transmission of religious doctrines but to the pursuit of knowledge through disinterested inquiry. My goal in launching the academic freedom campaign was to stop the erosion of these academic standards and the steady transformation of liberal arts departments into sectarian indoctrination centers for ideological causes.

The intellectual foundations of the modern research university were enshrined in a famous document called the "Declaration of the Principles on Academic Freedom and Academic Tenure," which was issued in 1915 by the American Association of University Professors. In the words of an authoritative account by two law professors, "The draftsmen of the 1915 Declaration sought to establish principles of academic freedom capable of ensuring that colleges and universities would remain accountable to professional standards...."[16] In other words, the cornerstones of both academic freedom and the modern research university were one and the same—the commitment to professional standards, based on scientific method, which were above party and faction.

The system created was self-policing, with faculty in charge of enforcing the standards. The two law professors warned that academic freedom "will collapse if faculty lose faith in the professional norms necessary to define and generate knowledge," and could only be sustained if academic peers "interpret disciplinary standards in a way that maintains the ... legitimacy of these standards."[17] Thus, the academic freedom protections in the Declaration were limited only to professors "who carry on their work in the temper of the scientific method," and thus only to professors who practice theoretical skepticism and encourage respect for empirical evidence. The Declaration denied academic standing (and academic freedom) to those who use it "for intemperate and uncritical partisanship."[18]

The impetus for our reform campaign was the erosion of these time-honored standards and consequent development of academic faculties whose political agendas were made possible by the failure of universities to enforce the principles in the Declaration. These faculties were concentrated in the newly created inter-disciplinary fields, which were based on the social critiques of the political Left. In place of the traditional disciplines—history, economics, philosophy—whose standards had evolved in the course of more than a century of scholarship, the new fields were inspired by ideologies such as feminism, whose intellectual scope was all-encompassing and whose methodologies were newly invented. An immediate consequence of this academic revolution was an epidemic of amateurism in academic classrooms.

Newly minted courses on "global feminism"—to take one example—now focused on the workings (and evils) of the international capitalist economic system, but were taught by professors whose academic credentials were not in economics or even sociology or political science, but in Comparative Literature, Education, and Women's Studies.[19] The primary credential for teaching such courses was not an academic expertise, but familiarity with left-wing ideologies.

This academic amateurism in the service of ideology wasn't confined to new fields like Women's Studies, moreover. The course "Marxism and Society" at Duke University, for example, is offered (and overseen) not by the Department of Economics or Sociology, but by the Department of Literature and—jointly—by the Education Program, which trains teachers for K–12 schools.[20] The course is taught by Michael Hardt, co-author of the book *Empire*. This is a text popular among academic radicals and has been described by other Marxists as "a Communist Manifesto for the 21st Century."[21] (Hardt's co-author, also a Marxist, is Antonio Negri, a convicted Italian terrorist.) According to the official Duke catalogue description written by Hardt, "The course considers the basic concepts of historical materialism, as they have developed in historical contexts. Topics include sexual and social inequality, alienation, class formation, impe-rialism, and revolution."[22] Hardt is a professor of comparative literature and has no peer-reviewed academic credential that would qualify him as an expert in history, sociology, economics, political science, or human sex-uality.[23]

The campaign I undertook in 2003 was an attempt to address these abuses by restoring the academic principles of the modern research uni-versity to liberal arts faculties. Its basic premise was that professors were obligated to behave professionally in the classroom, and that students had a right to expect them to do so. These were simple propositions that I spelled out in the "Academic Bill of Rights," which was based squarely on the 1915 Declaration. Where Buckley wanted to preserve the religious character of Yale, my concern was to defend and restore the professional standards of the modern research university that had been abandoned in its liberal arts divisions. In that sense, the reform I was proposing was con-servative as well.

What follows is the history of the campaign—the obstacles we encoun-tered along the way, the successes we achieved, and the prospects for mak-ing further progress. It is in some ways a personal story, because the campaign arose out of my concerns, and I have been its spokesman and the chief target of those who oppose it. But it is also a narrative that describes a disturbing development in America's liberal arts colleges and provides a guide for those interested in reversing it. This is a narrative, in other words, about the fate of higher education in America.

The possibility that this history might be of service to other reform efforts is the most important reason for publishing it. I am convinced that our campaign would have been able to achieve far more if liberals and con-servatives interested in the health of our universities (and our democracy) had joined our cause. Of course, I was aware that the political climate would make the recruitment of liberal allies difficult, even though our campaign was based on well-established liberal principles. For liberalism had undergone significant changes since radicals had mounted a systematic assault on the academic culture in the 1960s, seeking to make its curricula "relevant" and to politicize its educational programs. In the decades since, many self-identified "liberals" ceased to be committed to institutional process, or even to fairness. Many came to regard standards themselves as oppressive. So it was not difficult to understand why recruiting liberal support for the academic freedom campaign should be problematic.

On the other hand, I did not expect the lack of support we received from conservatives and libertarians, particularly since they had the most to gain from the restoration of these academic principles. Conservative texts and the viewpoints that inspired them were excluded from the newly politicized academic curriculum, and conservative and libertarian professors had become a vanishing presence on university faculties as a direct result of the newly politicized approach.[24]

Opponents of our campaign, however, were quick to portray me as a "pawn" of larger forces and to characterize our effort to restore liberal principles as "a well-funded project of the far Right."[25] This accusation served their political interests, but in the real world, the campaign we waged never became part of any conservative agenda. While Republican elected officials supported our efforts to pass legislative resolutions in more than a dozen states, they retreated quickly after the initial engagements, and only one such resolution—in Colorado—passed both houses of the legislature. Only one Republican Party (Maine) actually incorporated the Academic Bill of Rights into its platform, and only one Republican candidate (also in Maine) ran a campaign on our issue.

More inexplicable was the failure of conservative policy organizations—the Heritage Foundation, the CATO Institute, the American

Enterprise Institute—to embrace or promote our cause. For example, when the American Enterprise Institute held a conference on "academic freedom" well into our campaign, and later published a book, I was pointedly not included.[26] Although once a speaker at annual meetings of the National Scholars Association, the invitations stopped once our campaign was launched in 2003, despite the personal support of two of its leaders, Stephen Balch and Peter Wood. Even the California Association of Scholars, a branch of the NAS operating in a state where my offices are located, declined to invite me to its convention.

In the seven years of our campaign, not a single report on our efforts appeared in *National Review* or the *Weekly Standard*, the two most widely read intellectual journals of the Right, despite direct appeals to their editors. *Imprimus*, a publication of Hillsdale College with a million-and-a half conservative subscribers interested in higher education, ignored us while the president of Hillsdale publicly criticized our efforts. Only one of the four books I wrote on universities, documenting the abuses addressed by our campaign, was reviewed by *Commentary* or *National Review*, and none were reviewed by the *Claremont Conservative Review of Books*, the *Weekly Standard*, or the *Wall Street Journal*.[27] The *Journal* did, however, publish an editorial *attacking* the Academic Bill of Rights on the libertarian grounds that we appealed to legislatures for endorsements, which the writer regarded as a bad idea. The libertarian journal, *Reason*, printed several similar attacks on our campaign, but no report on the abuses we had uncovered or the progress we had made.

By contrast the *Chronicle of Higher Education*, a liberal publication unsympathetic to our cause, published a lengthy and reasonably balanced cover story on our efforts, as did *USA Today*. Both assigned reporters to follow me on campuses and report what they saw. Both the *New York Times* and the *Washington Post* published substantial and fair-minded articles as well, although the *Times'* "Education" supplement studiously ignored our efforts. In October 2005, an issue of the *Weekly Standard* did focus on higher education reform with a 10,000-word cover feature titled "The Left University: How It Was Born, How It Grew, How to Overcome It." The *Standard* even used our campaign logo featuring the three hear-no-evil, see-no-evil, speak-no-evil monkeys dressed in cap and gown for its cover design. But the story failed to mention our campaign or the Academic Bill of Rights, while the *Standard's* editors did not even bother to request permission to use our image.[28]

The calculated distance which the conservative establishment took towards our efforts reflected the same disposition that lay behind Buckley's failure to organize a campaign for reforming the university system, despite his prescient critique of its curriculum at Yale. While precise in their diagnosis of what is wrong with the university curriculum, conservatives have remained reluctant to pursue a course of action to correct the abuses. Conservatives are uncomfortable with organized movements generally and institutional reform efforts in particular. They are especially uneasy with conflicts that might bring them into collision with the intellectual establishment, or that would invite unscrupulous *ad hominem* attacks from the opposition. Ours involved all three.

There were significant exceptions. I did receive generous and important support for my campus appearances from the Young America's Foundation and the Leadership Institute, while the conservative publication *Human Events* gave attention to our efforts. The talk radio network and FOX News Channel did feature our cases and played an important role in raising the visibility of scandals such as the one involving Professor Ward Churchill, which greatly helped our cause. Sean Hannity, co-anchor of the *Hannity & Colmes* show, devoted an unprecedented five segments to my book *The Professors*, helping to put our concerns before the general public and induce our opponents to take us more seriously. But these media outlets were also viewed at a distance by the conservative intellectual establishment, and were regarded with ill-concealed contempt by the university audience we were attempting to reach.

The forces ranged against our university reforms were formidable, and regularly—even relentlessly—resorted to gross misrepresentations of the facts and personal smears to prevent a reasonable consideration of our proposals. Chapter nine, describing the academic freedom hearings in Pennsylvania, is particularly instructive in documenting the determination of teacher unions and the Democratic Party to block even an inquiry into whether academic freedom protections for students existed at any of the seventeen public universities in the state and then to obscure the committee's findings that at fifteen of those schools they did not. Chapter ten describes the faculty resistance to one student's efforts to use these protections at Penn State University.

While the facts presented in this narrative may seem discouraging, the campaign's successes suggest that if conservatives had embraced the Academic Bill of Rights and made curricular reform an integral part of their agendas, we would have been able to secure academic freedom protections for students not at two or ten universities, but throughout the higher education system. We would then have been able to proceed with the more difficult task of seeing that these protections were implemented as well.

I am convinced more than ever of the feasibility of the measures we have proposed as I am of the imperative of restoring integrity to the academic curriculum. This book is an effort to persuade Americans in general and conservatives in particular that the reforms described here can be achieved, to explain the difficulties involved, and to show how they can be overcome.

CHAPTER ONE

The Problem

OPPONENTS OF THE ACADEMIC FREEDOM CAMPAIGN HAVE ATTEMPTED to dismiss the Academic Bill of Rights as a "solution in search of a problem."[1] They have described our concerns as "manufactured outrage, manufactured outrage about Women's Studies, manufactured outrage about leftist professors," as though the abuses to which we have drawn attention do not exist.[2] In point of fact, long before I conceived the campaign, I spent more than a decade traveling to over a hundred college campuses where I met individually with thousands of students and listened to accounts of their classroom experiences.

At first, I was simply troubled by what I heard and marveled at how the academic world had changed since I had been a student forty years before, during what was, in retrospect, a golden age of the modern research university. I was born into a family of card-carrying Communists. My collegiate experience coincided with the Cold War and the tail-end of the McCarthy era. Because of these circumstances, I felt particularly fortunate when my professors treated me no differently from my classmates, and didn't single me out for my political views. I do not remember even one of my instructors expressing a personal opinion on the controversial issues of the day, or making remarks that would cast me in the role of a political adversary. This happy educational experience formed the background of my concern for the conservative students I now met.

During my campus visits, students recounted incidents with many professors who had not exhibited the same professional restraint as mine, but instead vented their political prejudices in the classroom, often with great—and intimidating—passion. These stories led me to wonder how my own education would have been affected if my teachers had behaved this way. How would I have reacted, for example, if one had turned to me in the middle of a class and said, "David, why don't you explain to us why Communists like to kill so many people?" Yet, students I interviewed had experiences not unlike this kind of professorial third degree.

In the spring of 2005, a student came to hear me speak in Connecticut and introduced himself as Nathaniel Nelson, an undergraduate at the University of Rhode Island. Nathaniel told me that he had been singled out as a Christian by his political science professor who was gay, and who asked him in front of the entire class, "Why do Christians hate fags?" The question upset Nathaniel, who didn't hate gays and didn't think most Christians did either. But under his professor's verbal barrage, which invoked Church history from the Middle Ages with which Nathaniel was unfamiliar, he was reduced to a humiliating silence. The subject of the political science course in which this incident occurred was neither Christianity nor homosexuality but "Political Philosophy: Plato to Machiavelli."[3] The professor, Michael Vocino, was not a political scientist but a film librarian with no Ph.D. After we published Nathaniel's story on our website (and only because we published Nathaniel's story), an embarrassed university administration barred Vocino from teaching a course for which he had no qualifications.[4]

Hearing Nathaniel's story, I found myself wondering how a student could learn from a teacher who displayed such personal hostility, particularly when it was directed at his religious faith. How could an instructor who has once confronted his student as a passionate adversary then function as his academic mentor? These were questions I thought about every time I encountered cases like Nathaniel's, and there were many.

One incident had a profound impact on all my thinking. I was on a speaking tour to St. John's College in northern Minnesota, a Lutheran school that had recently been transformed into a secular institution. As at other schools the faculty and curriculum were overwhelmingly liberal, and the students I questioned could only identify one professor whom they knew to be conservative. In the course of my lecture I said, "If your professors are not assigning texts with views that present more than one side of a controversial issue, you are being robbed of your educational dollar."

My next speaking engagement was scheduled for the University of Minnesota, which was in Minneapolis, a four-hour drive south. One of the St. John's students volunteered to drive me to a half-way point where I would be met by a student from the University of Minnesota who would then take me the rest of the way. During the drive, I interviewed her about her educational career. She told me that she was majoring in criminology and that her family lived in a rural area in eastern North Dakota near the Minnesota border. In order to pay the $15,000 tuition at St. John's, she had borrowed money from her relatives and was also working an eight-hour job after school. In the course of our conversation, she referred to the remark I had made during my speech and asked me, "Are there any articles or books that support the death penalty?" I said, "Of course there are;

didn't your criminology professor provide you with any?" "No," she replied, "he didn't."

Criminology was hardly my area of expertise, but I was aware that Ernest van den Haag had written a highly regarded book in support of the death penalty.[5] I mentioned it to her and asked how she had chosen criminology as a major in the first place. She told me she had a sister who was a year older, who had been murdered when she was eighteen. The killer was a transient who was tried and convicted by the state of Minnesota, which had no death penalty.

I realized then that this young woman had entered a college program to try to heal a wound that would never be healed, and that her request was part of her effort to deal with her pain. Yet she was being denied the means to do so by a criminology professor who thought it was more important to recruit her as an opponent of the death penalty than to be her teacher. This was an inexcusable betrayal of the educational mission. And in ways, it lay at the heart of my decision to take up the cause of students' academic freedom.

Receptions on Campus

Over the next few years, whenever I visited a campus, I tried to spend several hours meeting with the students who invited me and also with others who stayed to talk when my lectures were over. I questioned them about the subjects they were studying and the classes they were taking and the teachers who instructed them. Of particular concern for me was whether their instructors treated them respectfully if they disagreed with the instruction, whether their teachers distinguished between fact and opinion in their classroom lectures, whether they made students aware that there was more than one side to controversial issues, and whether they assigned texts that reflected those disagreements.

Since the students who hosted me were almost invariably conservative, it was also my custom to ask them how many professors they could identify who were likely to sponsor their group. The question provided me with a rough estimate of the number of conservatives willing to disclose their views and thus with the number of faculty conservatives available to counsel and support them. Almost invariably the answer was "two or three."

This was the case at large schools such as Ohio State University, which is a campus with 60,000 students, and at small schools such as Swarthmore with fewer than 5,000. Only twice in my academic travels, which took me to several hundred schools in forty-seven states, did I visit campuses with a significant number of openly conservative faculty members. The two were South Dakota State and Indiana Wesleyan. Only twice did I encounter a liberal professor who was willing to sponsor a Republican club when no Republican faculty member was available. One was a faculty adviser for College Republicans at Roger Williams, who told me that she was a Democrat married to a Republican. She then told me that after becoming a sponsor for the College Republicans her invitations to dinners and social events with her liberal colleagues had become increasingly rare.

On most university faculties conservatives constitute an average of 10 percent of the total.[6] But there are generally fewer on the faculties of their liberal arts divisions, which is where most undergraduates take their courses. There are even fewer in particular fields—sociology, psychology, communications, and usually none in Women's Studies, African American Studies, and Anthropology, whose focus is on political and social issues. "In my almost four years at Dartmouth," a senior named Dan Knecht observed, "... I have yet to meet one conservative professor."[7]

The absence of conservative viewpoints on faculties makes the reception accorded to visiting conservative lecturers an important indicator of a school's attitude towards dissenting ideas. I have spoken at schools such as California State College at Monterey where I was the only conservative invited to speak on campus in its entire eleven-year history. When I spoke for the first time at Emory University, an elite institution in Atlanta, I was the first conservative invited in four years. My predecessor, Ward Connerly, a regent of the University of California and an African American opponent of racial preferences, had been driven off the stage by violent protesters and was unable to complete his speech.

As I visited various campuses, I was always mindful of the lack of respect that was routinely shown to me by university faculty. It provided insight into the way conservative ideas were likely to be treated in their classrooms. I was the author of many well-received texts, had been nominated for a National Book Award, and was on a first name basis with senators, congressmen, and governors. An academic study identified me as one of the 100 most cited "public intellectuals" in the country.[8] But with a handful of notable exceptions, I was rarely invited to universities by administrators or faculty, even more rarely given an official welcome by either, and when I sat down to dinners with my student hosts, it was usually without a faculty member present. If a professor was there, he was invariably the lonely faculty conservative—the one conservative in the history department at the University of Delaware or the one conservative in the government department at Cornell.

I had been a fairly well known radical in the sixties, had edited *Ramparts*, the largest magazine of the Left, and written several books that were influential among activists. Since many radicals from that era were now college professors teaching courses for which the books I had written should have been relevant texts, the lack of interest in my visits was hardly without significance and provided a striking contrast to the receptions other figures from that era received whose politics had not changed. In the early nineties, I visited Dartmouth to speak in behalf of the editors of the *Dartmouth Review* who were under attack from the school administration over an editorial they had written. No Dartmouth faculty attended the event. Several weeks earlier, however, the campus had been visited by Angela Davis, a much honored professor at the University of California, but also the recipient of a Lenin prize from the East German police state and still a fervently anti-American Communist as she had been in the 1960s. Four deans of the college attended her speech, as well as other faculty who showered her with praise and treated her as an academic lion.

This wasn't unusual. Shortly after Ward Churchill became a nationally despised figure for calling the victims of September 11 "Nazis," I was invited to speak at the University of Hawaii in Honolulu. My appearance was boycotted by faculty and my speech obstructed by student radicals. My student host was particularly embarrassed by the failure of his teachers to meet with me as he had requested. But only weeks earlier, the very same professors, including department heads, had lined up for the privilege of joining the select circle around Churchill whom they held in high regard in spite of—and indeed because of—his public disgrace.[9]

Many of the reactions to my university visits were actively hostile, requiring a substantial police presence to ensure that no one was hurt. When I spoke at Portland State University, an editorial in the student paper began, "We all know that that some of us would like to snuff David Horowitz...." University administrators studiously avoided me while I was there, but assigned six armed guards to maintain order when I appeared. In the auditorium, where I spoke to 150 students, a history professor also named David Horowitz scurried around the hall handing out flyers which explained that he and I were not the same person, and that he was appalled by my views.[10] Twenty years earlier, I had spoken in the same hall as a radical, and called on the students to burn it down; the same professor, David Horowitz, came up to me then and told me how honored he was by my presence.

The attitudes reflected in these faculty boycotts were inexplicable for teachers in a university setting and antithetic to the very spirit of higher education. I made it a practice to refer openly to these boycotts in the lectures I gave. Even if professors disagreed with my point of view, why would they not encourage students to attend my lectures and disagree with the opinions I expressed? I was likely to be the only conservative adult that students might hear in an academic year or possibly in their entire college careers. My presence should have afforded students an opportunity to prepare their own critiques of conservative ideas, which were evidently so different from those of their professors.[11] Wasn't that the goal of an education—to show students how to analyze various perspectives and develop their own? What better way to do so than by confronting a contrarian point of view?

My academic opponents routinely defended extreme views like those of Angela Davis and Ward Churchill by claiming that the purpose of an education was to challenge conventional beliefs. But the argument cut two ways. There was probably no greater demonstration of the monolithic attitude that prevailed in these universities than the failure of liberal faculty to welcome and engage conservative intellectuals when students invited them to campus.

Sometimes the disapprobation of faculty "liberals" took the form of passive resistance, as when professors withheld the extra credit they otherwise routinely provided to students who attended lectures by speakers who shared their views. Sometimes it took a more aggressive form, as when faculty circulated poisonous e-mails over the university Internet to warn students not to attend my talks and to spread misleading and defamatory claims about my agendas and beliefs.[12]

In 1997, I was invited by students to speak at the University of Pennsylvania. I had just published an autobiography called *Radical Son* which was well-received in publications like *The New York Times*. I had also co-authored a widely-praised critique of the radical sixties called *Destructive Generation*. One might have expected professors teaching the sixties to take an interest in the work of a former editor of *Ramparts* and the most prominent critic of the decade. At the time, there were actually hundreds of courses on the sixties in schools across the country. Yet, with one exception—which I initiated—I received no faculty invitations to lecture, and my books were not assigned in their classes.[13] My experience, like that of other conservatives, contrasted sharply with the profusion of invitations extended to radicals such as Angela Davis, Noam Chomsky, and Bill Ayers, and the assignment of the books they had written to celebrate the political excesses of the time.

When the Penn students called to invite me, I asked them if the university offered a course on the sixties and was told there was a popular one with an enrollment of several hundred students taught by three professors. I contacted each of the professors in turn and invited them to participate in my event either as a debating partner or a critic of my text. All three refused, and then circulated an e-mail warning students not to attend the event.

The efforts to prevent students from being exposed to viewpoints like mine were not always passive and did not always take place behind closed doors. During a controversy sparked by my book *The Professors*, an academic friend asked how many times my campus speeches had been disrupted. This was my reply:

> I was once hit with a pie, at the beginning of a speech at Butler University in Indiana. I once had to terminate a talk prematurely despite the presence of thirty armed police and four bodyguards at Berkeley. I had to be protected by twelve armed

police and a German Shepherd at the University of Michigan. I was rushed by clearly deranged individuals and saved only by the intervention of a bodyguard, twice—at M.I.T. and Princeton. I was not able to begin my speech until activists from the International Socialist Organization, a Bolshevik cult, were removed by police on at least four occasions (and probably more but I can no longer remember). I had a talk delayed for twenty minutes by demonstrators at the University of Chicago and had to deliver my speech while a large undergraduate stood in the middle of the room with her back to me in protest (she was not removed by the Dean and police officers present because she was black, and they feared adverse publicity). I had talks delayed and disrupted at Portland State, the University of Texas, Indiana University, the University of California (Davis) the University of Washington, the University of Hawaii, the University of Illinois, the University of Delaware, UCLA, San Francisco State, Boston U., Harvard, Wisconsin, Arizona State, and Bowling Green. I had silent demonstrations directed at me in the auditorium where I spoke at the University of North Carolina and the University of Rhode Island. I was streaked by a protester at Purdue University. I had university e-mails circulated to students and faculty by hostile professors insinuating that I was a racist at Gonzaga University, the University of Pennsylvania, and the University of Missouri. I have had to have campus security present routinely, but not always in force (i.e., five or more officers) ever since the first Berkeley speech I gave against reparations in March 2001. I now have a personal bodyguard whom I share with conservative speakers Ann Coulter and Michelle Malkin.[14]

While college administrators did little to secure a civil atmosphere for conservative speakers, they readily instituted elaborate regulations restricting students' speech to protect the sensitivities of liberals. These "speech codes" were theoretically designed to protect minorities from harassment but in practice had been stretched to constrain the expression of conservative views on issues such as racial preferences and to condone behavior that was just plain rude. In one celebrated case from the early 1990s, a student at the University of Pennsylvania was threatened with suspension for yelling "water buffalo" out of his dorm room window when his studies were disturbed in the middle of the night by a group of raucous females who happened to be black. The student was threatened with suspension and formally tried by an administrative court. Deference to the Left by administrators on contentious social issues and a reluctance to even discuss such issues became a matter of simple prudence for students and faculty alike in the face of left-wing intimidation.[15]

The fear of retribution for being associated with conservative opinions on certain issues became so severe that even nationally prominent, liberal faculty members could not be assured of immunity from career-damaging attacks. In 1993, I hosted a show on public radio station KCRW in Santa Monica and interviewed Harvard Law Professor Alan Dershowitz.[16] In the course of the interview, Dershowitz observed that the atmosphere at Harvard Law was so antagonistic to the free expression of ideas in areas that were politically sensitive, and student radicals were so liable to exaggerate and distort what was actually said, that he would no longer lecture about rape law without video-taping his presentation.[17] The precaution was designed to provide him with an evidentiary basis for defending himself against a potential charge of creating a "hostile environment" for women in his class. Dershowitz also reported that one of his law faculty colleagues, who was a leading expert in the field of rape law, had simply stopped giving lectures on the subject. If one of the most prominent legal defense attorneys in the nation was wary of giving an undocumented public lecture at the Harvard Law School because the subject was a flashpoint for political radicals, what did that say about the freedom of expression for others, particularly students, in university environments?

Student Orientation

Attempts to indoctrinate students in the radical worldview actually preceded their entry into the classroom, as "politically correct" dogma was the central theme of "student orientation" sessions that universities required of entering freshman. "A central goal of these programs," as one commentator described them, "is to uproot 'internalized oppression,' a crucial concept in the diversity education planning documents of most universities."[18] In other words, the controversial and questionable idea that an open and upwardly mobile society such as America's is "oppressive" is an *assumption* of the university curriculum from the start and is almost never examined critically in the curriculum itself.[19]

Thus, liberal students attending my campus lectures often complained that in talking about America as a place of opportunity, I was ignoring the "hierarchies" of race, class, and gender—doctrines routinely instilled by their liberal arts professors. Because of the lack of conservative viewpoints on university faculties, and because of the lack of intellectual respect accorded these viewpoints, students had no inkling that the existence of such hierarchies was itself a controversial claim. Nor did they realize that these were concepts central to Marxism and its derivative ideologies, and to campaigns against free market societies that had resulted in the deaths of tens of millions of people in the twentieth century and the impoverishment of whole continents.

When I spoke at Carleton College, one of the top-ranked liberal arts colleges in the nation, I asked the conservative students if they felt their liberal professors were indoctrinating them in left-wing ideologies. Their answer, without exception, was that they did not think they were. I then asked, "How many of you have been taught that there are race, class, and gender hierarchies in America?" There were about twenty students present and every hand went up. In other words, a sectarian opinion of the Left had been presented to them as a scientific fact, and though they were conservatives, they had failed to recognize it as indoctrination. The instilling of the doctrines of race, gender, and class oppression had become part of the intellectual fabric of their university education.

At freshman orientation sessions, students were often divided according to their membership by ethnicity and race into "oppressed" and "oppressor" groups. They were instructed through training films which bore titles such as "Blue Eyes" and "Skin Deep," in which blue eyes and white skin were presented as symbols of the oppressor group, and brown eyes and brown skin as those of its victims. Students were also singled out if they came from more prosperous backgrounds. This, it was explained to them, was part of their inherited "privilege," as though such privilege were not itself earned by someone from whom it was inherited, and as though the possession of privilege in a democracy were not fluid, so that it could be gained by others and lost as well.

Students were taught that America—a free society based on voluntary contracts—was actually a status society based on tribal identifications primarily of race and secondarily of gender. "Programmatic differentiation by race is now typical in higher education," observes Professor Alan Kors, co-author of *The Shadow University*. "Half a century after the defeat of Nazism, our universities distinguish by blood and equate blood with culture.... The justification for this submergence of the individual into the tribe is the same as it was under fascism: the individual is a function—politically, morally, and historically of genetic and cultural collectivities. Campus life begins with the sorting out of students into oppressors and victims."[20]

In the 1990s, this collection of left-wing attitudes was codified in an orthodoxy so rigid that it acquired a name: "political correctness." Responding to this development, Richard Zeller, a tenured sociologist at Bowling Green State University, proposed a course focusing on "political correctness" as a subject. Among the questions he wished to pose was whether the idea of political correctness was at odds with intellectual pluralism and academic freedom. Zeller had come up with his proposal after hearing stories from students about professors who used grades to force them to agree to progressive orthodoxies, for example that whites were inherently racist, or to reverse their positions on emotionally and ideologically charged issues like abortion.[21] Zeller submitted the course for approval to his peers in the Sociology Department, who voted to reject it. He then sought an administrative home in other departments but was similarly rebuffed. Dr. Kathleen Dixon, Director of Women's Studies, was perhaps not aware that she sounded like a character out of Orwell when she told the Bowling Green student newspaper, "We forbid any course that says we restrict free speech."[22]

Far from being unique, Dixon's attitude was alarmingly common among Bowling Green faculty. An Ethnic Studies professor explained that Zeller's course would prompt students to "feel good about the ruling paradigm, which since the inception of the United States has said that genocide is good, racism is better, and exploitation of women and the poor is the best way to go." According to this view, any attempt to question a prevailing left-wing orthodoxy was to align oneself with the oppressor.[23] The Department of Sociology chairman Gary Lee completed the anathema on

Zeller by commenting: "Unfortunately, tenure protects the incompetent and malicious; [Zeller] has tenure, so he cannot be fired without cause."[24]

The transformation of Professor Zeller from a respected colleague into an academic pariah was now complete. The shunned academic decided to retire rather than continue his career as a heretic. In his letter of resignation, he wrote,

> Don't cry for me. I'm doing just fine, thank you. Cry out, instead, for the students who regularly get intellectually mugged on the Bowling Green State University Campus...the traditionalist who believes that marriage is between a man and a woman, but can't say so for fear of failing; the conservative who believes in minimizing government interference in our lives and says so in a sociology class, the woman who believes that abortion is murder, but must write a pro-choice essay to pass English, and all of those who have "adjusted" and "self-censored" their ideas so that they can pass their classes.... Bowling Green has sold its soul to the thought police of political correctness. There was a time that honorable people could disagree honorably; now, any challenge to the campus sacred cows—feminism, affirmative action, and multiculturalism—is denounced as evil.[25]

The Controversy Over Reparations

The tour of campuses I took during the years when political correctness was becoming an entrenched academic attitude culminated in February 2001, when I attempted to place an ad in seventy college papers called "Ten Reasons Why Reparations for Slavery Is A Bad Idea And Racist Too."[26] The ad did not oppose the idea of reparations for actual slaves.

What it opposed was the idea of reparations paid 137 years after the abolition of slavery to individuals who had never been slaves and by individuals who had no involvement with slavery, or whose ancestors had laid down their lives in the war to end slavery. The call for reparations was a movement that seemed to me both divisive and unjust.

The inspiration for the ad was the announcement of "Reparations Awareness Weeks," organized by radicals on college campuses. These featured academic panels which presented only one side of the issue, suggesting that the interests of the African American community and the reparations radicals were one and the same, and that decent people could have only one point of view on this issue. In point of fact, when the idea of reparations was first proposed in 1969, it was not supported by a single major civil rights organization, whose leaders regarded it as unwarranted, divisive, and extreme.

Forty student newspapers rejected the ad I submitted on political grounds. The effort quickly became a national scandal when the *The Daily Californian* at Berkeley published the ad, and its editorial offices were besieged by forty African American students and their faculty adviser demanding an apology. The intruders denounced the paper's "institutional racism," accused its editor, Daniel Hernandez, a Hispanic, of "betraying" his race, and demanded a retraction. The next day's issue featured a lengthy *mea culpa* from Hernandez, who explained his turnaround to a reporter from the *Los Angeles Times* in these words: "I think people are too quick to dismiss political correctness. . . . Latino and African American students whose ancestors [were persecuted] are now in a position to say, 'We don't have to listen to that.' This is a reversal of fortune, a reversal of suppression."[27] In other words, having once been the victims of discrimination they would now become perpetrators. Upon his graduation the following semester, Hernandez was hired as a reporter by the *Times*.

As the controversy spread to more campuses, I was invited by students to speak on the Berkeley campus. I wrote to Chancellor Robert Berdahl asking him to be present and introduce me as a measure that might discourage potential violence. Through one of his assistants, Berdahl peremptorily rejected my request, saying that I had "provoked a dialogue that no one wanted to hear"[28]—an odd position for an educator. In point of fact, Berkeley professors were already promoting the reparations movement in their classes as part of the "Reparations Awareness" campaign. Instead of attending the event, Berdahl assigned thirty armed campus police to maintain order.

It was not the only campus where an armed presence was authorized by university officials. University of Michigan administrators provided twelve armed police and a German shepherd to watch over my speech, which 1,000 students attended. My appearance was preceded by weeks of agitation by a radical group called the "Defend Affirmative Action Party," which had a reputation for obstructing speakers with whom it disagreed. At first the group threatened to boycott my talk, but when that failed, their followers appeared *en masse* at the event. I spoke from a platform flanked by several officers, while three university vice presidents sat in the balcony and observed the surreal scene without comment. Not one of them attempted to contact me before or after my address. Nor was any discipline administered to the student leaders and organizations whose verbal threats and generally threatening behavior required such precautions.

While I may have been the eye of this storm, however, I was not its chief target. This dubious honor belonged to the conservative students who invited me and the liberal students whose newspapers ran my ad, and who were denounced by campus radicals as "racists" for not censoring it. At the University of Wisconsin, the *Badger Herald* ran the ad while the other student paper, *The Cardinal*, rejected it and also provided the radicals with a free page to respond. Instead of attempting to answer the arguments I had made against reparations, they used the space for an indictment of the *Badger Herald* editors. Their banner headline screamed, "*Badger Herald*: UW Madison *Independent* Racist Propaganda Machine," and the text that followed was mainly a stream of racial invective directed at its editors.

Not content with mere verbal abuse, the radicals gathered around the editorial offices of the *Herald* in protest until campus police advised the student staff to take refuge in their dorm rooms. In their *Cardinal* ad, the radicals reminded readers that "black students [had] stormed the office of the *Badger Herald* on several occasions over the past couple of years," revealing inadvertently how the administration had in effect encouraged their bad behavior by not disciplining them on prior occasions. The organizer of the demonstrations and the racial attack was Tshaka Barrows, an African American student who was also the son of the Vice Chancellor for Student Affairs. Barrows had actually been praised by the liberal editors of the *Badger Herald* the year before "for his work as an advocate for diversity."[29]

A parallel scenario took place at Brown University where radicals denounced the liberal student editors of the *Daily Herald* as "racists." They then stole and trashed an entire issue of the paper, threatening to continue to do so until the editors yielded to their demands. These included turning over the tainted payment I had made for the ad to the campus Third World Center and providing free space in the *Herald* for a rebuttal. They also demanded that one of their members be appointed to the *Herald* editorial staff to monitor its opinions and decisions.

When Brown president Sheila Blumstein reminded the protesters that freedom of the press was still an honored principle, she was rebuked in a statement signed by sixty professors who supported the theft as a "symbolic protest."[30] At a campus meeting of the protesters, an African-

American senior complained that Brown had failed to prepare its students to be able to answer the ad and "condemned Brown as a racist institution with no interest in African-Americans." She was then berated by Professor Louis Gordon, the black faculty advisor to the radicals, who told her that if she couldn't answer the ad, that was her fault not his.[31]

In all these episodes, I was struck by the fact that virtually no administrators or faculty members had stepped forward to deplore the anti-intellectual attitudes that the attacks on the ad displayed. Apart from one or two isolated instances, such as president Blumstein's intervention, no attempt was made by university authorities to insist on civil intellectual discourse as a norm for dealing with controversial issues in a university setting.[32] No attempts were made to discipline student organizations that organized disruptions or defamed other students for printing the ad.

Despite the unprecedented attention the controversy received on campuses across the country, it never led to anything that might be described as a serious intellectual exchange about reparations or response to the objections I had raised. And how could there be such an intellectual dialogue if the price for disagreeing with the leftists was to be called a racist in the pages of the college newspaper? Instead of encouraging—let alone demanding—a civil discussion, university administrators confined themselves to marshaling campus police to prevent actual violence and limit their legal liabilities. Otherwise, they maintained a strict distance from the controversy itself. The failure of university officials to defend academic values created a vacuum, which allowed a small minority of political ruffians to dominate—and debase—the campus environment.

CHAPTER TWO

Beginnings of the Campaign

T HE CHANGES I WITNESSED ON UNIVERSITY CAMPUSES HAD BEEN decades in the making, while the radicals who had worked to politicize the curriculum in liberal arts faculties were so entrenched it was difficult to see how academic values might be restored. In the 1990s, I had spent many hours thinking about this problem without coming up with an answer. But during the reparations controversy, the campus situation presented itself in a way that for the first time suggested a concrete step that might be taken for reform.

One lesson I had learned was that those responsible for the name-calling and general intimidation of opposing viewpoints comprised a small, if effective, minority of the campus community. Political activists were able to exert a disproportionate influence over its public square through their aggressive tactics. But I knew from my campus experiences that in their absence, even a school with a reputation like Berkeley could be an entirely different environment. Before I became a targeted figure through the reparations controversy, I had been invited on two occasions to give guest lectures at Berkeley to political science classes of about 500 students. The professor who invited me was not a conservative, and ironically, the course itself was about "activism." Other invited lecturers included sixties radical Tom Hayden and former governor Jerry Brown. The discussion I gave reviewed the lessons I had learned in my activist career, including a capsule summary of my political transformation from radical to conservative. The students received my presentation attentively, and there were no incidents. Nor was any campus security necessary. Unlike my receptions during the reparations controversy, the atmosphere remained academic throughout.

Even during the reparations controversy, the confrontational atmosphere dissipated as soon as the activists chose not to attack. In November 2001, I spoke about reparations to 1,100 students at the University of North Carolina. The campus radicals came, but in a chastened mood. The spring disruptions at Berkeley, Wisconsin, Brown, and other campuses had backfired when they were seen as an attack on the freedom of the press. This had led to a public relations fiasco that put them on the defensive. Consequently, they adopted a new strategy in the fall. Instead of disrupting my speech, 100 of them staged a silent walkout ten minutes after I had begun. Once they had departed, I was able to proceed without incident. The experience for the thousand students who remained was entirely different, and when my speech was over, they gave me a reasonably warm reception. In short, when campus radicals decided not to pursue a strategy of disruption, an academic atmosphere prevailed.

This experience was repeated at other campuses as well. From Chapel Hill I went on to the University of Wisconsin, where I had been invited by a liberal student group that hosted a "Distinguished Lecture Series."

Before the event, I met with fifty undergraduates who were perfectly civil and eager to hear the other side of the story. The speech itself was attended by 1,200 students who were mainly polite, and the environment contrasted sharply with the angry demonstrations and verbal attacks that had taken place only months before. Once again, the campus Left had made a decision to lie low and allow an academic normalcy to return. The *Daily Cardinal* even printed a semi-apology for its behavior during the spring conflict, defending my right to speak and the responsibility of students to hear me out.[1]

Thinking about these reactions, I began to see the outlines of a solution to the problem. In the university's public square, administrators had abdicated their responsibility for ensuring that an atmosphere of civility and academic openness prevailed. This abdication made it impossible to conduct an intellectual dialogue on any issue that was deemed important by the Left. Since the disruptions could be traced to easily identifiable campus groups, restoring civility to campus discussions did not seem a particularly difficult task. The problem of politicized classrooms was a more difficult challenge but could also be seen as one of academic manners. If an authority was there to see that faculty behaved professionally, treating opposing viewpoints with scholarly respect, students would be able to make up their own minds after weighing the arguments.

These reflections led to my initial idea for a reform effort. I called it the "Campaign for Fairness and Inclusion in Higher Education," and came up with the slogan, "You can't get a good education if they're only telling you half the story." It was a version of what I had told the students at St. John's nearly a decade before. Fairness and inclusion were ideas I believed few members of the academic community would be likely to oppose. The intent of the campaign was to get liberal universities to live up to their professed ideals. If I could win support from liberals while isolating the radicals, as I had been able to do during the reparations campaign, success did not seem out of reach.

To recruit organizational allies, I reserved a couple of hours at an annual event I was hosting over Labor Day Weekend at the Broadmoor Resort in Colorado Springs. Among those I invited to discuss the campaign were Stephen Balch, the president of the National Association of Scholars; Ron Robinson, the president of the Young America's Foundation, which had underwritten many of my campus speeches; and Eli Lehrer, an editor for the *American Enterprise Magazine*, who had conducted a study for us on the lack of political and intellectual diversity on university faculties.[2]

On September 9, I sent a letter to various conservative campus organizations inviting them "to participate in a campaign to promote fairness and inclusion in higher education," which would "focus on four problem areas and demands." These included a call on university administrations "to conduct an inquiry into political bias in the hiring process for faculty and administrators" and also the selection of speakers. It also called for "a zero tolerance policy towards the obstruction of campus speakers and meetings and the destruction of informational literature distributed by campus groups," which was a common practice of the campus Left.[3]

While these overtures led to pledges of support for my campus appearances from Young America's Foundation and the Intercollegiate Studies Institute, I was unable to induce other organizations to make the campaign part of their programs. Hence the conduct of the academic freedom campaign was left to my own organization, the Center for the Study of Popular Culture, a non-profit foundation I had created more than a decade before.[4]

The reparations controversy had demonstrated that there was no constituency inside the university community that was both willing and able to defend the principles of intellectual diversity or fairness as a matter of course. On the other hand, these were principles were embraced by a majority of Americans. It was imperative therefore to put the academic problem in front of the broader public and hope that their concern would influence the response of university administrators.

Two days after I sent the letter announcing our campaign to other organizations, Islamic terrorists attacked the World Trade Center, and I realized that the campaign would have to wait. For many months to come, it would not be possible to get the American public to focus on anything besides the newly launched war on terror. I contacted everyone to whom I had sent the letter and told them I was postponing the campaign at least until the following year.

When the 2002 school term began, I returned to the project, publishing a pamphlet called *You Can't Get A Good Education If They're Only Telling You Half The Story*, along with a statement proposing the same measures I had described in my letter the year before.[5] On September 3, the Center for the Study of Popular Culture also published "The Problem with America's Colleges and the Solution," an article I had written, outlining these reforms.

The Academic Bill of Rights

Shortly after the statement was published, the chairman of the Center's board, Wally Nunn, called to suggest I get in touch with his friend, Tom Egan, who was the chair of the State University of New York's board of trustees. The SUNY system is a massive educational enterprise, encompassing sixty-nine colleges and universities with over 400,000 students. Wally thought I should talk to Egan about the possibility of securing some campus speaking opportunities for myself on the SUNY campuses. The prospect of meeting with so powerful a university official, however, caused me to consider using the opportunity to advance my educational reforms, which would mean putting Wally's idea on hold. I already knew the first proposal I would make to Egan—a policy of zero tolerance for students and student organizations that obstructed campus speakers who had been invited by officially recognized campus groups.

On December 4, 2002, I met with Egan in his administrative offices in midtown Manhattan. Provost Peter Salins, Vice Provost Donald Steven, and trustee Candace de Russy were also present. During the discussion, it occurred to me that we could streamline the other items in our agenda into a single document, which the SUNY administration could adopt. Before I left, I promised Egan I would come back to him with that proposal.

While my potential allies on the SUNY board were outwardly powerful, they were politically and culturally isolated, not only in the university but also in the surrounding environment. All the trustees had been appointed by a Republican governor operating in a state where registered Democrats outnumbered Republicans by more than 1,000,000 votes. Even though Egan occupied a position at the top of the university pyramid, he was severely constrained by his obligation to protect the governor who had appointed him, and who harbored presidential ambitions.

The last thing a governor seeking a national stage would want was a faculty revolt at his state university, particularly over an academic reform whose issues would be easy to distort to the voting public. A conflict pitting teachers against "right-wing activists" and "politically interfering" administrators, which is how the professorial unions could be counted on to frame the debate, was not calculated to appeal to Egan's advisers (as I had already observed in our meeting) or to his patron in the state capital.

Despite forebodings, I proceeded with my proposal, basing it on the 1915 Declaration, and designing it to be so firmly set in the framework of existing university principles as to be virtually unassailable.[6] Within a few weeks of our meeting, I sent Egan the new "Academic Bill of Rights."[7]

There were only two real innovations in the document I had written, but they proved to be more than the faculty unions would tolerate or the SUNY administrators could handle. The first was to formulate the already established principles of academic freedom as "rights." The 1915 statement was discursive and its principles often buried in layers of archaic prose. By distilling the principles and codifying them as rights, I made them harder to ignore (but also—as I later discovered—easier to attack).

The second and more important innovation was to frame the principles as rights for *students*. This was not an entirely new idea. Although the 1915 Declaration was conceived as a protection for professors, it also took note of the academic freedom of students, which it called "the freedom to learn" and not to be indoctrinated. The Declaration instructed faculty to avoid "taking unfair advantage of the student's immaturity by indoctrinating him with the teacher's own opinions before the student has had an opportunity fairly to examine other opinions upon the matters in question, and before he has sufficient knowledge and ripeness of judgment to be entitled to form any definitive opinion of his own."[8] My innovation was to say that if this was a faculty responsibility, it should also be a student right. Since students had no formal representation in university matters, academic freedom policies based on the Declaration were generally incorporated into the faculty union contract or the "Employee Handbook," and were thus unavailable to them.

In the Academic Bill of Rights, the protections for students against indoctrination were articulated in three separate clauses, which stipulated: 1) that students would be graded solely on their academic merits and not their political beliefs; 2) that curricula and reading lists should reflect "the uncertainty and unsettled character" of human knowledge;

and 3) that students should therefore be provided "with dissenting sources and viewpoints where appropriate."

Since my goal was to appeal to the majority of professors who were not radicals, I drafted the bill with careful regard for the institutional independence of the university—a fact cynically ignored by its critics throughout the campaign that followed. I was aided in this task by Stephen Balch, president of the National Association of Scholars, to whom I submitted the text for editorial review. I also submitted the document to UCLA law professor Eugene Volokh, a libertarian and nationally recognized expert on First Amendment rights, who recommended a single word change, to which I readily agreed.

I anticipated that many of our opponents would not address the specifics of the bill. Since my conservative credentials were well-known, the Left was likely to frame any proposal of mine as a plot to eliminate "liberal bias" in education by firing left-wing faculty members and hiring conservatives. To forestall such attacks, I made the first two principles of the Academic Bill of Rights the protection of *all* faculty from being hired or fired because of their political views. I did this, even though I knew it was redundant, since faculty already enjoyed such protection.

To make the bill as bullet-proof as possible, I then sent the draft to three well-known members of the academic left for their comments.[9] The three academics were Todd Gitlin, Michael Bérubé, and Stanley Fish. Gitlin was a journalism professor and former president of the radical organization, Students for a Democratic Society. Bérubé was an academic leftist active in the American Association of University Professors. Fish was a renowned Milton scholar and academic liberal, who had written extensively on free speech issues. He had authored a book, titled *Professional Correctness*, arguing that ideological concerns were distinct from and often at odds with scholarly interests, and he had recently published an article in the *Chronicle of Higher Education* called, "Save The World On Your Own Time," which advised professors to limit their classroom activities to their professional expertise. The article also counseled universities and academic associations to maintain strict institutional neutrality on controversial issues, a principle I incorporated into the bill.[10]

Gitlin was the first to respond. He was unhappy with minor wordings, which I agreed to change, and he objected to one entire clause, which would have required that tenure and hiring committees record their deliberations and make them available to "appropriately constituted authorities empowered to inquire into the integrity of the process."[11] The clause was designed to prevent tenure and hiring decisions from being affected by the non-academic prejudices of committee members. I inserted it because of abuses such as that reported by Michael Adams, a professor of criminology at the University of North Carolina (Wilmington). Adams had served on a hiring committee whose members described one candidate as "too religious," because he had attended a religious academic institution, and another as "too conservative," because he had written for a conservative publication.[12] I wanted candidates to have a means of appeal if they believed they were penalized for attitudes and opinions unrelated to academic merit. I left the appeals authority deliberately vague so that universities themselves could decide on an appropriate grievance process.

Gitlin objected to this clause, saying that that it would put a "chill" in committee deliberations. My view was that the only chill would be to the expression of judgments unrelated to academic merit. But his response showed me that I would not be able to persuade him, and when Bérubé and Fish agreed with him, I dropped the clause in its entirety. This concession earned their approval of the version I eventually published.

Bérubé's e-mail offering his approval is instructive because he would later become one of my most prominent antagonists, ridiculing the document and attacking me personally on Internet blogs, in books, and in influential publications, including *The Chronicle of Higher Education*, InsideHigherEd.com, and *The New York Times*:

Hi David—

The Academic Bill of Rights looks fine to me in every respect but one: the taping of all tenure, search, and hiring committee deliberations. It's a poison-pill clause, for one thing; completely unenforceable, for another; and last but not least, it would lead to all manner of ugly unintended consequences, none of which would necessarily have to do with anyone's political or religious beliefs. Simply put, when people deliberate over such things and they know their deliberations won't be confidential, they don't speak freely or honestly—they speak in code, so as not to offend X's colleague whose student, Y, is among those being considered for Z. (And again, it doesn't matter whether Y is a Stalinist or a Freeper or a Free-Soiler. People will simply clam up.) Besides, many of the conversations I've had with fellow search-committee members have taken place casually, in the mode of saying "what did you make of that writing sample?" to a colleague as we head to the men's room or to the bar. Otherwise, everything else looks fine. I especially like point 4, since I regard all questions in the humanities as unsettled, and have often complained about the academic mode in which people write, "as Foucault has shown...." After all, this ain't mathematics, and we don't deal in proofs. "As Foucault has argued" is a better way to proceed, followed by "Foucault's critics, however, contend...."

Michael[13]

After I eliminated the tenure clause, I sent an e-mail to the American Association of University Professors with a copy of the text and asked for their support or comment. There was no response.

At the time, the Academic Bill of Rights was strictly a proposal directed to university administrators and faculty. It was not then my intention to take it to legislatures in any form. Although the public had a legitimate interest in the operation of state universities and community colleges, I had always leaned to the libertarian side of conservative issues and was mindful of the dangers that legislative oversight entailed. Moreover, I was excited by the prospect that, with Egan's support, the sixty-nine campuses of the State University of New York might adopt the proposal. I was certain that if this happened other state university systems would follow.

Although I had secured their endorsement of the text, the three liberals declined to join a formal committee to support the bill, no doubt because it was associated with me. I succeeded in gaining the endorsement of one left-wing academic, Phil Klinkner, a government professor at Hamilton College in upstate New York, and subsequently Dean of Students at Hamilton. But Klinkner was the only one.

When Egan first saw the bill, his reaction was enthusiastic, and he explained to me how he was going to pass it through his Board of Trustees, specifying the precise committee he would assign to accomplish the task. But the weeks passed and nothing happened to move the agenda or fulfill his promise. Eventually I connected this inaction to a political situation I had glimpsed at my first meeting in the undertones between trustee Candace de Russy and the others present, but the implications of which I hadn't appreciated at the time.

From the moment de Russy was appointed a SUNY trustee in 1995, she had revealed herself to be an active proponent of university reform.

She had pressed the university to re-adopt the "core curriculum" in western civilization that had been pushed aside by interdisciplinary programs such as Women's Studies, Black Studies, and Queer Studies, and by the demands of their advocates to make classes from these departments "multicultural" requirements for all undergraduates. In 1999, de Russy's proposal was implemented by the SUNY board and a new core curriculum emphasizing more traditional disciplines was adopted. But this produced an adverse reaction from the politically active faculty that resulted in waves of paranoia and resentment that eventually had adverse consequences for my more modest reform. De Russy wrote to me,

> After the resolution was adopted almost all (if not all) of the faculty groups on campuses passed votes of no confidence in the Administration, claiming there had not been proper consultation with "shareholders," that there had been "micromanagement," usurpation of academic freedom, etc. The Governor's Chief of Staff came down on Tom Egan *"What were you thinking of, Tom?"* and from that moment on this regime caved to faculty pressures and almost every substantive proposal to raise intellectual standards was successfully resisted. Provost Salins once said to me, "We have to write off the humanities and social sciences." That about describes this regime's fatalism. It has not in any shape or form taken on the faculty radicals, who have been given everything they want, academically and financially. In return they agree to refrain from causing controversy.[14]

It had already become clear in our conversations that Egan wanted to avoid a confrontation with faculty at all costs. He asked me if I couldn't find some faculty representatives to request the adoption of my proposal.

But thirty years of winnowing out conservatives, along with the intimidating tactics faculty progressives had made routine, ensured there would be no dissenters to step forward. I called Stephen Balch to see if the National Association of Scholars had any members in the SUNY system who might submit a formal request to the board of trustees. He was able to come up with one professor who divided his time between teaching assignments at the University of Buffalo and the University of Heidelberg, and another who lacked tenure and was fearful of the career consequences if he stuck his neck out. And that was it. In the vast educational complex that was the State University of New York, we were unable to locate a single faculty candidate willing to stand up to the Left and sponsor the reform. After months of this futility, I stopped looking.

The political situation at SUNY was even worse than I imagined. The largest teacher union in the SUNY system, representing 30,000 of its employees, was "United University Professions" headed by William Scheuerman, someone of whom I was unaware when I had conversations with Egan, but who was about to become one of the most unprincipled opponents of our efforts. His attitude was reflected in a denunciation which appeared in his union paper. "The Academic Bill of Rights," he wrote, "is nothing more than a quota system for political extremists so they can deliver their right-wing political sermons in the classroom."[15] There was little chance that Egan or any academic administrator would be inclined to risk confrontation with 30,000 of his employees whose leader was prepared to use this kind of rhetoric.

I was aware that my public persona contributed to the problem—not only my conservative profile, but also the racial smears that campus radicals had employed to demonize me during the reparations controversy. The legacy of these attacks made me a poor candidate to lead a campaign for academic reform. On the other hand, if I did not undertake these efforts, who would? Many of the abuses I was concerned about had been documented over decades but with little practical result.[16] No individual or organization had stepped forward in all that time to organize a movement to correct them.

CHAPTER THREE

Devising a Strategy

W HILE WE FINALLY HAD A PROPOSAL FOR REFORM, THERE WAS STILL no strategy for getting it adopted. The SUNY experience showed it was unlikely that any impetus for change would come from within the university community. The conservative campus organizations, as mentioned, were reluctant to pursue an activist agenda and, while providing us with support in the form of sponsorship for my campus appearances, were not about to make the campaign for an Academic Bill of Rights one of their priorities.

At the beginning of the nineties, during the height of the era of campus "speech codes," I succeeded initially in organizing a group called "The First Amendment Coalition" to oppose them. Not a single one of the conservative organizations I approached was willing to get involved in funding a student movement. I managed to hold two campus conferences, including one at Harvard with representation from ten Ivy League campuses, before I had to abandon the effort for lack of resources.

This experience was one reason it took me so long to come up with a practical plan for dealing with academic abuses. Given the immobility (or absence) of crucial actors in the university community, it was obvious to me that students were the necessary constituency to initiate reforms. I had a small organization, and I had to figure out a way to engage students and mobilize them. A solution finally presented itself during a visit I made to the University of Missouri in the spring of 2003.

Identifying a Network

On April 10, I arrived in Columbia, Missouri, where I was met at the airport by a group of College Republicans. They immediately informed me that a biology professor named Miriam Golomb was offering her students academic credits if they would protest my scheduled speech. Golomb had already achieved notoriety among the Republican students for claiming on her academic website that conservatives were genetically inferior to liberals and for inviting left-wing activists to address her biology classes on non-biological issues such as the war in Iraq.

One student had asked Golomb if she would provide credit for attending rather than protesting my speech. Golomb responded, "No, why would I, since I don't like what he has to say? He's a racist." Then she said, "But I will give you twice as many credits if you go to protest." After class, Golomb, who is white, went to the black students' association, which at the university is called the "Legion of Black Collegians," in an attempt to incite the group to protest my appearance. Her appeal failed.[1] Golomb also sent a general e-mail to students over the university web urging them to protest, and devised a leaflet featuring a photograph of me, and calling me "A Real Live Bigot," while accusing me of being "on the payroll of a right-wing foundation."[2]

I was accustomed to malicious accusations from campus opponents, but coming from a faculty member this seemed egregious. The university administration had responded to these assaults, not by reprimanding Golomb, but by increasing the security measures for my event, assigning seven armed guards to maintain order. A lone but determined radical professor had thus transformed my visit from an occasion for intellectual debate into a political confrontation. The college TV station supported Golomb's offensive by running political ads describing me as "an extreme right-wing conservative."

Upon my arrival, my student welcoming committee had intended to take me directly to the hotel where I would be staying, but I told them to take me to the administration offices instead. The president of the university was out of town, but the Vice Chancellor of Administrative Affairs was in and agreed to see me. I asked her if slander was a customary discourse for her faculty. She agreed that the flyer Golomb had sent out, as well as her reported comments, were inappropriate. I also pointed out, to her distress, that these attacks were directed not merely at me but at the students who had invited me. I had come to campus, I said, to talk about academic freedom. In my view this included civility and respect for intellectual differences. The Vice Chancellor assured me that the university supported both principles. I suggested that an apology from Professor Golomb would be appropriate, along with a university statement laying down appropriate guidelines for academic behavior.

My chief concern was the impact Golomb's behavior might have on the students who had invited me. Although I was the ostensible target of her attack, they were its real victims. I would be leaving Columbia in the morning, but the stigma of Professor Golomb's slander would remain with these young men and women and follow them throughout their college careers. They would be known for having invited a "racist" to campus, however absurd the accusation. How could students who did not share Professor Golomb's prejudices feel free to express themselves in an environment where dissent could be so casually stigmatized?

The Vice Chancellor was intentionally vague when I pressed her on actions the university might take. I was not looking to punish Golomb, but to have the university set guidelines regarding academic behavior, or more accurately, enforce those that were already in place. The Vice Chancelleor's tepid response gave me the clear impression that once I left the campus nothing would be done. In fact, the administration did worse than nothing. It embarked on a bureaucratic cover-up, conducting a cursory review of the matter and then dismissing the students' testimonies about Golomb's behavior, while giving her a clean bill of health.

After leaving the Vice Chancellor's office, I gave a couple of local television and radio interviews to promote the evening talk which was scheduled to be held in the business school theater. When I arrived, the 500-seat auditorium was filled to capacity, and the audience, which was about half adults not connected to the university, gave me a standing ovation as I entered. I was introduced by Professor Richard Hardy, who was the faculty adviser to the College Republicans and the only conservative on the Missouri faculty the students could identify when I asked them.

I began my lecture by describing who I was and thereby answering Golomb's malicious charge that I was a racist. I described how I had marched in my first civil rights demonstration in 1948, when I was nine years old, and had continued my efforts for racial equality ever since. I repeated our slogan, "You can't get a good education, if they're only telling you half the story," adding, "even if you're paying $8,000 a year"—which was the tuition to attend the University of Missouri. I talked about "the longest, most successful blacklist ever conducted in America," by which I meant the exclusion of conservatives from university faculties. I also talked about the political harassment of conservative students and the creation of a "hostile learning environment through the open hostility that professors expressed for conservative figures and conservative ideas, and the need for more representation of "under-represented viewpoints," deliberately using the catch-phrases of the Left for maximum effect. I talked about the need for "intellectual diversity."[3]

I concluded by attempting to show the students another way to look at American history, in an effort to correct the negative curriculum devised by their professors. I used the history of African Americans as an example, since the oppression of African Americans was the favorite example the Left used to make its case. I pointed out that slavery had existed for a thousand years in black Africa before a white person had ever set foot there. It had been considered a normal institution and had existed at some time and in every society for three thousand years. Every person in this room, I said, regardless of skin color or ethnicity, was descended from slaves if you went far back enough in time.

The proper way to look at America was not just that it shared in a crime committed by all nations, but that it was a pioneer in ending the crime and a beacon of freedom for all. As a result of America's pioneering efforts in expanding the realm of freedom, blacks in America were now the freest and richest black people anywhere on earth including all the nations ruled by blacks themselves. I pointed out that America's secretary of state was black, and that its national security adviser in the war on terror was black. In conclusion, I said that America was a country to be proud of, and that it was important to learn to be proud of America, because "if you are not proud of your country, you cannot defend yourself."

This flourish resulted in another standing ovation. It was personally encouraging, particularly after the attacks by Golomb, but it also made me consider the contrast between the support I had received in this remote city in the American heartland and the hostility I encountered from university faculties wherever I went.

As the conservative students were taking me back to my hotel, one of them introduced me to her roommate, a member of the Legion of Black Collegians who had attended my talk. As a black student in an educational system that had become hostile to America's past, she was the most vulnerable victim of the radicals' efforts. She thanked me for coming and said, "Everything I have been told all my life, has been a lie."

Before I left Missouri, the College Republicans informed me that Rod Jetton, the Speaker Pro Tem of the Missouri legislature, had heard my comments on the radio and had called to ask if there was anything he could do to help. They also informed me that, as an undergraduate nearly twenty years before, Jetton had attended a campus event at which I had spoken. The event had been organized by Morton Blackwell's Leadership Institute, one of the campus conservative groups with which I had become acquainted. The students themselves knew Jetton because of their volunteer work on his and other Republican legislators' staffs.

Thinking about this and the network it represented on the flight to my next engagement, I began to see exactly how I would organize my campaign. It occurred to me that if I shifted my attention from university administrators to legislators like Jetton, and sought resolutions endorsing the Academic Bill of Rights, and if I were able to organize the Republican students who usually invited me to campus into a cohesive movement, I would have the force for reform I was looking for.

When I returned home, I began to work on creating a new organization, which I called Students for Academic Freedom, whose main task would be to persuade universities to adopt the Academic Bill of Rights. Because of my experience with the SUNY system, I decided to launch a parallel campaign to persuade legislatures to pass resolutions endorsing the Academic Bill of Rights and urging their state university systems to adopt them. I had extensive contacts among Republicans and could easily reach legislators in the state houses. The members of College Republicans whom I recruited to work with me would be perfect for informing legislators about the conditions on their campuses and instrumental in pressing them to act.

Students for Academic Freedom

Because I was aware how closely the Democratic Party was tied to the unions and their interests, I knew that College Democrats would be extremely unlikely to offer a helping hand, and I was comfortable with the fact that the network I was building would be mainly drawn from College Republicans. But this did not mean I was about to abandon the non-partisan goals or character of the campaign, or that we would give up on encouraging liberals and Democrats to join us, however challenging the task might be. Our campaign was—and would remain—about academic rules that were non-partisan and that would serve all students. I was determined to position the campaign as an effort that would defend both liberal and conservative students against faculty abuses and create an educational model that did not discriminate against any viewpoints, regardless of their position on the political spectrum.

It occurred to me that a campaign for academic freedom might be a little unorthodox for the conservative students who would be involved. They were accustomed to accepting their outsider status while complaining about "liberal bias" when left-wing faculty over-reached. This put them in the traditional conservative position of saying "no" to the excesses of the Left and to practices they did not like. There were several things that concerned me about this attitude. First, in attempting to change a situation, it is always better to offer a positive solution. Second, a negative call for ending "liberal bias" looks (or is made to look) like "censorship." It would also be dismissed by claims that the "best remedy for bad ideas is to expose them to the sunlight of better ideas." Of course, conservative ideas were already so conspicuous by their absence in the academic curriculum—or so routinely derided and ridiculed—that from a conservative point of view, there was no chance of exposing bad left-wing ideas to sunlight in a university setting. But the "no" position was still a losing one. By contrast, a movement for "intellectual diversity" had the potential to be a winner, particularly since the idea of "diversity" in ethnic and gender matters had already become a gold standard in university circles.

I didn't like the hallmark phrase of the conservative complaints for another reason. Everyone has a "bias," conservatives included, and there was no way to eliminate one man's bias without instituting its opposite. The real problem we were attempting to address was one of missing diversity. I also didn't like the word "liberal" applied to individuals who were intolerant and who expressed such ill-concealed contempt for the ideas of others. *Illiberalism* was the problem—not "liberal bias."

I needed to explain these ideas to our students so that the campaign could be framed correctly. I wanted to ensure that a chapter of Students for Academic Freedom would not revert to the "no" position and call for the expulsion of leftist ideas from the classroom. To guard against this possibility, and to ensure that all of the campus organizations we created adhered to these principles, I wrote a pocket-sized handbook called *Students for Academic Freedom*.[4] In it, I distilled the campaign into four points:

1. To promote intellectual diversity on campus
2. To defend the right of students to be treated with respect by

faculty and administrators, regardless of their political or religious beliefs

3. To promote fairness, civility and inclusion in student affairs

4. To secure the adoption of the "Academic Bill of Rights" as official university policy

To make sure everyone understood the points—and to insulate the campaign against efforts to misrepresent it—I summarized them in a sentence:
"The campaign is about Intellectual Fairness, Diversity, Civility, Reasoned Intellectual Pluralism, Inclusion and Respect for Intellectual Difference."

I devoted particular attention in the guide book to the issue of faculty
perspectives, distinguishing between legitimate bias, which merely
expressed a professorial point of view, and bias that infringed the academic freedom of students because it was either: 1) irrelevant to the subject matter of the class and not within the professor's professional
expertise; or 2) was partisan advocacy urged with passion in the classroom
making the instructor an adversary of his or her students rather than an
instructor.

To make sure the students understood these distinctions, I provided
answers to questions I anticipated might arise.

Question: Can a teacher express his or her personal opinions and
political views in class? Should professors be denied the right to
give their opinions on controversial issues?

Answer: Professors are citizens and have the right to express
their opinions like everyone else. However, in the classroom they
have a responsibility to stick to the subject matter of the course
and to the field of their expertise.... It is unfortunately not

unusual for professors ... to declare their political affiliations in inappropriate contexts and to invite students who disagree with them to drop their courses. This is unprofessional. Too many professors say proudly, "My teaching is an extension of my politics." This is a violation of the professional responsibility of a teacher.

The handbook warned students not to seize on disagreements they may have with their professors, leaping to the conclusion that their academic freedom had been violated.

Feelings are subjective and can be an unreliable standard of judgment. Feelings alone should not be used as a standard by which to judge professorial conduct. If students feel personally disrespected or abused, it is important for them to disclose their discomfort to the professor. A professor who is honestly presenting his or her subject matter—and not pursuing an agenda of political or religious indoctrination—will be receptive to a discussion of these matters and will take steps to assure students that no personal discourtesy is intended.

It is noteworthy that not once in the course of the academic freedom campaign did any of our critics acknowledge the efforts we made to protect teachers from unjust accusations and to instruct our students to respect faculty even when they disagreed with the students' opinions.

In the pamphlet, I also addressed the question of whether there was a conflict of interest in appealing to legislatures for help "since the principles of academic freedom seek to protect the university from political interference." I argued that there was no conflict in the approach we were taking since there was "a world of difference between asking the legislature to defend principles of academic freedom, intellectual diversity and student rights, and asking them to interfere with universities' proper academic functions."

Legislators had responsibilities to the tax-paying public that supported the state university systems. Among them was the responsibility "to insure that these institutions serve the whole community and not just a partisan political or philosophical faction. If public universities become politically partisan, they act to subvert the democratic process, which is not what their creators intended. It is illegal under state patronage laws to use state-funded institutions for partisan purposes. No one has the right to create a closed political fiefdom at public expense. Such exclusionary practices are the very opposite of academic freedom.... Defending the non-partisan character of public institutions is a responsibility of legislators."[5]

Another section of the guide dealt with the idea that universities had become a "hostile environment" for conservative students and conservative ideas. This was a term of art for feminists who had also incorporated it into law. I liked the idea of using the Left's catch-phrases to oppose its abuses, particularly in a case where the term accurately described the oppressive situation in which conservative students found themselves. But when I sent the text of the pamphlet to Professor Alan Kors, head of the Foundation for Individual Rights in Education (F.I.R.E.) and a noted defender of academic freedom, he strongly objected. The term was a weapon, he said, with which feminists successfully persuaded certain courts that protection of female sensitivities took precedence over constitutional guarantees of free speech rights. I assured him that I had no intention of using the "hostile environment" concept in court or as part of any legislation I would support. But when he insisted that the phrase itself be removed or he would not support our campaign, I readily yielded and it was removed.

Along with the guide, I thought it was important to create a document that would draw attention to the increasingly politicized nature of university faculties and thus dramatize the need for reform. The partisan composition of liberal arts departments was obvious to anyone familiar with a college campus, and was an offense to the principle of pluralism that should have been basic to an educational institution. Yet when I confronted liberals with this exclusion, I was surprised to encounter skepticism and apparent disbelief. Their typical response was that I was inventing a problem that didn't exist. It was apparent to me that some kind of formal demonstration of this obvious fact was a necessary prelude to our campaign.

I enlisted Eli Lehrer, who was then on staff at the American Enterprise Institute, and we put together a report called "Political Bias in the Administrations and Faculties of 32 Elite Colleges and Universities."[6] It took us a while to figure out how to go about demonstrating the political selectiveness of liberal arts faculties, since we didn't have the resources for elaborate scientific studies and wouldn't be able to secure the cooperation of university faculties in conducting them. Eventually, we decided to look at the political party registrations of faculty members who had voted in primary elections. This was a crude measure—and we conceded as much—but given the polarization of the political culture, it could be taken as a reasonable measure of faculty perspectives across a broad range of issues.

We selected party registration for our study because other indices of bias would be highly subjective. The meanings of "liberal" and "conservative" are notoriously indeterminate, reflecting as much the prejudices of the cataloguer as they would the preferences of those being studied. Although the terms "Republican" and "Democrat" may seem inappropriate in the context of academic pursuits, they have the advantage of reflecting the self-identifications of the individuals under scrutiny, and they are clearly identifiable. Moreover the terms "Republican" and "Democrat" can reasonably be said to reflect a predictable spectrum of assumptions, views, and values that affect the outlooks of Americans who finance, attend, administer, and teach at these educational institutions. This is why we chose them.[7]

Our report, released on August 28, showed that the ratio of Democrats to Republicans on the thirty-two faculties was extreme. We reported as much in our study.

> In our examinations of over 150 departments and upper-level administrations at 32 elite colleges and universities, the Center found the following: The overall ratio of Democrats to Republicans we were able to identify at the 32 schools was more than 10 to 1 (1397 Democrats, 134 Republicans). At Brown University the ratio was actually 30-1, at Bowdoin and Wellesley 23-1, at Bates 18-1, at Columbia and Yale 14-1. At four schools—Williams, Oberlin, MIT and Haverford, we could not identify a single Republican on the faculty. In another study I had my office conduct specifically for Colorado, we found that 94 percent of the professors in the social sciences at Boulder were Democrats and only 4 percent were Republicans. Of 85 English professors who had registered to vote, none were Republicans; of 39 professors of history, only 1 was a Republican; of 28 political science professors, only 2 were Republicans.[8]

Our report was followed by others, the most important of which was conducted by Daniel Klein and his associates, using far more sophisticated techniques.[9] These studies revealed the same basic monolith in an environment where the pluralism of ideas should have been a primary value. The data were alarming enough to warrant an effort to address the problem, but instead, there were more scholastic arguments by academics to explain away the facts. When conservative students at Duke University, who had been inspired by our example, published an article showing that conservatives were a rarity on the Duke faculty, the chairman of the philosophy department, Professor Robert Brandon, said: "We try to hire the best, smartest people available. . . . If, as John Stuart Mill said, stupid people are generally conservative, then there are lots of conservatives we will never hire."[10]

While launching Students for Academic Freedom, I hired Sara Dogan, a recent Yale graduate who had worked for Accuracy in Academia, as the national campus director of the campaign. I also put up a website, at www.studentsforacademicfreedom.org, where we posted all our literature, studies, reports, proposals, and media accounts of our activities, and a bulletin board for student complaints. We didn't have the resources to evaluate the complaints. They were there to indicate that students who had what they felt were justified grievances continued to be ignored by their administrators. We invited the professors named by the students to respond to their complaints.

In July, I traveled to Washington to address three conferences and recruit students to organize chapters of our new organization.[11] The conferences were organized by the Young America's Foundation, the College Republicans, and the Association of Legislative Exchange Commissions, a bi-partisan group of more than 2,500 state legislators and administrators who received our proposal warmly. This encouraged me to think that there was still a chance that we could enlist bi-partisan support.

I also dropped in on Al From, the chairman of the Democratic Leadership Council, the centrist wing of the Democratic Party. I told him that on my visits to campuses I had observed how radical the College Democrats, or at least the leaders I encountered, had become. I attributed this to the lack of intellectual diversity on campuses, which had become an echo chamber for the ideas of the Left, pushing the liberal spectrum towards the extreme. I suggested that he had an interest in helping me with my academic freedom campaign. A more diverse intellectual conversation on campus would strengthen the political center. He listened thoughtfully to what I had to say, but nothing ever came of our talk. Nevertheless, by fall we had signed up students from seventy campuses who were willing to organize chapters of Students for Academic Freedom, and we were ready to launch our campaign.

CHAPTER FOUR

The First Test: Colorado

W HILE SARA DOGAN WAS BUSY SIGNING UP STUDENTS, I TOOK STEPS to move resolutions in states where I thought the political balance would favor our agenda. I engaged the services of Brad Shipp, who was working for a political consulting firm, to help me with my legislative overtures and later hired him full time. I contacted Rod Jetton and Peter Kindle, two Missouri legislators who had offered to help, and also Jack Kingston, a congressman from Georgia and the head of the Republican conference in the House. Jack offered to sponsor the Academic Bill of Rights in congress and gave me a contact in the Georgia Senate, Eric Johnston, who said he would carry the legislation there.

Colorado was our first target state. I knew its popular governor, Bill Owens, who had been a conservative student leader and understood the conditions we were trying to change. I had my assistant Elizabeth Ruiz call his office to arrange an appointment in the Denver Capitol. His views leaned to the libertarian side of the conservative spectrum, and I was confident he would be receptive to our goals and would have a feel for the complex issues we were bound to face.

The Legislation and the Attack

When I arrived in his office on June 13, the Governor was cordial and reacted enthusiastically to my proposal. He said he wanted to take the lead on the issue at both the national and state levels. He even expressed a little pique that I had already met with his lieutenant governor and a dozen Republican members of the state legislature. To acquaint them with our proposal, we had arranged a breakfast at the Brown Palace, which is Denver's most celebrated hotel and a favorite meeting spot for its civic leaders.

I left his office greatly encouraged, but was soon to be reminded of the lesson I had apparently failed to learn in my encounters with Tom Egan. *National Review* had recently named Owens America's "best governor," and there was a growing presidential buzz around his name. This translated into caution in his political calculations, and he chose not to play a role in our campaign.

Although I should have known better, I had half convinced myself that the Academic Bill of Rights was unassailable, so perfectly liberal was its design. Americans were committed to fairness, inclusion, and diversity. How could a proposition based on these values fail? This was the focus of the pitch I made to the legislators who attended the breakfast at the Brown Palace. I also stressed the importance of keeping our universities from becoming any more partisan than the Left had already made them, and I emphasized the latent power that Republicans and conservatives had in regard to these issues. Conservatives were the chief private funders of universities and, in states like Colorado where they were a majority in the legislature, determined the public funding as well. How was it possible that conservatives had become such beleaguered minorities on their faculties and their students such harassed minorities? The fact of the matter was that while conservatives funded universities and serviced their needs, they had stayed far away from the curriculum and hiring process—and with good reason. If they ever exhibited concerns in these areas, faculty would respond with cries of "political interference!" and alarms about "academic freedom."

I addressed this concern in my talk to the legislators. In all our documents I had made it clear that our campaign was not an effort to get rid of faculty leftists or leftist ideas. It was a campaign for increased diversity and inclusion. If the legislators understood that our goal was greater intellectual diversity they would position themselves as the angels of academic freedom, and their opponents as its obstructers. The condition for a successful campaign was to embrace the goals of fairness and inclusion, and to avoid making it a campaign against faculty radicals.

For this reason, I had made the first tenet of the Academic Bill of Rights a ban on firing professors for their political opinions. It was a protection for all professors, including radicals, and it was also a protection (or so I thought) for our campaign. Our proposed reform was not about personnel, it was about academic *manners*—an attempt to change the collegiate atmosphere by putting a damper on partisan passions. The idea was to encourage the academic majority, which was not ideological, to open the doors to intellectual influences currently absent from the curriculum or derisively dismissed.

My remarks were well received by the legislators. They had all been students themselves and therefore had first-hand knowledge of the problems I described. John Andrews, the president of the Colorado Senate, was in attendance and said he would sponsor the bill.

Colorado's state legislature, like many others, is a part-time enterprise that only meets during the first six months of the year. Its next session would start in January 2004, which was six months away. To prepare for the continuing campaign, I hired a second year Denver University law student, Ryan Call, who organized chapters on eight campuses and helped me navigate my way around Colorado's institutions and elites. Ryan also organized speaking engagements so that I could promote the campaign. The first one, scheduled for the last day in September, was at Metro State College in Denver.

Two weeks before the speech, and before we had even issued a press release on our campaign, a front page story appeared in the *Denver Rocky Mountain News*, which was designed to blow us out of the water. The story was based on a leak from two interim workers in our campaign. When I hired Ryan and Sara as my staff for the academic freedom campaign, I antagonized two individuals who helped me set up my June meetings in Denver, and who expected permanent jobs as a result. They had taken their grudge to a left-wing reporter at the *Rocky Mountain News* named Peggy Lowe, who embellished what they told her with charges that came from union activists. On September 6, the paper ran her story with the headline "GOP Takes On Leftist Education." This was exactly the story line I had worked so hard to avoid and that the Left would want to see in print. But the report that followed was far worse than the headline.

"Top Republican legislators," Lowe's article began, "are working on a plan that would require Colorado colleges and universities to seek more conservatives in faculty hiring, more classics in the curriculum and more 'intellectual pluralism' among campus speakers." Two of these claims were patently false. The Academic Bill of Rights forbade political hiring, and thus could not require Colorado universities to seek more conservatives. All that it said about the curriculum was that more attention should be devoted to including diverse viewpoints.[1] As if these distortions were not enough, there was a second article by Lowe in the same issue of the paper, which bore the headline "Campus Ideology Under Fire," attacking us through the surrogate of a local conservative think tank, which, in response to our request for help, had created a "Campus Accountability Project" to deal with the issues that concerned us, including the one-sided composition of faculties.[2]

Three days after these attacks, the *Rocky Mountain News* ran yet another story by Lowe in which she reported that Colorado Democrats were denouncing our bill as "McCarthyism."[3] The article began, "Democrats lashed out Monday at a GOP plan to get more Republicans on Colorado's college campuses, calling it academic McCarthyism and quotas for conservatives." The Democratic Senate Minority Leader, Joan Fitz-Gerald, was quoted in the article as calling the bill "affirmative action for conservative Republicans, to get them into universities," and warning, "There is something chilling and troubling about a movement like this. They're going to create a climate of fear in our universities, fear of being the professor who says the wrong thing."

Anyone familiar with our agenda would have to pinch himself to believe that this was actually the attack our opposition was making—and through the "news" section of a major metropolitan paper no less. Nowhere did Lowe's story mention that the very first principle of the Academic Bill of Rights banned affirmative action hiring based on political viewpoints, or that no punishments were suggested (or even discussed) for professors who said the "wrong thing," nor did the bill include such a concept as saying the "wrong thing." The Democrats' attacks were an expression of political paranoia based on Lowe's false report and misinformation fed to them by the left-wing faculty unions.

There was not a scintilla of truth in the claims. We had proposed a bill that was viewpoint neutral, that protected faculty on the Left equally with faculty on the Right, and that was designed to promote academic freedom guidelines liberals themselves had created. But we were being attacked as though we were ideological witch hunters and thought police. The hopes I had that our proposal might be given a reasonable public hearing—let alone garner bi-partisan support—were rapidly disappearing.

In an attempt to counter these distortions, I called the editorial page editor of the *Denver Rocky Mountain News*, Vince Carroll, whom I had met years before, and who had once written a *Wall Street Journal* article about the exclusion of conservative viewpoints from the faculty of the University at Boulder. Carroll was a libertarian, and when I contacted him, he quickly realized that his reporter had made a mistake. On September 9, the surreal media circus was briefly interrupted by an editorial he wrote under the headline, "Tone the Rhetoric Down." Carroll pointed out that the Academic Bill of Rights proposed none of the reforms that its critics were complaining about. "The Academic Bill of Rights," he wrote "advocates precisely the opposite of political litmus tests." To prove the point, the *Rocky Mountain News* also printed excerpts from the Academic Bill of Rights—the first time the public in Colorado had seen the text.

The next day, Colorado's other major newspaper, the *Denver Post*, also ran a fair-minded article about us, written by its education reporter Dave Curtin. The article was accompanied by an interview Curtin conducted with me called "Horowitz Corrects Critics: I Don't Want Quotas."[4] This was a bracing development, but proved to be the last dose of reality—or fairness—that the press in general or the *Post* in particular was going to provide. Four days later, the *Post* ran a lead editorial ignoring what its reporter had written and what I had said (and written), while repeating the canards of the *News* article by Peggy Lowe. It even upped her ante.

The editorial was called "Absurdity In Higher Ed," and began by asking, "when is a quota not a quota?" It answered, "When it benefits Republicans, it seems." According to the *Post* editors, "The same party that's been squawking over race-based college admissions now apparently wants universities to check voter-registration rolls when hiring faculty to ensure more conservatives are added to the ranks."[5] The *Post* editors had simply invented the claim to further their partisan agendas. Or, more likely they had deliberately distorted our study of the composition of faculties to assert that we had proposed using voter-registration roles to balance them.[6] We had done no such thing.

A day later, a regular *Post* columnist named Gail Schoettler, who was also a former Democratic lieutenant governor of the state and a former Democratic nominee for governor, went further off the rails in a piece titled "Mind Police Are At It Again":

> Colorado's mind police are at it again. Now the Republican political leaders, including Gov. Bill Owens, Senate President John Andrews and House Speaker Lola Spradley, want to dictate political ideology at our colleges and universities. They couch this in benign language we can all accept. But their intent is far from benign .... Republican officials met last June with David Horowitz, a conservative who founded Students for Academic Freedom and the Center for the Study of Popular Culture—which isn't about popular culture at all, but is about investigating the political views of college faculty. Horowitz's goal is to force institutions of higher education to hire conservatives who reflect his point of view.[7]

Mind-reading was to become a feature of the attacks in the weeks that followed—which depended on total disregard for what we actually said and proposed in favor of the writer's interpretation of what we allegedly intended. Columnists from the Left—who far outnumbered conservative columnists in Colorado—had a field day spreading similar falsehoods while attacking the idea of quotas which no one had proposed, and which in fact our bill specifically outlawed.[8] A lone conservative columnist, Mike Rosen, countered with a defense of the bill and support for our efforts on his popular radio talk show.[9] But Rosen's commentary was virtually unique, and liberals continued to flood the opinion columns and news pages of the Colorado media, repeating the same false claims about the bill and its contents.[10]

So powerful was the myth the unions and their allies had created, and so determined were our opponents to stick to these talking points no matter how many times they were refuted, that six years later Cary Nelson, the president of the AAUP and a man whom I had debated and confronted over these charges on three occasions, published a book with this claim: "Horowitz's first effort to stigmatize progressive faculty involved efforts to get state-by-state 'Academic Bill of Rights' legislation passed mandating political balance in faculty appointments."[11] Not a single piece of legislation with which we were associated was ever proposed—let alone mandated—such a result.

At the same time that this distortion of our agendas was taking place, the press was also reporting public protests against our efforts organized by our union opposition. At Metro State College, where I had been invited to speak, the faculty union specifically added the Academic Bill of Rights to its list of formal work grievances. At a demonstration organized by the union, their leader, Joan Foster, who was also head of the Faculty Senate, called for an investigation into a "secret meeting" I was alleged to have had with Governor Owens to discuss the bill. The secret meeting had been insinuated in Peggy Lowe's original story and was as mythical as the quotas that were alleged to be embedded in the legislation. Nothing was secret about my meeting with Governor Owens. I had used the front door to gain entry to his office like any other citizen.

Confrontation at Metro State

Two weeks after the *Rocky Mountain News* broke Lowe's initial story, I arrived in Denver to give my speech at Metro State. The Auraria campus was built on the site of a defunct gold mining camp and housed three academic institutions—Metro State University, Colorado Community College, and the University of Colorado's Denver campus. As was frequently the case, the political Left had arranged a preemptive protest of my speech. In organizing this event, the opponents of my bill were illustrating the exact problem it was designed to address.

The leader of the protest was an African American student named Felicia Woodson who was also the Metro State College student body president. "Why was he even allowed to come to campus to speak?" Woodson asked the assembled crowd. To which one heckler responded, "Free speech."[12]

It was one thing for students to think it appropriate to protest a speech they hadn't heard and to call for banning of speakers they didn't agree with. But where were the adults? In fact, they were on the same platform as Woodson, cheering on the protesters. Most prominent among them was Joan Foster, head of the Faculty Senate, and alongside her Jim Martin, a trustee of the University of Colorado. Their presence showed just how confused some educators had become about the nature of the educational mission.

I used the spectacle as material for my talk to the 800 students who gathered in the Metro Student Union to hear what I had to say. "One would expect an educator to encourage students to listen to an invited speaker," I said in my opening remarks. "One would expect an educator to say, 'If you disagree with what you hear, prepare a reasoned and civil answer to it.' That is what an education is about, or should be. It should be about using one's brains, instead of just wagging one's tongue. It should be about learning to use logic instead of simply relying on raw emotions. This is a university, not the *Hannity and Colmes Show*." This last comment drew laughs of recognition.[13]

To illustrate what I meant by a politicized academic culture, I described a tour of the campus I had made before my speech with the students who invited me. Among our stops, we had visited the University of Colorado Political Science Department, which was a narrow hallway flanked with offices whose doors and bulletin boards were covered with newspaper clippings and cartoons.The only time students needed to visit such offices was when they were seeking guidance from their professors. Perhaps they were falling behind in their grades and wanted advice that would aid them in improving their scores. Perhaps they were contemplating a professional career and wanted guidance in pursuing it. Whatever the reason, they were seeking a counselor—someone they could trust. Yet every bulletin board in this narrow hallway and as many as two-thirds of the wooden office doors that students would have to open in order to enter were plastered with anti-Republican, anti-Bush, anti-conservative cartoons and newspaper columns. There were no anti-Democrat or anti-Left postings that I could detect—not that I would find these any more appropriate. In my view, as I told the audience, no political propagandizing, from whatever perspective, is justified in such a setting.

"What impact would such messages have on the students who come for help?" I asked. "How would a leftist student feel if he saw a cartoon on his professor's office door referring to anti-war activists as traitors? Would the liberal professoriate be comfortable if such political vitriol directed at

their side of the political debate were posted on the office doors of virtually every faculty member in the political science department? Did professors feel so impotent in their own lives that they were compelled to
badger a captive audience of students who were looking to them for guidance? Did it not occur to them that inflicting their partisan viewpoints on
students whose education had been put in their trust was a form of harassment and unprofessional? If they did not recognize these issues in this
departmental setting, how would they conduct themselves in the classroom? How would they see to it that their students got an education in
their areas of professional expertise and not simply an indoctrination in
their political prejudices?

To underscore my point, I recalled the time President Reagan was shot
by a would-be assassin. When he was brought to the hospital and placed on
the operating table, and just before he was put under the anesthetic, he
looked at his doctors and said with a wink, "Are you gentlemen Republicans
or Democrats?" We can all laugh at the president's humor, I said, because
we trust our doctors to follow their Hippocratic oaths and to treat us equally
without regard to our political affiliations or religious beliefs. It is a basic
professional responsibility to do so. But while we can still trust our doctors
to be professional, we apparently can no longer have the same confidence
in our teachers. And that, I said, was the serious problem for universities and
for the country that the Academic Bill of Rights was created to address.

When I finished my remarks, I was given a reasonably generous reception by the large audience, followed by a vigorous question and answer
session. I knew that I had changed no faculty minds, and that little would
be done to rectify these problems in the absence of outside pressure. However, I didn't fully understand how bad the situation was until a day later
when I received the following e-mail from a student who had come to hear
my speech:

Dear Mr. Horowitz

I am a Special Forces soldier, former Marine, and currently a student at Metro State University. Today I heard your speech. While your views are not popular ones, I do feel they are the right ones, in regards to making the American education system more equally represented in view points. I have witnessed first-hand the abuse of a teacher's political rhetoric in classes at Metro State. As a service member I have served in Panama (Just Cause), Gulf War I, Somalia, Bosnia, Kosovo, and most recently Afghanistan and Iraq.

I have been told in classes by my professors that my views are aggressive, violent, racist, and offensive in regards to my opinions on world politics. I have even been told that the wearing of my uniform in class is inappropriate, and offensive.

My current duties are with the state of Colorado as an OCS (officer candidate school) instructor. I try to conduct myself as a professional at all times whether in or out of my classroom. The service has taught me to respect others, and their opinions, no matter what they are. I try to instill that in my students. Yet as a student myself in college I am forced to endure hours of political rhetoric about past wars which I have fought in, and lost friends in.

Most recently I had to endure hours of liberal rhetoric on how badly this administration is doing in the war on terrorism, and how the troops in Iraq are the reason other countries hate us. These viewpoints come from individuals who have never served their nation in a time of war, or had friends die in these wars they talk so knowledgeably about.

I endure this attitude and grief in order to get my degree. Like other veterans I am trying to improve myself by going back to school and getting a higher education. Or as I like to call it, a low education. I am proud of my veteran brothers who take on the challenge of raising a family and improving their knowledge base. I feel we have only learned not to spit on our vets as was done during the Vietnam War. We have not learned that their opinions may hold merit, or that maybe they have some real world knowledge we can learn from.

I would like to thank you Mr. Horowitz for trying to improve the system and make it a better place to learn and not just a liberal indoctrination program. On behalf of all my veteran friends serving and not, I would like to say you have our support, and thank you.

SFC Mark J. Elrod

USARMY 10TH SFG(A)Special Forces.

After my departure, the President of Metro State, Ray Kieft, rejected Joan Foster's request to have my "secret" meeting with Governor Owens investigated. But he went on in an e-mail to say that "the Academic Bill of Rights is not needed on Metro State's campus because the Board of Trustees has committed to academic freedom in [its] personnel handbook and policy manual."[14]

This was far from the case. Here is what the Metro State manual actually says about academic freedom:

> The Board of Trustees endorses the principle of academic freedom, which means the freedom to discuss academic subjects fully, engage in research and publish the results of research, and write or speak as citizens without fear of institutional censorship or discipline, provided individuals do not represent themselves as speaking for the College."[15]

Even the casual reader will note that this statement is about academic freedom for professors, not students. There is not a word in its text that would protect students from the abuses of faculty who use the university as a political platform and substitute indoctrination for education. Or who would describe their students serving in the military as "offensive" for wearing their uniforms in class. This was why the Academic Bill of Rights was necessary, and the Metro State president's curt dismissal of the problem and disingenuous presentation of the facts proved to be all too typical of administrative responses to our efforts, and was the reason why I was more firmly convinced than ever that legislative action was necessary to jump-start the process of reform. It was not going to be initiated by administrators such as President Kieft.

A Temporary Victory

Shortly after my appearance at Metro State, the Majority Leader of the Colorado Senate, John Andrews, proved good to his word and sponsored legislation for an Academic Bill of Rights. Senator Andrews' bill was framed as a resolution to express the sentiments of the Senate rather than as a statute with sanctions. The idea was to encourage college administrators to address these problems. The Andrews resolution would provide a model for all our subsequent legislative efforts regarding the Academic Bill of Rights. The fact that it was a resolution and not a statute reflected both the political realities (since state legislatures were cautious in their approach to such matters) and my own preferences. I did not think that government could provide a satisfactory solution to these problems. It could only be a catalyst for a solution that the universities themselves would have to institute.

In December, Andrews held a one-day hearing into the state of affairs on Colorado campuses. A *Rocky Mountain News* story summarized the testimony: "A group of college students told legislators Thursday they have been subjected to ridicule, hostility and bad grades because of their conservative views. They complained about conservative authors being left off required reading lists and about professors who talk in class about their own liberal politics and who deride conservative politicians."[16]

But as the legislature began its spring session, it became apparent that the Republicans' one vote majority was not going to allow Andrews to get the bill through. The caricature of our agendas had created a solid Democratic opposition, and Andrews realized that he could not count on the Republicans to be as unified in their support. A decision was made to turn the bill over to Representative Shawn Mitchell in the hope that he could secure its passage in the House.

In February, a hearing was held to discuss the legislation and to try to get it through the Education Committee, the first step in the process. This proved to be a dramatic turning point in our favor. At the hearing, Ian Van-Buskirk, a student from the University of Colorado, stated that he was testifying to represent "students who have been told, 'This is my classroom. I've got my Ph.D., therefore I decide what views are appropriate. I do not want your right-wing views in my class.'" The student told legislators that he hoped that passage of the Academic Bill of Rights would have a "chilling effect" on this type of abusive behavior. As Ian stepped away from the microphone, he was immediately confronted by a man who was subsequently identified as Professor Tim Gould, a professor of philosophy at Metro State. In front of over 100 witnesses, the professor jabbed his finger at the student and said in a loud voice, "I got my Ph.D. at Harvard. I'll see your f—ing ass in court. Then we'll see a chilling effect."[17]

Representative Keith King, a member of the committee, immediately volunteered, "Sir, you are the very reason we need this bill." Shawn Mitchell amplified the point, "If he behaves that way in a hearing room, in front of legislators and the press, imagine how powerful he feels in his own classroom." Even the liberal press was shocked by Gould's outburst. "Gould gave the Republican-dominated General Assembly the ammunition it needs to impose a legislative gag order on teachers at state colleges and universities," commented the *Denver Post's* Jim Spencer in a hyperventilating and once again factually challenged column titled "Prof's Mouth May Silence All Educators."[18]

When the hearing was concluded, Shawn Mitchell's resolution passed the Education Committee in a party-line vote of 6 to 5.[19] It was sufficient to convince university administrators they had a problem on their hands. After the vote was announced, Representative Mitchell was contacted by the most important educator in the state, University of Colorado president Elizabeth Hoffman, who asked Mitchell if he would withdraw the legislation if the state's universities would voluntarily adopt the provisions of the Academic Bill of Rights their regulations did not already cover. Mitchell contacted me to see my response. I told him this was precisely the result we were hoping to achieve. Mitchell then withdrew the legislation.

I had met with President Hoffman the previous September when I came to Colorado to speak at Metro State College. She was an imposing figure brimming with self-confidence, and gave me a cheerful welcome as we sat down for our meeting, presenting me with a University of Colorado jacket for the occasion. "President Hoffman," I said, "you have a problem. Our studies show that 95 percent of your faculty are on the political Left. We are in a war on terror. One of these days, some of your radicals are going to go over the edge and cause an adverse public reaction that will damage your institution." It was two years before Colorado professor Ward Churchill's infamous Internet article referring to the victims of September 11 as "little Eichmanns" caused a national scandal and led to Hoffman's resignation and the loss of tens of millions of dollars by the university in canceled applications and legal fees.[20]

"The American public," I continued, "is fair-minded and will understand that people on both sides of the political spectrum will go off the deep end. What they will not understand is a faculty that is almost exclusively left-wing, and that includes political extremists. If, on the other hand, the university makes a visible effort to include conservative views, even if they remain a minority voice, the public's attitude will be different. If they see a conservative presence, they will accept that the university is a marketplace of ideas and will be more tolerant of radical excesses at the far end of the spectrum." I was quick to point out that I was not asking her to hire conservative faculty. I said the university could insulate itself from attack by embracing the idea of intellectual diversity first by adopting the Academic Bill of Rights, but also by promoting a conservative lecture series, and bringing conservative academics to campus as visiting professors.

President Hoffman listened and then replied, "David, we have no problem here."[21] Not only did she deny that there was a lack of intellectual diversity on her faculty, like President Kieft, she insisted the university already had in place regulations to deal with any academic freedom problem that might arise. She invited me to check them on the university's website. In fact, I had already done so and seen that the references to academic freedom were impossibly vague and, as usual, applied only to faculty. Hoffman's dismissive response re-enforced my conviction that before I could get the attention of the university community I would have to go to legislatures first.

Six months later, this proved to be the case when Hoffman contacted Shawn Mitchell with her offer to implement his bill. A "Memorandum of Understanding" was then signed between the educators and the legislators in which Colorado's state universities pledged to provide academic freedom protections to students, emphasizing that "Colorado's institutions of higher education are committed to valuing and respecting diversity, including respect for diverse political viewpoints." The Colorado legislature as a whole—Democrats as well as Republicans—unanimously adopted Senate Joint Resolution 04-033, commending the university presidents who had joined Elizabeth Hoffman for their leadership and willingness to revise campus policies to provide these needed protections. The Resolution also instructed the administrators to report regularly to the legislature on their progress.[22]

What had produced this dramatic turn of events? Why was Elizabeth Hoffman's attitude towards the Academic Bill of Rights so different in March from what it had been in September before the academic freedom campaign became public? Obviously it was the threat of legislation by the Republican majority in the Colorado legislature. After our meeting in September, Hoffman could not have gone to her faculty and said, "David Horowitz has a wonderful idea to protect our university and reinvigorate its academic standards, and we should listen to him." If she had done that, she would have faced a faculty revolt. Her faculty radicals would have accused her of capitulating to a right-wing conspiracy to subvert the university and turn it over to the conservative thought police.

But now that the legislature had been engaged, she could go to them and say, "That right-winger David Horowitz and the Republicans in the legislature are planning to damage our university. I can save the situation by getting them to withdraw their legislation and allowing us to defend academic freedom in our own way." This was the precise result I had hoped to achieve from the outset: that universities would address the problem themselves. By going to the legislature I had changed the political dynamics inside the university, providing administrators with an incentive to take action and a cover for doing so. This was a significant step forward, but I did not kid myself that the administrators would continue to do the right thing. That would require a lot more attention and pressure from those wanting reform.

Once the Joint Resolution for the Memorandum of Understanding was passed, John Andrews followed up with a call to the presidents of each of the major state universities to appear before a joint legislative committee to report what they had accomplished. The hearing was held at the opening of the fall school term and the results appeared impressive.

Elizabeth Hoffman reported that a task force of students, faculty, and administrators had been appointed to incorporate protections and support for political diversity into the codes and policies of the entire University of Colorado system. During the summer, the faculty senate of the University of Colorado Law School adopted a new binding Rule on Political and Religious Non-Discrimination which included the provision that students would be graded on their merits and "not on the basis of their political or religious beliefs."

Larry Penley, president of Colorado State University, reported that the Fort Collins and Pueblo campuses had revised their policies to protect students from "discrimination or harassment on the basis of . . . religion, creed [or] political beliefs." In addition they had provided instructions to students on how to use campus grievance procedures in the event of a violation of the new policies. These guidelines were published in the 2004–2006 *Course Catalogue,* and according to the testimony were incorporated into presentations given to each student during orientation. The Memorandum of Understanding and the Senate Joint Resolution were published on the webpage of the Colorado State University president along with a letter in which Penley emphasized his personal "commitment to a campus environment that respects the rights of students and faculty to express diverse, and at times, unpopular opinions, [since] that is at the heart of what it means to be a great university." [23]

But our victory was Pyrrhic, as I knew it would be, blocked by the wall of hostility the faculty unions had created in the university community and the Democratic Party. There was no way the campus problems we were trying to address could be dealt with in the absence of a consensus about their existence, along with a broad base of support for the measures that were needed to deal with them. We had achieved neither.

In November, Colorado held elections and Republicans lost control of the Colorado House. As a result, there would be no more legislative hearings to determine if any actions followed the fine words and sentiments, no inquiries to see if students were being informed of their rights or if their grievances were being addressed. I had set out to change the university dynamic by using the legislature to induce administrators to enforce academic standards, and the strategy had worked. But once Republicans lost their majority, the impetus for action was gone, and the *status quo* reasserted itself, rendering the reforms we had spurred impotent, and uninteresting to those in authority.

CHAPTER FIVE

The Opposition

T HE STRATEGY I WAS PURSUING RELIED ON OUR ABILITY TO PUT THE Academic Bill of Rights before the public, which meant stimulating (or if need be provoking) a discussion in the national media and the education press. It also depended on finding support for our proposals in the university itself. Without support from the academic community, no real change could take place. Although the odds were long, it seemed to me that success was possible. Most professors were not ideologues but scholars who should be well-disposed to a reform whose purpose was to revitalize academic standards. Three well-known liberal professors had vetted the final draft of the Academic Bill of Rights and found it unobjectionable. In addition, there was a general institutional unease in the academic world over the continuing excesses of radical professors at a time when the nation was at war.

My next logical step was to seek a dialogue with the American Association of University Professors. Because it had gained generally recognized authority on the issue of academic freedom, it was a force I would have to reckon with. I was prepared to amend the Academic Bill of Rights to satisfy reasonable objections, as my negotiations with Gitlin, Bérubé, and Fish had shown. Consequently, before making the document public, I also sent a draft to Mary Burgan, the General Secretary of the AAUP, asking for an organizational opinion on the text. When I didn't hear back I called the AAUP offices in Washington and asked for a meeting, but there was no response. Six months into our campaign, I made the same appeal to Roger Bowen, who succeeded Burgan as General Secretary. I did so both in e-mail correspondence and in person when I debated him at Wheaton College in Connecticut. I made an identical overture to Cary Nelson after he was elected president of the AAUP in 2006, both in e-mail correspondence and in person when I debated him at an event I hosted in Washington. But while Bowen and Nelson were willing to debate me as adversaries in public, both refused to engage in private discussions that might lead to compromise and possibly even a joint effort to deal with campus abuses, a hope I made explicit when I approached them. Instead, they insisted that that the number of instances in which abuses took place was "minimal" and the problem I sought to address wasn't, in fact, a problem at all.

My decision to seek endorsements from state legislatures for the Academic Bill of Rights was also a sticking point, even though I had made clear I was fully prepared to give up my legislative efforts if the academic community showed an interest in addressing the problem instead of denying its existence. The legislative resolutions I had sought were merely instrumental—a way of getting universities to focus on the problem and take steps towards a solution. It was never my intention to seek government management of universities, as my opponents claimed (and continue to claim). I did not think such an arrangement would be feasible or—more importantly—desirable, as I made clear. My actions in Colorado confirmed these intentions. Once we were able to secure an agreement by university officials to address the problem, we dropped our legislative effort. I felt that reasonable people would understand that.

It quickly became apparent, however, that my optimism was misplaced. On December 3, just two months after the first misleading articles on our campaign appeared, the AAUP issued a formal statement denouncing the Academic Bill of Rights as "a grave threat to fundamental principles of academic freedom."[1]

The statement was issued by the AAUP's prestigious "Committee on Academic Freedom and Tenure." The committee had undergone a dramatic change in the last twenty years as a result of the leftward shift in university faculties following the Vietnam War. "Committee A," as it was called, was now headed by a tenured radical named Joan Wallach Scott, who had been a leading academic defender of convicted terrorist Professor Sami Al-Arian and now emerged as a fierce opponent of our efforts. In public testimony at the academic freedom hearings in Pennsylvania, Scott would claim that "The Academic Bill of Rights recalls the kind of government intervention in the academy practiced by totalitarian governments. Historical examples are Japan, China, Nazi Germany, fascist Italy, and the Soviet Union. These governments sought to control thought rather than permit a free marketplace of ideas."[2]

Disregarding the fact that the bill was modeled on its own classic statements on academic freedom, the AAUP followed Scott's lead, finding sinister omens in subtexts it purported to discover in the document, while attempting to discredit our efforts in the most extreme terms. The expressed goals of the bill—to restore academic standards and *prevent* the establishment of political orthodoxies—were portrayed in the AAUP statement as the opposite: an attempt to *undermine* academic standards and interject extremist orthodoxies into the academic curriculum.

According to the AAUP, the bill's concern to foster "a plurality of method-ologies and perspectives" would require departments of political theory to appoint "a professor of Nazi philosophy."[3]

This was not a plausible reading of the text of the Academic Bill of Rights, which explicitly ruled out political criteria in the hiring or evalu-ation of professors. Moreover, fostering a plurality of methodologies and perspectives was already an established academic practice if the method-ologies and perspectives reflected left-wing concerns. Thus virtually every history and law faculty was careful to recruit a gender feminist in its ranks by design, while English departments normally included deconstruction-ists, post-structuralists, gender feminists, and Marxists. In another bla-tant distortion of a statement in the bill, the AAUP claimed that "the Academic Bill of Rights seeks to transfer responsibility for the evaluation of student competence to college and university administrators or to the courts, apparently on the premise that faculty ought to be stripped of the authority to make such evaluative judgments." There is no such statement in the Academic Bill of Rights, which never mentions courts nor ascribes to administrators any such authority.

The AAUP statement further accused the bill of rights of justifying external control of the university curriculum through its "reference to 'the uncertainty and unsettled character of all human knowledge.'" This was particularly interesting since Michael Bérubé, a prominent AAUP figure, had applauded this clause when I submitted the original draft to him. "I especially like point four," he said, "since I regard all questions in the humanities as unsettled, and have often complained about the academic mode in which people write, 'as Foucault has shown....'"[4] Bérubé, who was shortly be elevated to the leadership of the AAUP, never commented on this key element of its opposition to our efforts.

According to the AAUP the view that knowledge has an unsettled character was tantamount to denying that there is any such thing as knowledge, "If there is no such thing as knowledge, then unqualified administrators and judges would be allowed to interfere in matters traditionally left to teachers." This was a non-sequitur since the Academic Bill of Rights did not deny the existence of knowledge nor an expertise based on it.

The AAUP statement continued, "This premise [that the character of knowledge is unsettled]...is [also] antithetical to the basic scholarly enterprise of the university, which is to establish and transmit knowledge." But the Academic Bill of rights does not deny the existence of knowledge. It merely says that there are many unsettled questions particularly in the humanities. Moreover, the view that there are unsettled questions is actually the foundation of academic freedom, something the AAUP statement (contradicting itself) affirms: "Academic freedom rests on the principle that knowledge is mutable and open to revision...."

The AAUP then attempted to absolve itself of the contradiction by inserting ideas into the Academic Bill of Rights that aren't there. "Although academic freedom rests on the principle that knowledge is mutable and open to revision," it says, "an Academic Bill of Rights that reduces all knowledge to uncertain and unsettled opinion, and which proclaims that all opinions are equally valid, negates an essential function of university education." But the Academic Bill of Rights proclaims no such things—neither that *all* knowledge is unsettled nor that *all* opinions are equally valid.

The AAUP's attack on the Academic Bill of Rights was so uncompromising that it included a blistering attack on a principle I had taken directly from Stanley Fish's article calling for neutrality of academic institutions, "Save the World On Your Own Time." The AAUP began by describing the implications of this requirement as "truly breathtaking."

> Academic institutions, from faculty in departments to research institutes, perform their work precisely by making judgments of quality, which necessarily require them to intervene in academic controversies. Only by making such judgments of quality can academic institutions separate serious work from mere opinion, responsible scholarship from mere polemic. Because the advancement of knowledge depends upon the capacity to make judgments of quality, the Academic Bill of Rights would prevent colleges and universities from achieving their most fundamental mission.[5]

But the clause referred to was not about "faculty in departments [or]…research institutes" and did not challenge the authority of individual professors to make judgments of quality about scholarly issues. The clause was quite clearly designed to prevent academic *institutions* and "professional societies" from passing *organizational* resolutions on controversial political issues, such as global warming or the war in Iraq, which divide their members.[6]

On December 5, two days after the AAUP issued its statement, I published a point by point rebuttal, which was ignored.[7]

The AAUP's War

The AAUP's rejection of an argument based on its own most celebrated principles was revealing, although the lack of attention to our side of the argument by the education press meant that few would notice. Because of the prestige the AAUP had earned in the past when its leaders were genuinely liberal and supported these principles, the distortions of our position by the radicals who now spoke in its name affected the entire media coverage of our campaign and the debate over the Academic Bill of Rights.

The AAUP's statement was in effect a declaration of war on our efforts. The origins of this war were described by an AAUP official named Marcus Harvey in an article that appeared in the AAUP book, *The Academic Bill of Rights Debate.* "The AAUP's west coast office," Harvey wrote, "had been monitoring Horowitz's efforts since the release of a study early in 2002 that purported to show that America's faculty members were politically and culturally out of sync with the American public."[8] Harvey was referring to a survey I had commissioned by pollster Frank Luntz that was published a year before we formally began our campaign. The Luntz study, which showed that university faculties in the Ivy League had become increasingly monolithic in their political and social outlooks, was called *Inside the Mind of An Ivy League Professor.*

Harvey continued, "From the moment that we heard that first salvo, several of us on the AAUP's national staff anticipated where Horowitz's campaign was headed and began working to decode the seductive rhetoric of diversity and inclusiveness being cynically deployed by Horowitz and Co." The employment of the term "decode" is instructive. It explains why the AAUP's response to the Academic Bill of Rights was so prone to distortion and searching for meanings that were alleged to be grossly misrepresented by the text. As radicals, the AAUP leaders regarded me as a political adversary in advance of anything I actually said about academic freedom or measures for academic reform. "Horowitz was waging political war and not engaging in serious scholarship," Harvey asserted. Yet, it was the AAUP who had mischaracterized their opponents as a threat to academic freedom and who had refused to sit down and negotiate the issues.

Although the AAUP had identified me as their enemy, they did not think I was the author of the campaign I had launched. In a recent book, the current AAUP president Cary Nelson describes the "true nature of [my] enterprise" as "a well-funded collective project of the Right," and concludes, "In the power dynamics of contemporary culture, Horowitz is only a pawn in their game."[9] This attitude echoed the AAUP position as described by Marcus Harvey—that I was merely the agent of the neo-conservative right: "A significant strategy in the neo-conservatives' war, has been to develop a populist stance and lament the disjunction between academicians and the common people."[10] As evidence of my alleged collusion in this war, Harvey cited a statement Luntz had made in his introduction to the poll he conducted for us. "Not only is there an alarming uniformity among the guardians of our best and brightest minds," Luntz wrote, "but this group of educators is almost uniformly outside of mainstream, moderate, middle-of-the-road American political thought."[11]

While Luntz may have formulated the results of his poll in terms of a disjunction between elites and masses, this was not my point of view. I don't recall ever having lamented the fact that professors were "outside of mainstream" opinion. Academic professionals are by nature an intellectual elite, and one would expect no less. Besides, our quarrel was not with the perspectives of professors, but with their professional conduct. The Academic Bill of Rights and the academic freedom campaign were not weapons in a neo-conservative war. If they were, our campaign would not have been ignored by the principal neo-conservative organs and institutions, and I would have received substantially more resources and support.

To "decode" and de-legitimize my efforts, the AAUP enlisted Graham Larkin, an art instructor at Stanford and a friend of Marcus Harvey's who was soon elevated to the position of state-wide AAUP vice president. In an article widely circulated on the Internet, Larkin characterized me as "an ultra-conservative intellectual" and "the brains behind the mischie-vously-named-and-crafted Bill of Rights," which he described as "a doc-ument which co-opts post-modern ideas on the situated nature of truth... to counter-act what Horowitz depicts as the stranglehold of pro-gressive politics on university campuses."[12]

The Academic Bill of Rights contained no post-modernist allusions.[13] As a viewpoint neutral document, the bill could *not* be aimed specifically at progressive politics on university campuses, as Larkin falsely claimed. As a document designed to restore academic standards it was antithetical to all ideological strangleholds on university campuses, from whatever quarter they originated.

Notwithstanding the facts, Larkin presented my agendas as an attempt to *impose* an orthodoxy—the exact opposite of what the bill of rights intended, which was *prevention* of the imposition of orthodoxies. "Despite all his mollifying talk of freedom and fostering diversity," Larkin said, "it is clear that Horowitz would just *love* to see knowledge policed." How was this clear? As evidence, Larkin cited an article I wrote objecting to the posting of political editorials and cartoons on faculty office doors. "And [Horowitz] knows how to get [thought-policing] done," he claimed. "Wit-ness the recent *Chronicle of Higher Education* article in which he takes deep offense at the UC-Denver political-science department for having 'office doors and bulletin boards... plastered with cartoons and state-ments ridiculing Republicans.'"[14] But questioning whether it was appro-priate for professors, to whom students looked for guidance, to post political statements on their office doors was hardly tantamount to call-ing for the creation of a knowledge police.

I had had extensive experience with the *ad hominem* tactics of the cam-pus Left. But even that unpleasant experience did not prepare me for the cynical manipulations and crass slanders of academics such as Larkin and the other AAUP critics of our campaign. In April 2005, a second Larkin broadside appeared in the influential educational journal InsideHigherEd.com under the title "David Horowitz's War On Rational Discourse." In the article, Larkin referred to me as a "liar extraordinaire" and as his "rabid opponent" and treated the academic readership to passages like this:

> [Horowitz] believes you should drown your political opponents in a steady stream of bullshit, emanating every day from newspapers, TV and radio programs, as well as lavishly funded smear sites and blogs. He also thinks you should go on college lecture circuits where you can use incendiary rhetoric to turn civilized venues into the Jerry Springer show, and then descend into fits of indignant self-pity when someone responds with a pie to your face.[15]

Larkin ascribed to me "Horowitzian techniques ranging from cooked statistics, race-baiting and guilt by association to editorial foul play and baffling logorrhea," and urged his audience to observe "the tide and eddies in an unending stream of bullshit," in order to "extract any number of dangerous lies."

Larkin accused me of lying about the three liberals who had vetted the Academic Bill of Rights.

> In the course of our exchange [on a local PBS show], Horowitz spewed a lot of the usual BS, but he also floated some audacious lies. For instance he tried to convince readers that his conservative-funded bill—basically just a guileful attempt to sanction the FOX News agenda in the nation's universities—was actually a non-partisan document with intelligent academic backing. To

bolster his case, he tried to make us believe that three "left wing" professors (Todd Gitlin, Michael Bérubé, and Stanley Fish) and one avowed libertarian (Eugene Volokh) actually told him that they didn't mind the bill.

Larkin claimed to have "debunked that lie (simply by asking the four professors what they thought about the bill)." But what Larkin asked the four professors was not what they thought of the contents of the bill, but whether they supported the *legislation* inspired by the bill. I had never claimed that Bérubé, Fish, Gitlin, or Volokh supported *legislation* even in the toothless form of resolutions that I had sponsored. What I did claim was that they found the actual text of the Academic Bill of Rights satisfactory, and they had.[16]

The fact that InsideHigherEd.com would publish such a gutter assault was indicative of the direction in which the opposition against the Academic Bill of Rights was heading. Larkin's article appeared at a moment when the opposition's smear campaign had just moved into high gear as a result of an incident in Colorado connected with our efforts.

The Case of the Colorado Exam

The "Memorandum of Understanding" agreed to by both houses of the Colorado legislature had called for a progress review. In September 2004, Senate president John Andrews conducted one. "Some follow-up is timely as the new school year begins," he told the *Rocky Mountain News*. "Just this month, we've heard about a Marxist instructor at Colorado State University berating a young woman veteran, a law professor at the University of Colorado saying Republican students are racists and Nazis, and a Metro faculty member telling her class that conservatives can't think. Such incidents may be unavoidable, but legislators will want to know how the universities are handling them."[17]

Among the four university presidents appearing before the Andrews committee was Kay Norton of the University of Northern Colorado. In her testimony, Norton referred to an incident that our opponents would soon turn into a *cause célèbre* and use to stigmatize me and our campaign. "Actually last year," Norton said, "a young woman did raise a question about what she thought was an inappropriate examination question. I referred her to our procedures, she followed them, and I'm pleased to report to you that the original version of what would have been an inappropriate examination question proved not to be what was actually on the examination, and so the process worked."[18]

We had become aware of the student's complaint through one of our Colorado volunteers, Erin Bergstrom. The student was afraid to have her name made public, and it was never revealed. She had complained about a failing grade—or what she regarded as a failing grade (the actual grade was also never disclosed) on a final exam in a criminology class. The exam was given in May 2003, two months after the war in Iraq began, and the student told Bergstrom that one of her exam questions required her to "Explain why George Bush is a war criminal." She told Bergstrom that she had answered the question instead by explaining why Saddam Hussein was a war criminal and had been given a failing grade by her professor.

We had our volunteer, Erin Bergstrom, write a formal account of her conversations with the student, which was published on our website.

My name is Erin Bergstrom. I am a 45-year-old businesswoman and free-lance writer. I am also a student at REGIS University. In the 2003–2004 term I was a volunteer activist for Students for Academic Freedom. I interviewed students on several differ-

ent campuses regarding their first-hand experiences with academic bias and discrimination. In November, 2003, a young man
told me about a woman at the University of Northern Colorado
who had a distressing experience in one of her courses. He contacted her, and she agreed to talk to me. She and I talked over the
phone on several occasions, and I also met her at the Greeley
campus. I found her to be a warm and personable young woman.
She is articulate, and seems intelligent and sincere.

I have my original notes from our first conversation. I interviewed her for more than an hour. She described her criminology
professor, and how he asked her and her classmates to describe
why President Bush is a war criminal on an exam. She did not
believe that her test question was fair or reasonable. She was not
willing to dishonor her President—someone she greatly admired.
Instead, she wrote why she considered Saddam Hussein to be a
war criminal. The professor gave her a zero on her test. She was
an 'A' student, so she formally appealed, but was not able to
change her grade.... She said: "I just kept thinking if I took it
higher someone would make it right. None of them did anything.
The school just kind of pushed it under. They said that I just
needed to move on ... I love this university, but I am angry, and
disappointed."[19]

The student pressed on, however, and was finally able to get a formal
adjustment of her grade. This was exactly the kind of abuse our campaign
was designed to correct, which is why I included it among the cases we
were using to illustrate our concerns. I had referred to the case in several
articles, but it did not become a target of attacks until I testified in support
of the Academic Bill of Rights at legislative hearings in Ohio, where

Senator Larry Mumper was sponsoring Senate Bill 24, based on the Academic Bill of Rights. I testified before the Education Committee on March 15, 2005, and used the Colorado incident as one example among others.

> It is not an education when a final examination contains a required essay on the topic, "Explain Why President Bush Is A War Criminal," as did a criminology exam at the University of Northern Colorado in 2003.[20]

Even before the Ohio hearings began, the local press was hostile to our efforts. A headline in the *Cleveland Plain Dealer* informed readers about the legislation in this fashion: "Legislator Wants Law to Restrict Professors, Political and Religious, Political Discussions Targeted."[21] Both accusations were false, but they reflected the views of the powerful coalition that had been assembled to oppose the bill. On March 3—two weeks before hearings on the bill—the AAUP sent out a memo to all its members in Ohio that warned, "Our academic freedom is under attack. The national campaign for an 'Academic Bill of Rights' has made its way to Ohio in the form of Ohio Senate Bill 24. The bill would, among other things, outlaw 'persistent' discussion of controversial topics."[22]

This was flatly untrue. A clause in the Senate bill did prohibit the introduction of "controversial matter . . . *that has no relation to the course's subject of study and that serves no legitimate pedagogical purpose"*—quite different from "outlawing" controversial topics. Moreover, the sentence in the bill was itself taken nearly verbatim from the AAUP's own classic statements on academic freedom, which is why the academic freedom provisions of Ohio State, the largest of Ohio's public universities, included the precise formula as part of "The Rules of the University Faculty of Ohio

State University." There it was stated as a "responsibility of teachers to...
(5) refrain from persistently introducing controversial matters that have
no bearing on the subject matter of the course..."[23]

It would be hard to imagine more damning proof of the AAUP's bad
faith in misrepresenting the Academic Bill of Rights than this cynical
attack on its own principle. The evident purpose of all the AAUP's attacks
was not to argue the issues but to destroy the credibility of our campaign.
Our opponents seized on the case of the Colorado exam to accomplish this.

On the same day the AAUP sent out its memo attacking the Senate bill,
a column appeared in the *Cleveland Plain Dealer* under the byline of an
AAUP professor named Mano Singham. Singham's column was about the
Colorado student, whom he characterized as "the poster child for the
nationwide movement that argues that college faculty are liberal ideologues who will go to any lengths to stifle opposing (i.e., conservative)
views and thus indoctrinate students to think like them."[24]

Singham was not content to challenge our interpretation of the incident, but claimed it had been invented out of whole cloth. This followed the
standard opposition script, claiming that we had invented the problems we
sought to address. Singham's column was titled "That Liberal Fiend Can't
Be Found," and claimed that the student and her exam did not exist.

> I decided to track down the professor to ask what the full story
> was. And this is where things started to get interesting, because
> the professor seems to be more elusive than the scarlet Pimper-
> nel.... I called the acting head of the political science depart-
> ment, the dean's office and the provost's office at the University
> of Northern Colorado and asked them if they knew anything
> more. They had never heard of this story and were all surprised
> to hear that they were supposedly harboring this fiend...."[25]

The Colorado student wasn't our "poster child" as Singham claimed. We had posted hundreds of examples of this kind of harassment. The identification of the professor as a liberal was more political spin. Our reforms were viewpoint neutral, and we had never characterized this professor as a "liberal," let alone as a "fiend." There were plenty of conservatives and Republicans who had strong moral objections to the war in Iraq. We were not objecting to the exam because it required a *liberal* answer to a controversial question. We were objecting to it because it required a *single* answer to a controversial question.

Two days after the column appeared, the left-wing website "Media Matters" ran an article accusing the general press of repeating "unsubstantiated Horowitz tales of anti-conservative bias on campus," giving the Colorado case as an example. It was followed by an InsideHigherEd.com feature titled "The Poster Child Who Can't Be Found," picking up on Singham's malicious attempt to stigmatize our campaign.[26] The article was written by InsideHigherEd.com's editor-in-chief Scott Jaschik, who reported that "a number of blogs and columns have noted in recent days that neither the student nor the professor can be found." Jaschik quoted an academic blogger who was speculating that Horowitz had "been caught up in an urban legend that he can't let go of."

In writing this article, Jaschik was being coy and not a little disingenuous. He had already investigated the story and knew very well that the student and the professor existed, and that I was the target of a campaign whose sole purpose was to discredit our efforts. The next day, he published a story called "Tattered Poster Child" in which he used the information he had uncovered to suggest that even though the student did exist, I still had invented the case.

Jaschik's investigation of the facts was limited to interviewing the university's public relations representative, Gloria Reynolds, and asking her for the school's official account. He did this without bothering to check whether what she told him was an administrative cover-up to protect the university from further embarrassment. He made no attempt to speak to our contact Erin Bergstrom, who had interviewed the student who by now was too frightened to talk to anyone.

Jaschik presented his new indictment to the academic readers of InsideHigherEd.com this way:

> Over the last week, a number of bloggers have questioned whether the student really exists. But just because that question has now been answered in the affirmative does not mean the controversy is going to fade. Because while a Northern Colorado spokeswoman acknowledged Monday that a complaint had been filed, she also said that the test question was not the one described by Horowitz, the grade was not an F, and there were clearly non-political reasons for whatever grade was given. And the professor who has been held up as an example of out-of-control liberal academics? In an interview last night, he said that he's a registered Republican.

We had not presented the case as an example of "out-of-control liberal academics," and the fact that the professor, whose name was now revealed to be Robert Dunkley, was a Republican was completely irrelevant, except as a pretext for making us look bad.[27] The university's claims that the grade was not an "F" and that there were non-political reasons for it were deceptive. The university's spokesperson was never specific about which grade she was referring to—the grade on the exam or the exam question, or the grade for the course. When our office called to try to get an answer from her, she refused to provide any particulars "on advice of university legal staff."

But the distinction was crucial. Although the student was unable to change the grade on her exam, her appeal of the final grade was successful, and she received a "B" for the course. The fact that she was able to get her grade changed undermined the university's cover story that there had been no problem, which is why the university spokeswoman concealed it. Later, the student wrote an explanatory note to our staffer Ryan Call explaining her own understanding of what happened. "I did fail the final exam," she wrote, "at least that is what I was told, however, based on Dunkley's and the school's comments you never really know what is truthful. It has always been my understanding and my story that I got an 'F' on the exam but a 'B' in the class. I dont think Dunkley disputed that, but he is such a manipulative person you never really know."[28]

Gloria Reynolds' claim that the exam question was "not the one described by Horowitz" was also misleading because Dunkley had destroyed the original exam—itself a violation of university rules. Having destroyed the exam papers, Dunkley had to reconstruct the exam questions to present them to the official inquiry into the student's complaint.[29] It was in this reconstructed form that the controversial exam question was produced by the university's spokesperson, Gloria Reynolds.

The reconstructed wording was altered slightly from what the student had told Bergstrom, but even its new version clearly violated the academic freedom standards we were concerned about—and in exactly the same way. The reconstructed exam question was, "Make the argument that the military action of the US attacking Iraq was criminal." How was this different in substance from what the student had claimed? If the war was criminal, so was the commander-in-chief who had ordered it. In either version the question required students to take the professor's point of view on a controversial issue.

Moreover, the university's grievance committee had adjusted the student's grade on appeal. Why would they have done that if not, as the student claimed, because of the inappropriate nature of the question on the exam? This was itself a crucial fact concealed by the university authorities, by Jaschik, and by our other critics.[30]

If Jaschik and the AAUP had been genuinely interested in the issue of academic freedom, they would have acknowledged that abuses existed and focused their disagreements on the question of how they were interpreted and how we proposed to remedy them. Instead, their entire agenda was to discredit me as the academic freedom campaign's spokesman, to attack my credibility by stigmatizing me as a "liar" and "loose with the facts."

To set the record straight and refute the false claims made by Singham and the others, I summarized the evidence in an article which I called "The Case of the Colorado Exam."[31] I submitted the article to Jaschik, who refused to print it—no explanation offered—and also refused to post a correction of the false claims he had published. Jaschik did agree, on the other hand, to provide a link to the article when I published it on my website. This had no effect on the reputation I was getting in the liberal press of being factually challenged and brazenly dishonest.

By now, I was an urban legend. This legend held that I had made up the problem of faculty abuses, and my campaign was a solution for which there was no problem. It would have been politically untenable for the AAUP or InsideHigherEd.com and my other critics to call students liars, so it was convenient to call the person who brought attention to their complaints a liar instead. On academic websites and in educational media venues such as InsideHigherEd.com and *The Chronicle of Higher Education* I had become typed as an unreliable witness. It had become widely accepted that nothing I reported could be trusted. This was a more effective means of thwarting our campaign than confronting the issues or dealing with our arguments. It was also a tacit acknowledgment that the case we had made was in fact unanswerable.

I was of course hampered throughout this episode by the reluctance of the student to come forward. The reasons for this, as reported by Erin Bergstrom, provide some clarity:

> This young woman allowed me to begin using part of her story in December, 2003, and it received nation-wide exposure. In March of 2004, she asked me to stop using it. I presented some of the positive benefits if she was to go completely public with her story, but she decided against this. She recognized the value of speaking out about this issue, but was afraid to be in the public spotlight. She was afraid that it might somehow hurt her chances of getting into law school. She said that she wanted to move on with her life, and just put it behind her. In our conversations she expressed the type of ambivalence that I have often heard in other 18- to 22-year-old conservative students—or even students who are much older. They want to stand up for their rights, but they are easily intimidated. They are afraid of possible negative consequences, such as ridicule, contempt, lower grades, or missed academic opportunities. They are uncomfortable in the role of whistle-blower, or protestor. The students want to believe their authorities will respond in an honorable way, and will present a just solution. So even if professors and administrators are unreasonable or self-serving, students will still talk about wanting to please them, and act in a loyal manner.[32]

Having initially approved the Academic Bill of Rights, Michael Bérubé had emerged as one of its chief and most unprincipled opponents (a reversal he never bothered to explain). A year after the dust had settled on the Colorado case, Bérubé, who was now an AAUP national council member, published a book which was well-received in the liberal press and was substantially an argument against our campaign. It was called *What's So Liberal about the Liberal Arts?* and was an attack on what Bérubé called the "anti-academic Right" and an extended argument in defense of the academic *status quo.*

In his book, Bérubé offered the Colorado case as a model of how our campaign operated. Bérubé explained,

> [It] involved a student at an unnamed Colorado college who was allegedly compelled to write an essay on why George Bush is a war criminal, and who allegedly received an "F" when she turned in an essay on why Saddam Hussein is a war criminal instead. Horowitz wrote about this case in his online magazine *Frontpagemag.com* on December 5, 2003 … [In Horowitz's telling] it is a cautionary tale about academic liberal bias so virulent as to punish innocent students for failing to impugn their President during a time of war. The only problem with the story is that it is false; no such essay was required, the professor in question was a registered Republican, and the student did not receive an "F."[33]

Bérubé then quoted at length the misleading article "Tattered Poster Child," which Scott Jaschik had written and never corrected. My opponents had created a loop of misrepresentations designed to prove that I was "fact-challenged" and my accounts of academic abuses were fictions, which was played non-stop and never changed.

CHAPTER SIX

Intellectual Diversity

ALTHOUGH OUR CAMPAIGN WAS SET BACK BY THE RELENTLESS ATTACKS, we had achieved considerable success in our most difficult task—drawing attention to the problem of classroom indoctrination and also to its solution in an Academic Bill of Rights. Our success was largely due to our strategy of seeking legislative action. Legislatures in a dozen states were already considering resolutions on behalf of the Academic Bill of Rights, which we were making our own efforts to publicize.[1] This triggered alarm among unions in states across the country, prompting hundreds of articles about the Academic Bill of Rights, many of them op-ed columns written by our opponents. The negative attention given to our campaign also spotlighted our complaints which might have otherwise remained obscure.

Because the coverage made our proposals the topic of heated conversations in faculty lounges and university offices across the country, professors became more mindful of their responsibilities in the classroom. But there was also a downside. The legislative measures gave our opponents the opportunity to misrepresent our efforts. In Ohio, for example, faculty senates throughout the state had followed the ACLU's lead, calling the legislation "chilling" and claiming that it involved "serious and unnecessary restrictions," while in fact it merely quoted word for word the text of the American Association of University Professor's own statement on academic freedom.[2]

The relentless distortion of our agenda was so politically driven that no amount of effort to correct the facts or blunt the *ad hominem* assaults could counter them. Nonetheless, I opened my testimony before the Ohio Education Committee with an ecumenical offering, "Ohio Senate Bill 24...is not about Republicans and Democrats, liberals and conservatives, left and right. It is about what is appropriate to a higher education, and in particular what is an appropriate discourse in the classrooms of an institution of higher learning."

I elaborated on this statement with a passage from the 1915 AAUP Declaration, which had warned faculty against "taking unfair advantage of the student's immaturity by indoctrinating him with the teacher's own opinions before the student has had an opportunity to fairly examine other opinions upon the matters in question, and before he has sufficient knowledge and ripeness of judgment to be entitled to form any definitive opinion of his own." My remaining testimony was entirely devoted to a discussion of the academic process, along with a correction of the misrepresentations of our agenda that had preceded these hearings.[3]

When my testimony was over, the first Democratic legislator to question me, Teresa Fedor, ignored everything I had said and proceeded to attack me personally, using a dossier provided by the teacher unions. It purported to show that I was the leader of a right-wing plot with hidden agendas and was funded by sinister "right-wing" foundations. Her line of questioning into my funding and motives was so unusual in such proceedings—I was testifying about educational policy and was not on trial—that one of the Republicans on the committee objected and the chairman asked her to withdraw her question.

In point of fact, my funding was modest compared to that of the ACLU and the unions who opposed the legislation and whose budgets exceeded half a billion dollars annually.[4] The resources available to me were provided by the contributions of 40,000 individuals, while foundations, whatever their character, contributed less than 10 percent of the total. Moreover, as I have already pointed out, there was no concerted right-wing campaign to support our efforts or take up the Academic Bill of Rights as a cause. No other conservative organization had joined us in our attempts to pass this bill or any other. The campaign had begun and remained our initiative alone.

These union attacks were ultimately successful in blocking most of our legislative initiatives. If legislation had been our goal, our campaign could be said to have failed. But that wasn't the case. The purpose of the legislation was always to focus public attention on a serious problem in order to induce university administrations to seek a remedy. In *this* agenda we were making some progress. Even professors who feared and despised us were now forced to deal with the issues we had raised. An article in InsideHigherEd.com describing a panel on how to deal with classroom controversies at an annual meeting of the American Sociological Association reported, "Horowitz was for much of the discussion the elephant in the room that no one was talking about."[5]

Intellectual Diversity at Georgia Tech

While we had come a long way, we were still making no progress in getting the university community to take concrete steps towards reform.

Consequently, nine months into our campaign, I tried a new tack based on the diversity policies the Left had instituted in previous decades.

It was ironic that the very academics who were now claiming that our legislative resolutions represented unwarranted intrusions into the academic process had previously welcomed massive political intervention in the form of federal mandates about sexual harassment and ethnic discrimination. Multi-million dollar bureaucracies had been created within universities to comply with these mandates. Contracts had been signed which allowed government officials to decide who universities could hire, what salaries they could pay, who they could admit as students to their institutions, and even what kind of statements teachers could make in the classroom. [6]

In the 1990s, under Clinton appointee Norma Cantu, the Department of Education aggressively pursued perceived violations of its diversity mandates with a $50 million budget and 850 staffers and lawyers. Cantu's department took on more than 4,000 cases in a single year without protest from the academic organizations that were now conducting an open war against the very modest Academic Bill of Rights.[7] Because they enforced prejudices held by the faculty Left, these government interventions were tolerated and even encouraged, despite their infringement of academic freedom. Although I was not a supporter of this government intrusion, they prompted me to think about the ways in which an existing diversity template universally accepted by the academic community could be put to advantage in regard to the problems that concerned us. At the very least, it would reveal how serious the university was when it came to living up to its stated principles about diversity.

Ruth Malhotra, an honors student at Georgia Tech University, had come to us with a case that provided an opportunity to test such a strategy. Malhotra had been forced to drop a public policy course required for her major after telling her professor, Georgia Persons, that she would be attending an event sponsored by a conservative group. In a written memorandum, Malhotra recounted the facts in her case: "I told the professor that I would miss one day of class because I would be in Washington D.C., and asked if there was anything I needed to do in advance. When asked why I was going to D.C., I replied, 'to attend the Conservative Political Action Conference.' Professor Persons responded, 'Well you're just going to fail my class.'"[8]

In the following weeks, Professor Persons proceeded to return Malhotra's papers and exams with failing grades even though Malhotra was a Dean's list student and had received "A" grades in her public policy classes previously. In classroom discussions, Professor Persons, who was African American, made her contempt for students who disagreed with her point of view abundantly clear, referring to them as "rich white kids that grew up in privilege," and inferring that people from the South were ignorant and dumb. When students dissented from her opinions, she often told them, "You are ignorant."[9]

When one frustrated member of the class complained, saying that he didn't appreciate having his professor laugh at students who disagreed with her opinions, Persons told him, "I don't laugh at you. I may ignore you and I may snicker, but that's only because you don't know anything." On one occasion, Persons told Malhotra, who is Filipino, "You are not an individual, you did not make it here on your own, but because of society." On another occasion, when Malhotra defended President Bush's economic policy, the professor reprimanded her, "You don't know what you're talking about. George Bush hasn't done anything for you. He's too busy pimping for the Christian Coalition."[10]

At the end of one classroom session, Malhotra made an effort to reason with Persons, suggesting that the class would benefit by discussing different points of view rather than by having them ridiculed. Persons replied, "This class is unique because it has [my] liberal ideas in it . . . and you don't like me because I am not a white, male Republican."

Persons' behavior provided a troubling example of our academic concerns. When the Georgia Senate held hearings on the Academic Bill of Rights in February 2004, we invited Malhotra to testify about her experiences.[11] The following day, Malhotra received her first test back with a failing grade. She immediately made an appointment with Diana Hicks, chair of the Public Policy department, who met with her on March 5 and expressed her "deep concern" over what Malhotra had reported and promised to find an "appropriate remedy."[12]

On March 22, the Academic Bill of Rights passed the Georgia Senate by a vote of 51 to 4. The following day, the *Atlanta Journal Constitution* published a story about Malhotra on the front page of the Metro section. It was called "Students Fight Alleged Political Prejudice."[13] Other Atlanta media quickly joined the discussion, including AM radio talk show hosts Kim Peterson, Martha Zoller, and Neal Boortz.

The university administration was furious—with Malhotra. On March 24, she was summoned to a meeting by her academic advisor, "who tried to intimidate me, and said that 'because of your actions here, people will no longer trust you.' She also said that this story was bad for recruiting new students and that I was to blame. She tried to pressure me not to do any more interviews." The next day Malhotra was called in by the Dean of Students, "who advised me to make a statement saying that the *Atlanta Journal Constitution* report had misquoted me and misrepresented my situation. She also told me specifically to not go on Neal Boortz's radio show."[14]

Malhotra was not about to be intimidated. The following day, March 26, she went on the air with Boortz to discuss her case. Following the show, the Department Chair, Diana Hicks, suggested that Malhotra withdraw from the class. The deadline had passed for dropping courses without forfeiting the tuition and without having the withdrawal noted on her academic record. Malhotra submitted a "Petition to the Faculty" to seek relief from the tuition penalty and to have the black mark on her record removed. As a result of the hearings and the publicity around her case, she felt she had strong support from public officials, her Christian community, fellow students and alumni, but no support from the school itself.

In April, I went to Atlanta to deliver a speech. While I was there, I made a point of meeting with Malhotra. I then took her to see the education advisor to Governor Sonny Perdue and also to the office of Dr. Stephanie Ray, the Diversity Dean at Georgia Tech. Stephanie Ray, who was also African American, was entirely sympathetic and supportive of Malhotra. I began by asking her whether it wasn't the case that a goal of diversity programs such as hers was to teach students respect for "the other." She agreed that it was. I asked her if she would take up Malhotra's case and see that she was not penalized by having a permanent notice on her record or by forfeiting the tuition funds she had paid for the course, because she had been forced to drop it. Ray assured me she would do this, and she did.

This sequence of events confirmed my belief that there was good will inside the university if enough attention was focused on these issues and enough pressure was brought on universities to do something about them. It could not be left up to outside organizations such as mine. If there was to be a remedy for these problems, it had to come from inside the university and include formal grievance procedures for academic freedom complaints and a significant effort by the administration to provide students with information about their right to academic freedom.

Testing the Waters

One result of the Malhotra incident was that it confirmed my supposition that many of the problems we were concerned about could be promptly addressed if universities would simply incorporate "intellectual diversity" into their existing diversity programs. Diversity offices and personnel were multi-million dollar line items in university budgets, with diversity deans and staffs to administer them. Although I was not an enthusiast of these programs, being familiar with their abuses, I was not a purist either. If this institutional arrangement was acceptable to universities, I was pragmatic enough to work with the system. The intervention of Stephanie Ray at Georgia Tech had demonstrated that the university bureaucracy could be used to good ends.

There was another attraction in a diversity strategy: it wouldn't have any particular association with me. The teacher union attacks had made me so toxic in academic circles that even those who sympathized with the liberal sentiments of the Academic Bill of Rights were unwilling to support any measure I had devised. Incorporating the reform in existing diversity mandates would circumvent this problem.

Consequently, I decided to test the sincerity of university administrations by asking them to apply the diversity principle to intellectual issues. I had my national campus director, Sara Dogan, draft a letter with such a request. Sara, a Yale alumna, suggested we use the Yale diversity statement as a model for our proposal. In the summer of 2004, Sara and my other staffer, Brad Shipp, sent a letter to eighty-eight college presidents in seven states, including Georgia:

> Dear President [X],
>   I am the national campus director of Students for Academic Freedom, a student organization dedicated to promoting aca-

demic freedom, intellectual diversity, and civility on American university campuses. We currently have chapters at over 135 institutions of higher learning nationwide.... I would like you to consider incorporating intellectual, religious and political diversity in your institution's diversity mandate. This would protect all students at [NAME OF SCHOOL] from being treated as second class citizens and would promote a climate of intellectual.pluralism that is essential to a liberal education.

In her letter, Dogan included the text of a statement she had drafted based on the policy at Yale. She added the adjectives "intellectual," "ideological," and "political" to the "cultural," "ethnic," and "religious" diversity categories in the Yale template. She asked each president to adopt the following paragraph in their existing diversity office mission statements, and to do so before the fall term (the words in italics represent Dogan's additions to the existing university policy):

This office was established with the premise that expanding diversity within the university enhances the educational experience and furthers the understanding of the entire scholarly community. An atmosphere of civility and mutual respect towards difference is indispensable to the educational process and enables the free interchange of ideas that is the basis of scholarship. These differences may be immutable or changeable, cultural, ethnic, religious, *intellectual, ideological or political*. Each of these qualities is integral to the identity we form as individuals, and all are essential to creating a vibrant university community composed of individuals with unique perspectives and backgrounds. The university must commit itself to a policy of inclusion, respect for difference, and fairness, and guarantee the same rights and freedoms to all its members to ensure the fullest degree of intellectual freedom.

The proposal seemed reasonable enough, but even though we followed up the letters with phone calls, we received only two responses from the eighty-eight schools—a blunt indication that without legislators directly interceding, our concerns would simply be ignored.

One of the responses we received was a "thank you" from the president of Emory University, the other a more extensive reply from Robert McMath, a vice-provost at Georgia Tech who had handled the administration's inquiry into the Malhotra case. We had copied the letter we sent to McMath to a number of legislators from Georgia including congressmen Newt Gingrich and Jack Kingston, U.S. Senator Zell Miller, and state senators Eric Johnston and Bill Hamrick, perhaps encouraging his reply.

McMath's letter, which was sent on July 8, was formally polite, but its gist was that we needn't have bothered. "For over ten years," McMath wrote, "Georgia Tech has published in our catalog a 'Statement on Human Relations' which is similar in tone and substance to the document you shared with us."[15] Thus, in McMath's view, Georgia Tech had an existing policy that already dealt with our concerns. It was one of two standard replies made by representatives of the academic community throughout our campaign—first, "there is no problem"; and second, if a problem should happen to arise we already have policies to deal with it.

On July 19, Dogan replied to McMath, attempting to correct his account of Georgia Tech's standing policies. "While the [Georgia Tech Statement on Human Relations] notes the importance of religious diversity," she observed, "it fails to mention intellectual or political diversity. If this Human Relations statement were sufficient to protect students from discrimination, then why have a campus office dedicated to diversity issues at all?"[16]

Dogan was referring to the Georgia Tech diversity office headed by Stephanie Ray, which the university had obviously created because it felt that the "Statement on Human Relations" did not sufficiently cover such concerns. Our complaint was that the template of the diversity office did not include intellectual or political diversity. If I had not visited Georgia Tech and asked Stephanie Ray to intercede, the diversity office would not have been involved, because intellectual diversity was not part of its mandate.

The very existence of a diversity office suggested, as Dogan pointed out, "that the university deemed such an office (and the regulations and enforcements that accompany it) to be necessary to protect students from discrimination due to their race, sex, or other protected characteristics. We are merely asking for equal treatment for students who may be disrespected or harassed on the basis of their intellectual, political, or religious beliefs, and ask that these characteristics be explicitly mentioned in the mission statement of the Office for Diversity."

In his reply to this letter, McMath reiterated his satisfaction with the *status quo*, but did not respond either to Dogan's question or to her request. What he said was this:

> You disagree with my affirmation that our Statement on Human Relations is similar to your sample statement on diversity. (Note that I said "similar" not "identical.") The right to disagree intellectually, and the ability to do so in a civil fashion, goes to the heart of the principles of academic life that I believe we share. We at Georgia Tech are always interested in improving the ways we operate. In that spirit I am forwarding your letter and statement to the faculty co-chair of our Diversity Forum, a student-faculty

group charged with promoting diversity on our campus, from
which our Statement on Human Relations was issued several
years ago.[17]

In her response, and out of frustration with McMath's failure to respond
directly to her points, Dogan brought up the Malhotra case:

> I was pleased to hear that you are raising the issue of intellectual
> and political diversity on campus with your student faculty com-
> mittee. However, I was somewhat disappointed in your letter.
> The situation at Georgia Tech is difficult to understand given
> what you say is your commitment to intellectual diversity and
> fairness. You have a professor who is extremely vindictive
> towards conservative students, who has ridiculed their beliefs in
> class, and even gone so far as to fail them for their conservative
> views. The same professor accused a student of being "ignorant"
> for having a positive view of the economic policies of the President
> of the United States. This class, moreover, was a required course
> for the student's major. Since to my knowledge nothing has been
> done to discipline this professor and no apology has been made to
> the student in question, it is difficult for an outside observer to see
> what practical support your administration is actually giving to the
> idea of intellectual diversity in your classrooms.

This provoked McMath to a testy reply that effectively ended the dialogue:

> Georgia Tech has a history of commitment to protecting intel-
> lectual and personal freedom. Our policies related thereto have

been in place for more than two decades.... Thus I am disappointed by your dismissal of our policies, the questioning of our motives, and your extended monologue on the shortcomings of a university with which you have little knowledge. That is indeed unfortunate, as it cheapens the dialogue and insults the intelligence of all of those whom you draw into it....

Ignoring our active role in the Malhotra case, McMath continued:

Your letter restates the essence of a six-month-old newspaper account of a student disagreement with a professor on campus. We took the allegations seriously and as soon as it was directly reported to us, we launched a thorough investigation by an independent reviewer to determine if there was indeed political, religious, or cultural discrimination in this particular classroom. After interviews with the principals and more than half the students in the class, the investigation found no credible evidence of any such discrimination.[18]

In fact, the university's investigation displayed the very deficiencies in the existing policy that we were seeking to remedy. There were no provisions at Georgia Tech protecting students' academic freedom rights. Consequently, McMath's investigators focused exclusively on issues of ethnic diversity and on whether equal opportunity laws had been violated by Professor Persons. They did not inquire into whether she had behaved in an unprofessional manner that violated Malhotra's academic freedom.

Following the investigation, Malhotra had been given a "Summary of Findings" by the Public Policy Chair, Diana Hicks, and Pearl Alexander, the Chief Investigator from the Office of Diversity Management. In a

statement regarding these findings, Malhotra wrote: "On close examination, it was clear that my core concerns and the fundamental issues have
not been addressed, and the matter remains unresolved. It seems that in
the investigation, the focus shifted from addressing the real problem of the
academic environment, to the issue of Equal Opportunity policy, which
was never a part of my grievance."

Malhotra continued:

> I believe that the school (Georgia Tech) has circumvented the
> central problem and needs to provide further clarification. The
> chief investigator (Pearl Alexander) concluded that, "There is no
> conclusive evidence or indication that discrimination resulting
> in an Equal Opportunity policy violation was committed by Dr.
> Persons." I am not familiar with the legal terminology; however
> this seemed to be a very narrow clause and one that did not
> address the core problem. When I discussed this at the meeting,
> school officials essentially admitted its weaknesses; the investi-
> gator stated that, "academic environment is a separate issue from
> Equal Opportunity," and went on to say, "it was not possible to
> address the academic freedom issue with the limited amount of
> information and time constraints, so we focused on the Equal
> Opportunity policy."[19]

This was the bureaucratic universe we were dealing with, in which our
concerns about academic freedom did not formally exist, in which administrators pretended that they did, and in which the professor unions were
determined to see that they never would.

Despite the failure of university officials to address the academic freedom issue in the Malhotra case, we managed to achieve a positive out-

come. Thanks to the attention given by Georgia legislators, the publicity provided by local and national media, the efforts of Dean Stephanie Ray, and the concerns of faculty members associated with the Georgia Tech Diversity Forum, including the public policy chair Diana Hicks, a significant (but in the end only temporary) change in the academic environment was achieved. A new teacher was assigned to the public policy course from which Malhotra had withdrawn. Malhotra re-enrolled and received an "A" for the course.

In an account of her experience, Malhotra reported:

> The professor truly generated spirited discussions, encouraging students to articulate their beliefs and defend the reasoning behind their positions. It was evident that personal ideology would not interfere with one's academic performance. The way the professor presented the material was very relevant, as there was emphasis on the basic foundations and connecting it to current issues/examples. There was a very diverse group of students in the class from different backgrounds and experiences, and the professor allowed and encouraged each one to express themselves individually whether through their presentations or general class discussions. She also offered words of affirmation and constructive feedback for improvement, which is to be appreciated.[20]

The improved atmosphere was not limited to the public policy department.

> I am very encouraged at the change of atmosphere I've noticed in my humanities classes (Public Policy and International Affairs), with many professors paying particular attention to the

issue of academic freedom and the need to encourage diverse thought in discussions. There is a marked change and the progress is definitely evident in the classroom. . . . In my Political Philosophies class, the professor devoted an entire segment to discussing the concept of academic freedom and intellectual diversity in the classroom. She even made Horowitz' "little red book"[21] on the Academic Bill of Rights required reading for the segment, distributing them to the entire class of about 90 students. (Thanks to Students for Academic Freedom for providing these!) Although the professor is a self-professed "liberal feminist" and does not agree with Horowitz and the Academic Bill of Rights, she did a good job of presenting both sides of the issue and encouraging student discussion on the topic. It was encouraging to see that so many students were passionate about this issue and recognize the need for balance and accountability. The fact that academic freedom is recognized as a critical issue is in itself encouraging, as one year ago you would probably not hear issues like this being discussed on campus.[22]

We had won a battle, but it involved no structural reform. The fact was we were still losing the war. Without an institutional change—without formal university support for students' academic freedom—there was little chance that other students facing politically motivated or ideologically hostile teachers would be able to find redress in the university system.

CHAPTER SEVEN

A National Victory

O UR CAMPAIGN AMONG STUDENTS WAS NOT WITHOUT ITS SUCCESSES. We had signed up volunteers across the country and established chapters on over a hundred campuses, encouraging each of them to press for the adoption of an Academic Bill of Rights. This had proved to be an uphill struggle, because student governments were dominated by the political Left, and campus radicals were actively supported by faculty. Moreover, the campus Left were able to create and fund many more organizations than conservative students. Their inherent advantages were reinforced by the ferocity of the campaign the unions had incited against us. In order to support a liberal document requiring instructors to assign texts on more than one side of controversial issues, our students had to withstand attacks that stigmatized them as "McCarthyites," "extremists," and opponents of free speech. I was always impressed with the students who took up this cause. At Brown University, the student government adopted a version of the Academic Bill of Rights. Although it was watered down to secure its passage, the adopted version included important provisions including one which read, "The obstruction of invited campus speakers, destruction of campus literature, or any other effort to inhibit the civil exchange of ideas should not be tolerated."[1] Other schools that passed our bills included East Carolina University, the University of Texas San Antonio, Georgetown University, Bowdoin College, Tufts University, Brooklyn College, Bates College, Middle Tennessee State University, Pennsylvania State University, Wichita State University, the University of Montana, Occidental College, Utah State University, and the University of Wisconsin-Superior (where it was initially passed, then retracted because of certain language issues, with the proviso that it would be adopted later). At Princeton University, the Academic Bill of Rights was passed in a referendum of the entire student body.

On the other hand, the opposition was largely successful in frustrating our efforts, even when we were gaining ground. When student legislators attempted to pass the Academic Bill of Rights at Brooklyn College, the university administration disbanded the student government. Protests from students, alumni, a few faculty, and lawyers representing the Foundation for Individual Rights in Education (F.I.R.E.) forced the University to retreat from its legally untenable position. David French, a noted First Amendment lawyer and president of F.I.R.E., commented at the conclusion of the case, "While we are pleased that Brooklyn College has reinstated its duly elected student leaders, it is appalling that the administration was so fearful of true academic freedom that it took such extreme steps to derail the democratic process."[2] But the administration's draconian move had sent a powerful message to students about the administration's attitude towards such measures and essentially rendered the student government's new code ineffective.

In one bizarre but illustrative turn of events, the student legislator who introduced the bill of rights at the University of Montana was charged with "plagiarism" by the leftists in student government for "copying" our document, so that we were forced to write a letter giving him permission to use our text.[3] The student legislator had not initially disclosed the fact that it was our initiative, having deduced—correctly—that it would not pass if this information was known. When the left-wing student senators discovered its authorship, they were unhappy at being "duped" into supporting a "Right-wing cause" and consequently initiated the plagiarism charge. Jason Mattera, the student who introduced the bill at Roger Williams University in Rhode Island, had to defend himself from a similar accusation.[4]

The limited authority of student governments and the hostile attacks from student leftists effectively precluded any attempts to enforce the rights and made our victories only symbolic. Our greatest success took place in Maine where Nathaniel Walton, the student body president at Bates University, was able to get our bill adopted and then, with the help of Bowdoin student Daniel Schuberth, to organize a statewide academic freedom campaign. The two succeeded in persuading the Maine Republican Party to put the Academic Bill of Rights into its official party platform. But again there were no practical results, since the reform we were seeking ultimately had to be the work of the academic community itself.[5]

The Ward Churchill Affair

Amid these successes and frustrations, events were unfolding at two universities thousands of miles apart, which brought the problems we were trying to highlight to the attention of the American public. When I had met with University of Colorado president Elizabeth Hoffman a year earlier, I had warned her about the dangers to her university posed by its radical faculty while the nation was engaged in a war with terrorists.[6] I had suggested then that a damaging incident was bound to take place, and in January 2005 it did.

The scandal involved an Ethnic Studies professor named Ward Churchill at the University of Colorado, who had been invited to speak at Hamilton College in upstate New York. Churchill was the tenured chairman of his department at Colorado and a well-known speaker on the campus circuit. He had written a series of books characterizing America as a "genocidal" nation, comparing it to Nazi Germany and urging armed revolution. Among his "academic" titles were, *A Little Matter of Genocide: Holocaust and Denial in the Americas 1492 to the Present* (2002); *Fantasies of the Master Race: Literature, Cinema and the Colonization of the American Indians* (1992); and *Struggle for the Land: Native North American Resistance to Genocide, Ecocide and Colonization* (1993).

As an academic resume in the contemporary university, this was—sadly—not exceptional, and the invitation to Churchill would normally have gone unnoticed by university officials. The faculty committee at Hamilton that had extended the invitation was actually headed by professors who had personal ties to the Weather Underground, a terrorist group that had bombed the U.S. Capitol in the 1970s.[7] As Churchill's speaking date approached, the committee was already under fire for hiring a visiting professor named Susan Rosenberg, who was a convicted Weather Underground terrorist. Rosenberg had participated in the robbery of a Brink's armored car in Nyack, New York, in which three officers were killed. She had been given a 58-year sentence, but subsequently received a pardon from President Clinton.

Initially Rosenberg's appointment caused no concern for the Hamilton administration, but a student at the school named Ian Mandel was upset enough to protest. Mandel had grown up in Nyack, and had to pass a memorial to the officers slain in the Brinks robbery every day on his way to school. "Every day of my life until I left for Hamilton, I drove by the memorial to officers Brown and O'Grady located about one mile from my house," he recalled when he was invited to tell his story to the media.[8] Alerted by Mandel's protest, New York police officers staged a protest of their own at a New York fund-raiser for the school. The adverse publicity prompted university administrators to withdraw the offer to Rosenberg and put restrictions on the faculty committee's ability to invite future speakers. One outstanding invitation, however, was left untouched. That invitation was to Ward Churchill.

Churchill's university speeches had caused no stir in the past, but because of the Rosenberg episode, one Hamilton faculty member was on guard and turned up an article Churchill had written three years earlier praising the terrorist attack on the World Trade Center. The article was published the day after the attack, and was titled "Some People Push Back: On The Justice of Roosting Chickens." It contained this passage: "Let's get a grip here, shall we? True enough, [the victims of September 11] were civilians of a sort. But innocent? Give me a break. If there was a better, more effective, or in fact any other way of visiting some penalty befitting their participation upon the little Eichmanns inhabiting the sterile sanctuary of the twin towers, I'd really be interested in hearing about it."[9]

The article was perfectly consistent with the themes of Churchill's "scholarly" work over the previous ten years. It argued that America, like Hitler's Germany, was dedicated to the extermination of minorities. Therefore, the "civilians" who comprised its "technical core," the inhabitants of the World Trade Center, were in fact Nazis—cogs in a machine that churned out mass murder. In Churchill's view, there was no better way of punishing them for their participation in the workings of America's imperial—and genocidal—economy, than killing them in their place of work.

Even when attention was brought to Churchill's article, there was no particular concern among Hamilton faculty and administrators. Then another student named Matthew Coppo stepped forward. Coppo had lost his father in the World Trade Center in the September 11 attack. He appeared with his mother on FOX News channel with anchor Bill O'Reilly, who commented that that hateful comments such as Churchill's "should not be rewarded by any sane person." Hamilton's president promptly withdrew Churchill's invitation.

When the story became national news, Colorado's governor Bill Owens reacted by demanding that university officials fire Churchill. A chorus of academic defenders rallied to Churchill's cause, including the American Association of University Professors, which responded with an official declaration of support. The AAUP invoked "the right to free speech and the nationally recognized standard of academic freedom in support of quality instruction and scholarship."[10]

The claim that Churchill's rant about America's Nazi core reflected "scholarship" was absurd and reinforced our concerns about academic standards. On the other hand, the free speech issue was real. To clarify our own position on academic freedom and to underscore our concern for the freedom of ideas, I wrote a column for the *Denver Rocky Mountain News* defending Churchill's First Amendment rights.[11]

> It will probably come as a surprise to many people, both friend and foe alike, that I am opposed to any attempt to fire Ward Churchill for the essay... in which he denounces his own country as a genocidal empire, supports America's terrorist enemies, and says that 9/11 was a case of the "chickens coming home to

roost." We live in country whose cornerstone document is a Bill
of Rights that guarantees Americans a right to make fools of
themselves if they so desire. State institutions like the University
of Colorado are forbidden by our Constitution from firing people for expressing opinions, however offensive ...

Another concern I had was making readers aware that Churchill was not
an isolated individual, and his views, extreme as they were, sadly did not
qualify as aberrant in the current university curriculum.

Those who marvel at the current spectacle should keep in mind
the fact that there is absolutely nothing new here, nothing that
has not been publicly known for years. The offending essay itself
was published three years ago. Whatever sin he has committed
has not only been a matter of public record for more than 30
years, it has been reviewed over and over by duly constituted academic authorities at the University of Colorado. The opinions
that have suddenly catapulted this professor into the limelight
have been examined and applauded by his university professors,
the search-and-hiring committees that put him on the faculty of
CU-Boulder, the promotion-and-tenure committees that made
him a full professor, and the department that elected him chair.

The first casualty of the Churchill affair was Colorado president Elizabeth
Hoffman, who was fired at the end of the spring semester.[12] This sent an
important message to university administrators who were still of the opinion they could sweep the problem of faculty activism under the academic
rug. It signaled a change in the environment in which our campaign was
operating and helped to accomplish the first and most difficult task we had

set for ourselves, which was to draw public attention to the problems we were attempting to address. From the moment Ward Churchill became a headline item in the nightly news cycle, it was no longer possible to shield the general public from the knowledge that the universities they were funding had woefully inadequate standards when it came to the integrity of the curriculum, the professional demeanor of their faculty, and the scholarly nature of their enterprise.

A Breakthrough

Even as the Ward Churchill story was unfolding, congressional legislators were preparing the new Higher Education Re-authorization Act, the first in eight years. This legislation was the basis of all federal funding for higher education and an obvious opportunity to advance our agenda. I knew and had the respect of many key Republicans in Congress and had developed strong relationships with Republican House Conference Chairman Jack Kingston (who testified for us in the Georgia hearings) and California Congressman Henry "Buck" McKeon, Chairman of the Subcommittee on Higher Education.

I met with McKeon and asked him if he would include a resolution supporting our bill of rights in the Re-authorization Act. He encouraged me to speak with John Boehner, the head of the full Committee on Education and Labor, who ultimately agreed. After negotiations with other members of the Republican caucus, McKeon was able to include key points of the Academic Bill of Rights in a non-binding "sense of Congress" resolution to be incorporated in the Act.[13]

Even this expression of sympathy with the intentions of our bill was too much for the academic Left and its unions, who responded as if their worst nightmare were about to be realized. When I met with Boehner in his office, his chief of staff told him that the Democrats on the Education Committee were taking the position that four items in the bill were unacceptable and had to be removed, and that the demand was "non-negotiable." One of the four items was the "sense of Congress" resolution about academic freedom that we had inserted into the Act.

I looked around the room, which was filled with staffers and legislative aides, and began to think of the billions of dollars tied up in the bill that might not get to schools because of a resolution that was really only symbolic. I told Boehner that I knew there were a lot of agendas before his committee, and if he felt this was one cause too many, we could wait for another opportunity. "This is a battle I want," he said.

As it happened, there was a divergence of views on the other side of the controversy, which provided a way out of the impasse. A subsequent study conducted by the liberal Brookings Institute described the conflict between administrators and the faculty unions and guilds over our initiative. In a book that reported their findings, the Brookings researchers described me as the "gadfly-critic of the universities and *bête noire* of the campus Left," and also "one of the most prominent figures pushing for 'intellectual diversity' on campus." The study ascribed this prominence to the zeal of my adversaries. "Horowitz's singular influence," it said, "and unique status in the pantheon of conservative critics of the universities can be attributed . . . in part to the efforts of his enemies." These enemies, they said, had "inflated" my activities "into a serious threat to academic freedom," a position that was "happily suited to [my] talent for keeping in the public eye."[14]

This was a backhanded way of acknowledging the efficacy of the strategy I had devised for our campaign, which was based on the realization that the way to reach a liberal media was through the anxieties of the Left. The media would respond to alarms from the Left, where they would ignore the concerns of conservatives, particularly if these concerns focused on the failures of liberal institutions. As a result of the Left's attacks, I had become a symbol of the conservative critique of the university. This was of particular concern for administrators, according to the Brookings team.

> Pointing to Horowitz in order to rally one's allies, done at times as a conscious tactic and sometimes merely as an overreaction to one of his charges, made some educators uneasy. The concentration of critical fire on Horowitz could be seen as a tactical mistake, and, more broadly, as the failure of a close-minded establishment to address some of Horowitz's legitimate complaints. To build Horowitz up into a David battling the higher education Goliath was not a winning strategy.[15]

In the wake of the Ward Churchill scandal, university administrators had concluded that the unions' scorched earth approach to our campaign was counter-productive and becoming a threat. The Churchill scandal was making their position increasingly untenable, forcing them to concede,that "Horowitz's demands were, at some level, reasonable and indeed quite in line with deeply rooted academic values. What is wrong with viewpoint diversity? Who would seriously argue against the concept that students should not be browbeaten in the classroom?"[16]

The Brookings authors endorsed our view that student rights had always been a core element of the academic freedom tradition.

> In addition to viewpoint diversity, Horowitz has championed student rights. The main idea of his academic bill of rights is that students have been left out of the traditional concept of academic

freedom. This omission contravenes the original Weberian intent to include student rights under the concept of *Lehrfreiheit* and *Lernfreiheit* (the freedom to teach and to learn). Students need to be protected against intimidation and proselytizing by faculty members.[17]

The Brookings authors also acknowledged that I was willing to compromise with reasonable critics, and that the point of my legislative initiatives was to draw attention to the issue, not to impose government rule in university matters. I was not surprised by the refusal of the union opposition and their Democratic Party allies to acknowledge these obvious facts—which would have put a damper on their war against our efforts—but I found it difficult to explain on practical grounds, since no specific action was required by our resolutions. The only way to explain it was to acknowledge their determination not to make any concession that might be seen to confer any legitimacy on our critique of academic behavior.

The American Council on Education Steps In

I was able to confirm for myself the factors contributing to the changed attitude of the university administrators when I met with Terry Hartle, the senior vice president for government affairs of the American Council on Education. This organization represented 1,800 institutions of higher learning and scores of important academic associations. Hartle told me that their members, who were university presidents, felt they were being put in an increasingly unsustainable position by the unions' refusal to even acknowledge that a problem existed, and that a statement by them about the issues we were raising was in order. Explaining the readiness of the

Council to reach a compromise, Hartle made the following comment to the Brookings investigators: "It was clear to us that David had considerable traction, and while at some level we had no problem with what he was saying, we were uncomfortable with some of the language. We worried over how you could, for example, implement a requirement for 'balance,' in the classroom."[18]

Hartle's memory was faulty on this point, or perhaps the false statements of the unions had made their imprint. We had never asked for "balance" in the classroom, and I tried not to use the word itself in my formal statements about universities. It implied a demand for one-on-one trade-offs on all ideas presented in the classroom, which would have been both unworkable and undesirable. The actual sticking point for the coalition Hartle represented was an issue raised by the Council of Christian Colleges and Universities. During the negotiations over the Re-Authorization Act, I had met with their counsel, Bob Andringa, to discuss the matter. His concern was not "balance" but the fact that the Academic Bill of Rights forbade hiring faculty on the basis of viewpoint. This would be a problem for religious institutions, since they would want to hire faculty that shared their values and were willing to transmit them. I had no problem with this exception. The Academic Bill of Rights specifically exempted private institutions—provided they stipulated to the public what doctrinal restrictions they wished to place on academic freedom. This turned out to be the sticking point for the Christian Colleges. They did not want to "separate themselves" from the larger community of colleges who subscribed to the principle of viewpoint neutrality. In short, they wanted to have their cake and eat it too.

A compromise was reached when the Republican leadership in the Senate withdrew our resolution in light of a new statement on academic freedom by the American Council on Education. The Council statement,

issued on June 23, 2005, shared key principles with the Academic Bill of
Rights. The Brookings report described our victory in these terms:

> Perhaps the peak of David Horowitz's national influence came in
> June 2005 when a coalition of twenty-eight mainstream national
> education associations, led by the American Council on Educa-
> tion, approved a statement on academic rights and responsibili-
> ties that blended traditional concepts of academic freedom with
> an endorsement of intellectual pluralism and student rights as
> championed by Horowitz.[19]

It was also a vindication of our strategy of seeking congressional resolutions. There was no way the American Council would have stepped forward with this helpful declaration if it had not been for our legislative
efforts and the forthright support of congressmen Boehner and McKeon
who refused to back down under pressure from the union lobbies.

The ACE statement on "Academic Rights and Responsibilities" began,
"Academic freedom and intellectual pluralism are central principles of
American higher education."[20] In the original draft, supplied to me by congressional staff, the statement had referred to "intellectual diversity"
rather than "intellectual pluralism," but objections from the unions had
led them to change the draft. Apparently they felt that using the actual
language of the Academic Bill of Rights would afford us too great a vindication; or perhaps they feared that it would expose the sophistry in their
campaign against the term "intellectual diversity," which falsely claimed
that it would require the teaching of every point of view in the classroom,
however intellectually unworthy.

The ACE statement recognized that academic freedom for faculty
entailed a responsibility not to indoctrinate students. This was a

concession with far-reaching implications, and I described it as "a huge step forward." The educational establishment considered the ACE statement a victory for them as well, hoping that it would blunt our criticisms. By appearing to take the problems seriously instead of pretending that they didn't exist, and by removing the legislative issue, the educational associations felt they had removed the problem.[21]

The statement also called for the creation of grievance machinery for students who felt their academic freedom rights had been violated. "Any member of the campus community who believes that he or she has been treated unfairly on academic matters," it said "must have access to a clear institutional process by which his or her grievance can be addressed."[22] I regarded this as an important concession. Yet it was not without problems. The phrase "academic matters" did not specify academic freedom issues. "Academic matters" might refer to grades—and universities generally provided grievance procedures for students who felt they had been unfairly graded, or who had been discriminated against in class because of racial or gender issues.

Complaints about racial and gender discrimination were backed by an elaborate diversity apparatus and institutional staff informing students about their rights and ensuring that students who confronted such issues would receive an adequate hearing. Racial and gender discrimination guidelines were articulated and publicized to the entire university community, and were included in the orientation of freshmen classes. But there was no such information available about students' academic freedom rights. A common misunderstanding of the problem focused on unfair grading based on political discrimination, which did not begin to address the issues of indoctrination and political harassment in the classroom. The prime issue, as we saw it, was the quality of education being provided to students, not the treatment of individual students regarding their grades.

Finally, the ACE statement was merely a recommendation. There was no guarantee of an actual implementation of the policy at the university level, which had been the problem from the start. If individual universities did not create actual enforcement mechanisms, and if there was no institutional will to correct the problems as they manifested themselves in university classrooms, our victory was only symbolic.

CHAPTER EIGHT

The Professors

IT WAS CLEAR THAT IF THE NEW STATEMENT ON ACADEMIC FREEDOM WAS not supported by the university community, the status quo was not going to change. In their summary of these developments, the Brookings authors conceded as much, noting that "the [ACE] statement, in fact, passed largely unnoticed in the academic community."[1]

It would have been an empty victory if not for our legislative efforts.

Since our experience in Colorado, I had encouraged the sponsors of our resolutions to withdraw them once university officials agreed to endorse their principles. In Ohio, where Senate Bill 24 was still pending, the new statement by the American Council on Education provided the opportunity for this kind of compromise. Under ferocious attack from the Left, our legislation had run into serious trouble. Its sponsor, Senator Larry Mumper, despite having once been a teacher himself, had given our opponents powerful ammunition to oppose it. When pressed by a hostile reporter from the *Columbus Dispatch* as to why the bill was necessary, Mumper had responded that too many professors were "anti-American" and that "80 percent of them are Democrats, liberals, socialists or card-carrying communists."[2] It was a gift our opponents were quick to accept, despite Mumper's quick apology for the remark. An unfolding corruption scandal in the Ohio State Republican Party was also having a negative impact on the chances of the bill's passage. I suggested to Mumper that he immediately approach university officials with a Colorado-like compromise, which would have been my first option even if the bill had been going well.

The Ohio "Inter-University Council," which represented all seventeen state universities, soon accepted our offer to withdraw the bill in favor of a statement by them embracing the ACE principles. This was duly adopted on October 11, 2005. The statement, called "Resolution on Academic Rights and Responsibilities," essentially endorsed the ACE position, including the "principle of intellectual pluralism and the free exchange of ideas."[3]

This was a victory, but this success—from a practical point of view—also had many uncertainties hanging over it. The statement was a concession, regarded by the universities as damage control. It did not represent a genuine will to implement a new policy, since this would only have been possible with faculty support—and the organizations representing faculty had given no evidence of a change in their attitudes, even though the AAUP had signed the ACE statement. Their view of what had transpired was succinctly expressed by one AAUP contributor to *The Academic Bill of Rights Debate*, who described the compromise in these words: "In the end, not much happened. David Horowitz predictably declared victory, professors breathed a huge sigh of relief, and absolutely nothing changed."[4]

This summary went a bridge too far. As a result of our efforts, seventeen state universities, including major academic institutions such as Ohio

State and Ohio University had adopted a new academic freedom policy granting academic freedom rights to their students—the first universities in the nation to do so. Among the salient points in the new policies was the right of students not to be harassed for their political views: "In a learning context, everyone must respect those who disagree with themselves and also maintain an atmosphere of civility." Even more important was the recognition that "students do have a right to hear and examine diverse opinions."[5]

This was perhaps the most contested issue of our campaign, with the opponents of the Academic Bill of Rights contending that the principle of intellectual diversity would require faculty to teach the views of Holocaust deniers with respect. To meet this objection, the American Council on Education had inserted the qualifying clause, "Students do have a right to hear and examine diverse opinions, but within the frameworks that knowledgeable scholars—themselves subject to rigorous standards of peer review—have determined to be reliable and accurate."

The statement was problematic. If opinions could be determined to be "reliable and accurate," they wouldn't be opinions. But we did not raise any objections, regarding it as a matter that could be adjudicated in the event that it became an issue. What the new policy showed was that compromises were not difficult to reach if there was a will to acknowledge that a problem existed—something the arguments advanced by the faculty unions and their allies lacked.

One aspect of the new Ohio policy that was a particularly dramatic change in the status quo was its endorsement of a grievance policy specific to students' academic freedom rights and not, as had been previously the case, merely for unfair grades (although several of the universities that adopted the statement failed to institute the policy).

Academic Grievances

A student may grieve academic matters not involving grade changes. These issues may include course content and instructor behavior. Before pursuing such a grievance, students should familiarize themselves with the importance of academic freedom to the educational environment of the university. Ohio University supports the idea that protecting academic freedom at the institution is the responsibility of students and faculty alike. Ohio University takes the position that academic freedom protects faculty and students' research and scholarship activities as well as material introduced in the classroom and must be assured during the academic appeal process. However, instructors are expected to show proper judgment in the classroom and should avoid persistently intruding material which has no relation to their subject.[6]

Despite the unprincipled attacks and attendant bad press, we had achieved a huge reform of academic policy in the state of Ohio that would not have taken place without our legislative efforts.

Unfortunately, while the American Council on Education represented universities in all fifty states, the Council didn't lift a finger to see that its recommendations were actually adopted in any of them. The only reason the Inter-University Council in Ohio implemented the ACE statement and transformed it into university policy in seventeen state schools was because of the legislation sponsored by Senator Larry Mumper. The university community's passive resistance to actually correcting a bad situation was to continue, leaving our mission still far from accomplished.

The Ohio universities that adopted the new policy were large. Ohio State for example had a student population over 60,000. Consequently, without an aggressive campaign by its administration, virtually no students would ever be aware of the policy let alone understand how to pursue a grievance. Academic freedom issues were complex, and students without guidance would have a difficult time in an institutional environment that had shown hostility to these concerns.

By contrast, students seeking to file sexual harassment and discrimination grievances could count on broad faculty sympathy and a wealth of available faculty advice and support. Conservative students, who were the ones most likely to raise academic freedom issues, would have virtually none.

We were still facing the problem with which we had begun. One former college president, commenting generally on the institution of new policies provided this insight into administrator's attitudes: "'Policies are non-action,'...Usually, the least action a president can take is to adopt a policy. The adoption does nothing.' Action [to implement a policy] by contrast 'scares everyone, not just the actor.'"[7] It was action we wanted.

The 101 Professors

When the Ward Churchill scandal broke in January, I decided to take advantage of the opportunity to find a publisher for a book I wanted to write about activist professors. I wanted to profile academics who thought of themselves as proselytizers instead of scholars and who regarded the university as a platform for promoting their ideological agendas. Without the public interest that Churchill had aroused, however, no publisher was likely to underwrite such a project.

I was convinced (and said as much on several occasions) that the majority of professors were professional scholars who did not abuse their classrooms. My concern was a radical minority—in my book I estimated them to be 10 percent of any given faculty or 60,000 nationwide—who regarded themselves political activists and were willing to put aside professional restraints in the service of what was to them a "higher truth."[8] The activists were concentrated in liberal arts faculties and had been able to politicize entire academic disciplines such as the Ethnic Studies field, in which Churchill was a notable figure.

As a measure of their ability to shape university governance, faculty radicals had succeeded in imposing "speech codes," easily the greatest infringement on First Amendment rights in the modern era. Many speech codes had been struck down in a series of federal court decisions in 1992 to1993, but despite the legal risks and costs in maintaining such measures, administrators were reluctant to drop them. In the words of the Brookings Study authors, "Surprisingly, the campus speech codes did not disappear after what seemed to be this authoritative judicial resolution of their legal standing, rather the number of codes *increased* [emphasis in original]. By the end of the 1990s, more than 800 colleges and universities had them."[9]

Professor Jon Gould, the author of a well-regarded book on speech code regulations, explained the administrators' position, ascribing it to a fear of feminists, critical race theorists, and other campus leftists and the backlash they would create if administrators dropped them. By rewording the regulations, administrators calculated, they could withstand legal challenges.[10] Similar concerns prevented them from implementing policies to protect students' academic freedom.

This was why I decided to write the book which I called *The Professors*. By describing who these faculty activists were and documenting their radical views, I hoped to weaken their opposition to the Academic Bill of Rights. While they presented themselves as "liberals" and "scholars," an examination of their academic resumes, curricula, reading lists, and public pronouncements revealed a different picture. I realized that publishing such a study would invite charges that our campaign was part of a "right-wing" effort to purge leftists from faculties and replace them with conservatives. But the atmosphere was already rife with such baseless charges, and I assumed that things could hardly get worse. A description of the faculty activists who constituted our opposition was crucial to an understanding of the conflict itself.

The Professors opened with the story of the Ward Churchill affair and then posed a series of questions about the academic system. Given the elaborate procedures for reviewing candidates for university faculties, how could someone like Churchill have been hired in the first place, then promoted to tenure, and then elected department chair, where he was in a position to control new faculty appointments? Why did it take a national scandal to trigger a peer review of his academic credentials, considering that a panel of academics ultimately found them to be fraudulent?

I argued in *The Professors* that the answers to these questions lay in a system of academic governance that had been corrupted by political interests.[11] The argument, the core of which was ignored by its critics, was buttressed by a collective portrait of 101 professors who conflated political activism with their scholarly disciplines, introduced political agendas into their classrooms, and taught subjects that were outside their professional expertise (e.g., English professors who gave lectures on economic imperialism).[12]

Churchill was an obvious metaphor for such academic radicalism, but there were others who made the case equally well. William Ayers, the "Distinguished Professor of Early Childhood Education" at the University of Illinois, was also the unrepentant leader of the Weather Underground, a terrorist group that had formally declared war on "AmeriKKKa." He had continued his revolutionary work by other, academic, means as the editor of a series of teacher guides published by Columbia Teacher's College, which were blueprints on how to insinuate "social justice" agendas into K–12 education.[13] Professor bell hooks, "Distinguished Professor of English Literature" at City University of New York (and a fan of lower case letters) was the author of *Teaching to Transgress*, which explained that an educator—particularly a minority educator—"as a subject in resistance has a right to define reality." Of her own agendas she said, "My commitment to engaged pedagogy is an expression of political activism."[14]

Eric Foner, the DeWitt Clinton Professor of History at Columbia University, an eminent figure in the academic world and a long-time fellow-traveler of the Communist Left, wrote, "Scholarship and activism are not mutually exclusive pursuits, but are, at their best, symbiotically related." This remark was made in the "Foreword" to a collection of papers from a faculty conference at Columbia titled, *Taking Back the Academy: History of Activism, History as Activism*. The participants at the conference were dedicated to the idea that academic history should be a form of political action.[15]

When it was published, *The Professors* sold 40,000 copies and was well received by a general readership increasingly uneasy with the transformation of educational classrooms into radical recruitment programs. But the academic reaction to the book was anything but positive and anything but academic.[16] The American Federation of Teachers led the assault by organizing a coalition of left-wing groups called "Free Exchange On Campus" and funding a website devoted to attacking what it described as my campaign to stifle ideas, of which the book was the latest example.

The Free Exchange Coalition included the American Association of University Professors, the ACLU, the National Education Association, the Soros-funded Campus Progress, People for the American Way, and the Progressive States Network, providing an opportunity to assess the magnitude of the lobby we were up against. The collective budget of the coalition organizations was well over $500 million, and its members could field operatives in every state, every congressional district, and every university town in the nation.[17]

Playing ventriloquist to itself, the American Federation of Teachers issued its own press release about the organization it had created: "Free Exchange On Campus... has condemned a new book that attacks individual professors for their personal political beliefs. The book is *The Professors: The 101 Most Dangerous Academics in America*, by David Horowitz, who is also the author of the so-called Academic Bill of Rights legislation making its way throughout the states. The book is essentially a blacklist of academics, says Free Exchange On Campus, and is based on inaccurate and misleading information."[18]

Far from being a blacklist, *The Professors* explicitly defended the freedom of professors to hold unpopular political beliefs, stating in its introduction, "This book is not intended as a text about left-wing bias in the university, and does not propose that a left-wing perspective on academic faculties is a problem in itself. Every individual, whether conservative or liberal, has a perspective and therefore a bias. Professors have every right to interpret the subjects they teach according to their individual points of view. That is the essence of academic freedom."[19]

Ignoring the clear intention of the book, the Free Exchange website continued to describe *The Professors* as a McCarthy blacklist and published complaints from its faculty subjects in a document it called "Facts Count." This document purported to show that the book was filled with factual errors, was unreliable, and should not be taken seriously. It was another version of the union canard that we had made the problem up. On review, we found exactly six identifiable errors in the 110,000-word text that could be called factual, all of them trivial. In three mentions of a professor named Elizabeth Perez, for instance, she was referred to as "Emma Perez" once. Professor Dean Saitta was described as the director of a museum in 2005 when the year should have been 2003, and Victor Navasky was described as the chairman of the *Columbia Journalism Review*, when he was not. Not one among the handful of errors approached the level of the falsehoods endlessly repeated by Free Exchange and the teachers union, in particular their claim that the book was a blacklist seeking to remove professors from faculties because of their ideas.[20]

In writing *The Professors*, I had given one undeniable hostage to the opposition by allowing the publisher to subtitle it "The 101 Most Dangerous Academics in America." I did this reluctantly, and only because 30,000 covers had already been printed by the time I was made aware. I did not insist that the term "dangerous academics" be removed, because it would have required trashing all the covers and title pages, and would have thrown the publishing schedule off and created havoc with the marketing of the book.

The word "dangerous" did not, in fact, appear in the text, nor was it any part of the analysis that framed the profiles or informed the argument of the book. It should have been clear from reading the text that if the activist professors profiled were a danger, it was specifically to the academic process and the university whose funding base was threatened by Churchill-type scandals. But of course this was not what my critics focused on when they launched their attacks. Typical was the treatment of the book by InsideHigherEd.com, which greeted its appearance with the headline, "David Horowitz Has a List" and began its story:

> Caroline Higgins is 66 years old, and at 5'2" she's not a daunting figure. Walking on the Earlham College campus last week, she ran into one of her students, a football player who very much towers over her. She mentioned that she was about to be named to a list of the "101 most dangerous academics in America." Hig-

gins said that her student just started laughing—and that for anyone who knows her, "dangerous" just isn't the word that comes to mind. She teaches peace studies.[21]

Ridicule is, of course, a more effective weapon against a book than confronting its arguments or the evidence that supports them. The type of "list" InsideHigherEd.com had in mind was described in the same article by a Marxist professor named Joel Feagin, one of the academics profiled in the book. "This appears to be a new type of McCarthyism," he wrote. "I remember McCarthy made up dangerous people lists too. I never thought, as a 1930s baby who lived through the Depression and World War II, that I would live to see this country sink so low as to have public attacks on social science researchers because of their research."[22]

To be thought of as a victim of McCarthyism obviously tickled Feagin's fancy, as it did many of the radicals profiled in the book. But anyone who actually read the text would see that neither Feagin nor Higgins was singled out because of "research." Although the InsideHigherEd.com article never got around to mentioning it, both were included in *The Professors* because of their clear violations of academic standards and professional ethics, not for political opinions they expressed. Higgins' contention that she was teaching pacifism at a college whose students had a special interest in pacifism was disingenuous to say the least. Higgins was a Marxist whose views can be surmised from her praise for the book *Empire*, the polemical analysis of globalization by neo-Marxists Hardt and Antonio Negri (the latter a convicted terrorist). Higgins did not praise the book for its (non-existent) pacifism but "for its vision of putting an end to capitalist exploitation and ushering in a communist society based on cooperation and community."[23]

In noting her extreme political views, *The Professors* commented, "Professor Higgins is entitled to her private political views. The professional issue is that her political views are everywhere stringently enforced in her classroom. For example, her course 'Methods of Peace-making' amounts to a for-credit blueprint for left-wing activism. A syllabus for the course notes that it is principally concerned with 'social movements and initiatives which suggest new strategies for change.'"[24] But students are not only expected to study such movements and their strategies—they are actually expected by their professor to implement those strategies in the Richmond community. In the words of the syllabus, there is 'inevitably an intersection of practice and theory.' Students are informed that 'we shall be working for peace and justice.'"[25]

The Professors also examines Professor Higgins' senior seminar for Peace Studies majors, which she intended to be the "capstone" course of their experience at Earlham. One purpose of the course, which was called "Theory and Practice Revisited," was "to work together to produce analysis of a problem, development, challenge, or approach to social change, which is enlightening for peace theorists and activists."[26] However, readings for Professor Higgins' seminar did not reflect any kind of academic concern for critically analyzing the issue of social change. Nor were they particularly pacifist. They were comprised, without exception, of works by Marxists and other radicals not known for their pacificism, including Gore Vidal, Angela Davis, and even the Mexican Marxist guerilla leader, Subcomandante Marcos. No alternative social analysis, no conflict or debate with these views, was provided in Higgins' curriculum.[27]

Professor Higgins made no attempt to justify the absence of diverse views or scholarly skepticism in her required readings. On the contrary. "Against the approach of this course," she wrote in the syllabus of another she taught, "it can be objected that students get essentially one point of view, a point of view critical of mainstream thinking. This is a valid objection."[28] But rather than remedying this unprofessional curriculum, Professor Higgins suggested that students look elsewhere if they wanted a non-doctrinal discussion of philosophical issues, "my response is that rather than changing this course, I should urge all of you to take more courses and read more books."[29] This should have been a red flag to a reporter looking into the facts, but the editor of InsideHigherEd.com was apparently too interested in discrediting *The Professors* to notice.

Professor Higgins' refusal to provide students with an analytic framework for evaluating differing views of controversial issues was a clear violation of professional ethics and academic freedom prescriptions. Caroline Higgins' curricula were designed to indoctrinate students in her political prejudices, though neither her superiors nor the education press seemed to care. Her academic malfeasance was compounded by the fact that she also had no visible academic credential for teaching courses in "Peace and Global Studies" and no record of scholarship in these fields. Her one sole-authored book was a novel, *Sweet Country*, about a leftist underground movement in Chile after the coup of 1973, while her only other published work was an edited collection of essays in praise of "peace studies." This political professionalism and academic amateurism was why she was included in *The Professors*, not because of her specific views or any desire to draw up a list of left-wing professors who should be fired.[30]

It soon became obvious that the case put forward in *The Professors* was not going to get a serious hearing from the academic community. "Whether to laugh at the book, like Higgins's student, or to take it seriously, has been the subject of much discussion among academic groups and those who made the list in recent weeks," commented the editor of InsideHigherEd.com. "Some fear taking Horowitz too seriously will only legitimize his sometimes breathless attacks. (The book jacket promises information about professors who 'say they want to kill white people,' 'support Osama bin Laden,' and 'defend pedophilia.') Some professors worry that they really don't gain much by discussing a book that can have them explaining that, no, they are not murdering, pro-terrorist, child molesters."

It was a well crafted attack, relying on the fact that to people who had not read the book, the promotional copy on its jacket would seem surreal. But the jacket references, written not by me but by someone in the publisher's publicity department, were actually accurate to the letter. The first reference was to Professor Amiri Baraka, a well-known anti-Semite and racist who wrote (in a poem cited in *The Professors*): "Rape the white girls. Rape their fathers. Cut the mothers' throats."[31] In case any reader missed the genocidal message of his text, Baraka spelled it out for them: "We [blacks] must eliminate the white man before we can draw a free breath on this planet."[32] When a white woman once asked Professor Baraka what whites could do to help the black cause, he replied, "You can help by dying. You are a cancer. You can help the world's people with your death."[33] "Kill white people"—the jacket text was a reasonable rendering of these sentiments.

The reference to a professor's support for bin Laden was to the notorious speech by Columbia Professor Nicholas DeGenova, who called for "a million Mogadishus"—the site of a massacre of U.S. troops by al-Qaeda at a University "anti-war" teach-in. "U.S. patriotism," he went on, "is inseparable from imperial warfare and white supremacy. U.S. flags are the emblem of the invading war machine in Iraq today. They are the emblem of the occupying power. The only true heroes are those who find ways that help defeat the U.S. military."[34] The reference to child-molesting was to Professor Gayle Rubin, who has made an academic career out of promoting sex between adults and minors.[35]

It was immediately clear that the academics who bothered to comment on *The Professors* were not interested in how to engage its arguments but only in how to discredit it—and me. It was a strategy openly advocated by Michael Bérubé, who had emerged as an AAUP point man in the campaign against the Academic Bill of Rights. In a post on the academic blog, Crooked Timber, Bérubé wrote, "Late last year I had lunch with David Horowitz on the *Chronicle of Higher Education*'s dime.... Here's what I was thinking at the time: OK, I've agreed to meet David Horowitz. In this context—the *Chronicle*, as opposed to Hannity & Colmes—this grants Horowitz, and his complaints about academe, a certain legitimacy. My job, therefore, is to contest that legitimacy, and to model a way of dealing with Horowitz that does not give him what he wants: namely, (1) important concessions or (2) outrage.... Liberal and Left academics need to try (3), mockery and dismissal, and thereby demonstrate ... that person needs to be ridiculed and given a double minor for unsportsmanlike bullshit."[36] At the lunch Bérubé conceded that although he was the author of three attacks on *The Professors*, he hadn't actually read the book.[37]

In our lunch meeting, I pointed out to Bérubé that neither the AAUP nor any other academic organization had approached me to explore whether I would be willing to compromise on any specifics in the Academic Bill of Rights. As he well knew, I had begun my campaign by submitting the proposed text to him for vetting, and had been willing to change wordings and even to drop specific clauses to which he objected. I suggested that the AAUP invite me to discuss these matters, privately. But Bérubé was determined not to go out on any limb that might appear to legitimize our concerns, and he never took me up on my suggestion. His reluctance to discuss the issues in a non-confrontational setting was an entrenched attitude among the organizations of the Free Exchange coalition as well.

Nonetheless, over the next year I continued to make overtures to my adversaries. I invited the very hostile vice president of the American

Federation of Teachers, William Scheuerman, to a Student Academic Freedom Conference I held in Washington, D.C., during the weekend of April 6 to 7, 2006,[38] and then invited the president of the American Association of University Professors, Cary Nelson, to a second such conference on March 4, 2007.[39] Both invitations were accepted, but neither led to any reciprocal gesture.

Their denial that a problem of academic abuse even existed had been central to their case, so I was curious to see how they would respond to the student panelists I assembled when they related their experiences at the hands of unscrupulous professors.[40] Both Scheuerman and Nelson had a chance to hear these testimonies first-hand and evaluate the accounts for themselves, although we had posted similar reports on our websites and made them available to all parties involved throughout the controversy over the Academic Bill of Rights. Scheuerman passed on the opportunity to attend the student panel. Nelson did as well, but in the question and answer period after our debate, he had a chance to hear one undergraduate tell her story. This was Ruth Malhotra, the student from Georgia Tech, who spoke from the audience.

In an account he published three years later, Nelson described this encounter with Ruth (without mentioning her by name) in the following manner: "Horowitz will now ritually bring some brainwashed waif to his public performances, trained to testify to recovered memory of instructional abuse."[41] Oblivious to the fact that Ruth's complaints had been supported by the Dean of Diversity at Georgia Tech and by liberal faculty associated with the Georgia Tech "Diversity Forum," and that the university's investigation had led to the removal of the professor from the classroom, Nelson simply dismissed not only Ruth's testimony but by extension the testimony of any student who might be associated with me. With an attitude like this, it was not surprising that he made no attempt to follow up with Malhotra after she had appealed to him directly or to facilitate meetings between me and the leaders of the AAUP to discuss these problems. Instead, he rejoined his colleagues in promoting the popular claim that we were "a solution in search of a problem."

The AFT vice president, Scheuerman, who was a professor of political science, turned out to be a crude ideologue. He promptly repaid my cordiality in giving him a platform with an editorial in his union paper attacking the "Academic Bull [sic] of Rights" as "nothing more than a quota system for political extremists so they can deliver their right-wing political sermons in the classroom." He added, "In case you think this version of McCarthyism has no place in the United States, think again."[42]

Nelson, who was the author of *Manifesto of a Tenured Radical*, reviewed *The Professors* in the AAUP's official journal, *Academe*. His review began, "Please ignore this book. Don't buy it. Don't read it. Try not to mention it in idle conversation."[43] Strange advice from an educator, but not so strange for a political activist alarmed by the prospect that his agendas might come under scrutiny. Calling *The Professors* "a faculty blacklist," Nelson complained, "The entries...purport to be accounts of a hundred faculty careers. Yet most of them ignore the chief publications at the core of those careers. Horowitz's entries are fundamentally acts of misrepresentation and erasure."[44]

Evidently, Nelson, like Bérubé, had failed to read the book. In the 12,000-word introduction, I explained the rationale for the 101 profiles. If he had read it, he would have realized that the portraits didn't purport to be anything like an account of academic careers. They were compiled to illustrate particular attitudes and to identify specific patterns in the academic philosophies and practices of individuals who confused their political activism with the profession of scholarship. The profiles documented violations of academic behavior in four specific categories, but did not attempt to provide accounts of intellectual oeuvres, something that could hardly be accomplished in a format limited to four pages an entry.

During our debate at the conference, Nelson said, "You cannot take politics out of my classroom anymore than you can take it out of life. It's built into my subject matter, and it's been built into my subject matter for the whole thirty-seven years in which I've taught."[45] Nelson went on to criticize what he regarded as the timidity of his colleagues who refrained from expressing their political views in the classroom.

Whether Cary Nelson and others who shared his animus against the Academic Bill of Rights actually understood the distinction between a political and a scholarly discourse was itself unclear.[46] An "Afterword" Nelson wrote for a *festchrift* in his honor (pointedly titled *Cary Nelson and the Struggle for the University*) is instructive. It suggests a crippling confusion about this issue, which is central to the entire debate about academic standards and academic freedom.

Nelson, who is a Professor of English Literature at the University of Illinois, called his "Afterword," "Activism and Community in the Academy." In it, he focused on a book he had written twenty years earlier.[47] He described the book as a "Marxist and post-structuralist analysis," in which he proposed to "recover" poets worthy of inclusion in the literary canon who, in his view, had been left out not because of their aesthetic deficiencies but because of their political views. According to Nelson, the ideas of a literary canon and a literary history constituted "conservative and even reactionary political forces. . . . Working together canon formation and literary history reaffirm that the dominant culture is the best that has been thought and said, sanctioning the silencing of minority voices and interests not only in the classroom but in the society at large."[48]

For Nelson, these silenced voices consisted of poets who were Communists or otherwise politically Left, or who were black, female, or gay (and Left). His "Afterword" presented itself as the answer to a question about the changes he would make to the text ten years after he wrote it, particularly the additional poets he would include if he were to rewrite it. His answer: "I never thought of giving any space to Sara Teasdale, whom I dismissed as hopelessly sentimental. But now my student Melissa Girard has recovered Teasdale's uncollected and unpublished anti-war poems written on the eve of the U.S. entry into World War I, and Teasdale thereby becomes a different and newly powerful poet."[49]

This is an extraordinary statement for a professor of literature to make. Does a sentimental poet become a non-sentimental poet by being discovered to have a politically correct point of view about the First World War? Nelson's claim that, in taking a political stance on the war, "Teasdale becomes a different and newly powerful poet" reflects the attitude of a philistine rather than a connoisseur of literary values, which one would have thought was the prerequisite for an "expert" credentialed in literary studies.

It is more than likely that someone who cannot distinguish between good poetry and bad poetry that is merely politically correct would be hard put to understand the distinction between a discourse that is academic and one that is a political sermon. That was precisely what our academic freedom campaign was about.

CHAPTER NINE

The Pennsylvania Hearings

W E HAD ASSEMBLED OUR EVIDENCE AND MADE OUR CASE. SARA Dogan and I had written tens of thousands of words documenting instances of faculty abuse and responding to critics. These appeared mainly as articles on the web, but on one or two occasions in the *Chronicle of Higher Education* and InsideHigherEd.com. We also posted students' direct testimonies about their classroom experiences and the studies that social scientists conducted about the lack of diversity on university faculties.[1] In addition, we had posted a detailed history of every legislative action that we had taken and an archive of both critical and supportive news stories.[2] But all these efforts at transparency had no effect on our critics, who ignored the facts we presented and efforts we made to set the record straight, continuing their attacks and misrepresenting our actions and intentions.

On January 9, 2006, the American Historical Association passed a unanimous resolution condemning the Academic Bill of Rights, which it called an attack on academic freedom. The resolution read,

Whereas, So-called Academic and Student Bills of Rights legislation, investigations, and similar measures will give power over
such matters as curriculum, course content, and faculty personnel decisions to governmental authorities and other agencies
outside the faculty and administrations of institutions of higher
learning; Whereas, Such measures would violate academic freedom and undermine professional standards by imposing political criteria in areas of educational policy that faculty members
normally and rightly control; therefore, be it Resolved, That the
American Historical Association opposes the passage of Academic and Student Bills of Rights and all similar attempts to regulate the academic community.[3]

Despite the fact that those voting for the resolution were credentialed historians, each of its claims about the Academic Bill of Rights was false. The
bill was not a proposal for government action but for universities whom
we were asking to adopt its provisions. We did ask legislatures to pass resolutions supporting its principles, but the purpose of these measures was
to urge universities to provide students with academic freedom rights.
They did not call for—or entail—the imposition of political criteria over
any areas of educational policy, nor did they give control over course content, curriculum, or faculty personnel decisions to government.

The discussion preceding the AHA vote on our bill was, if anything,
even more misleading than the resolution condemning it. According to the
account in InsideHigherEd.com, "At the history meeting, debate over the
Academic Bill of Rights itself was fairly simple. Ellen Schrecker, a professor of history at Yeshiva University, called the Academic Bill of Rights
a 'cleverly written document' that was designed to pressure faculty members to hire more conservatives and to avoid topics and views that offend

conservatives. We should not seek to protect students from hearing uncomfortable views,' she said."[4] Contrary to Schrecker's claims, the Academic Bill of Rights specifically forbade academic institutions from hiring professors on the basis of their political views, and thus from hiring more conservatives as she claimed. Absolutely nothing in its text or in our statements could be understood to require or even encourage professors to avoid topics and views that offended conservatives or anybody else.

By misrepresenting the bill, the historians had avoided confronting its central concern, which was the need to extend academic freedom rights to *students*. Not surprisingly, the same AHA meeting rejected a resolution to oppose campus speech codes as restrictions on free speech.[5]

The meeting had not been attended by the 14,000 members of the American Historical Association. Only a tiny fraction of the AHA membership was present.[6] The vote was taken at a business session composed of a few hundred of its most political—and left-wing—members, who were generally the individuals most likely to show up for such events. It was at the business meeting that resolutions on non-scholarly issues were put to a vote. While the attendees put their opposition to the Academic Bill of Rights on record, they had not previously passed resolutions condemning government diversity statutes such as Title IX, which actually intruded federal authority into academic governance. The diversity statutes gave large government bureaucracies power over such matters as curriculum, course content, and faculty personnel decisions. But there was not a whisper of protest from the AHA, the AAUP, the AFT or any of the other professional associations which pretended to see a government threat in the Academic Bill of Rights.

In December and January, similar resolutions containing identical distortions of our agendas were passed by the American Library Association,[7] the Modern Languages Association[8] and, in a more temperate version, by the Association of American Colleges and Universities.[9] Not one of these organizations—or any academic body for that matter—made an effort to contact us to explore whether we had any flexibility on the issues that concerned them. None was interested in finding out if we were willing to negotiate modifications of the language in the Academic Bill of Rights that would make it more acceptable to them.

While the professional associations were condemning our efforts as attempts to infringe on the independence of scholars in the classroom, Arizona legislators were proposing a bill to do just that. It was a bill I opposed. The Arizona legislation, SB 1331, was called "Alternative Coursework and Materials," and was designed to guarantee students "an alternative course, alternative coursework, alternative learning materials, or alternative activity" if they were personally offended by the texts their instructors chose. Under the legislation, students would be given the right to select alternative texts "without financial or academic penalty" if they objected to the instructor's assignment "on the basis that [the material] conflicts with the student's beliefs or practices in sex, morality, or religion."[10]

Within weeks of the AHA resolutions condemning our efforts as an attempt to control classroom instruction, I wrote,

At first glance this legislation might appear to be authored by the academic freedom movement with which I am associated and which I have launched in the name of intellectual diversity.... But this impression would be wrong. In fact, I oppose the bill which is anti-intellectual and attacks the very core of what a liberal—or democratic—education should be about, which is to challenge students' habitual modes of thinking and teach them to think for themselves. The core mission of education in a democracy is to train a citizenry that thinks for itself." By contrast, I wrote, "under the proposed bill, SB 1331, students could avoid being challenged at all. This is not education. It is a form of self-indoctrination.[11]

The Arizona bill, I wrote, was exactly what the campaign for academic freedom was designed to *oppose*. The Academic Bill of Rights was "a challenge to the current imposition of intellectual orthodoxies by professors who have abandoned academic professionalism for academic activism. The politicization of the classroom, which is common today, the ridicule and harassment of students who are religious, who are white, and who have traditionalist beliefs, was undoubtedly an inspiration for the misguided Arizona legislation. But its sponsors have not taken their cue from my Academic Bill of Rights, which preserves the appropriate relationship between teacher and student."[12]

In framing their bill, conservative legislators had attempted to mirror the actions of the tenured radicals they despised. "The idea that students should avoid discomforting moments in their educational vocation," I pointed out, was "the precise philosophical assumption of left-wing diversity movements. What is 'political correctness' and what are 'speech codes' but attempts to enforce a political and ideological orthodoxy on members of the academic community by claiming that unorthodox ideas are offensive?"[13] My comments should have given my academic critics pause since it reflected views that were the very opposite of the ones they attributed to me. But it didn't. That would have meant giving serious consideration to our proposals and concerns.

The Hearings

Since we were getting nowhere in our efforts to find a university partner, we took the opportunities that presented themselves. Once again, these led us into the legislative arena. In March 2005, I was contacted by Pennsylvania assemblyman Gib Armstrong who was interested in sponsoring a resolution similar to Ohio's, based on the Academic Bill of Rights.

Armstrong was a former Army Ranger who had served in Mogadishu. He had been approached by a constituent at a Republican Party picnic who complained about a course she had taken at Penn State University. The student, Jennie Mae Brown, had served in the Air Force in Iraq, after which she returned home to resume her education. She had enrolled in a physics course at Penn State and was shocked when her physics professor devoted class time to rants against the military and the war.[14]

At this point in our campaign, I was of the opinion that we had achieved all we could through legislative resolutions. We had set out to raise public awareness of an issue which had previously received scant attention, and to make it a matter that university officials could not continue to ignore. In roughly two and half years, we had made academic freedom rights for students one of the most talked about issues in the academic world. Despite the Left's overwrought fears, Republican legislators had little appetite for these issues, and the ferocity of the opposition and its alarmist attacks were sufficient to stall most of our bills. We did not have the staff to push the resolutions through multiple state houses, and I had no real interest in pursuing this avenue any further. But Armstrong had already drafted legislation and was proceeding under his own steam, so I readily agreed to work with him.

At the same time, the factors that had confronted us elsewhere were present in Pennsylvania and would affect our efforts at every turn. Among them was the general disinterest Republicans showed in the issue itself and their ingrained reluctance to take on the unions. The only reason Pennsylvania's Republican legislators were willing to support Armstrong's legislation was that John Purzell, the Speaker of the Pennsylvania House who had been enlisted in our cause by a mutual friend, supported it.

Nonetheless, the lukewarm attitude of the Republican majority led to an immediate change in the nature of the legislation. Despite their dominance in the House, Armstrong's colleagues lacked the political stomach to confront the predictable opposition to a resolution supporting an Academic Bill of Rights.[15] On the other hand, they were willing to pass legislation which simply called for an inquiry into the state of academic freedom. I was relieved by this development, since we had already exhausted the possibilities of resolutions supporting the bill of rights, and I welcomed the new opportunity it presented.

The preamble to Armstrong's legislation (HR 177) was drawn almost verbatim from the Academic Bill of Rights. The legislation itself created a House Select Committee on Academic Freedom in Higher Education and authorized it to

> ...examine, study and inform the House of Representatives on matters relating to the academic atmosphere and the degree to which faculty have the opportunity to instruct and students have the opportunity to learn in an environment conducive to the pursuit of knowledge and the expression of independent thought at State-related and State-owned colleges, universities, and community colleges.[16]

When sent to the floor, Armstrong's bill passed in a bitterly contested party-line vote of 108 to 90, with about a dozen members of both parties switching sides. During the floor debate, the Democrats had denounced the proposed committee as "McCarthyism" and "thought-control," while Republicans tepidly defended it.

After the bill passed, the Democrats who had led the fight against it were selected by their party to represent the minority on the newly created Committee, where they continued their opposition. Democrat Lawrence Curry, an ally of the teacher unions and fierce opponent of the legislation, became the Committee's co-chair. Gib Armstrong, who was the bill's sponsor and our most committed advocate, was only a freshman legislator and was therefore not selected to be the majority co-chair. This responsibility was passed to Thomas L. Stevenson, a reluctant participant who never contacted me and whose primary concern throughout the ensuing battles was to survive the ordeal with as few scars as possible.

The Committee hearings began in Harrisburg on September 19, 2005. In his opening statement, Stevenson, sensitive to the attacks that had already been made on his committee, laid down rules that excluded the mentioning of the names of individuals and that focused the inquiry on university policy. I was actually pleased with his statement of these rules which were designed to insulate the hearings from the charge of being a legislative inquisition. "This Committee's focus," Stevenson said as the sessions began, "will be on the institutions and their policies, not on professors, not on students." University policies and the lack of enforcement were in fact our main concerns as well, so we were happy with this direction. On the other hand, Stevenson might have saved his breath for all the attention our opposition paid to what he said.

The first day of testimony was limited to a single witness, David French, a First Amendment lawyer who was head of the Foundation for Individual Rights in Education. French also served as the Committee's legal advisor. He discussed speech codes, which was his particular area of expertise. French had successfully sued the University of Shippensburg, which was part of the Pennsylvania state college system, and had persuaded the courts that the university's speech code was unconstitutional. French testified that fifteen of the seventeen colleges in the state system had speech codes similar to Shippensburg's, pointing out that these universities were risking taxpayer funds in order to deny Pennsylvania students their constitutional rights.

The next session took place on November 9 and 10 at the University of Pittsburgh and set the tone for what would transpire at venues across the state over the next nine months. It also made obvious that while the Republicans on the committee had been nervously preparing for an inquiry into policies and institutions, the Democrats and their union allies had been gearing up for a political war.

Mike Veon, the Democratic Whip of the Pennsylvania House, led the charge, creating a website which featured a petition campaign to stop the hearings. On behalf of the Democratic Party caucus and the teacher unions, or what he called "the education advocacy lobby," Veon denounced the new "Armstrong-McCarthy hearings" and legislative "witch-hunts." He described the Pennsylvania panel as an "attack by right-wing legislators and conservative special interest groups" whose targets were "open-minded professors and administrators" and whose aim was to "remove them from their jobs if they could, all in the name of so-called 'Academic Freedom.'" According to Veon, these forces found it "unacceptable that professors would tolerate discussions they find offensive; their version of 'freedom' would have schools locked into a curriculum straight out of Karl Rove's notebook."[17]

Playing from the same prosecutorial script, a group of leftist students showed up to interrupt the hearings with chants of "HUAC go away, let our professors stay!" an overt reference to the House Un-American Activities Committee of the McCarthy era, and an insinuation that professors were about to be fired for their political beliefs. Students might be excused for not knowing that the chairman of the Pennsylvania Committee had ruled out the mention of individual professors and thus any "witch-hunt," but members of the committee could not plead such ignorance. This did not prevent Democrat John Pallone, a member of the committee, from making the identical charge, saying of the hearings, "It's a plain and simple witch-hunt."[18]

On the first day of the Pittsburgh session, the committee heard testimony from Professor Burrell Brown who repeated the unions' principal talking point, that the Academic Bill of Rights (and by implication the hearings) was "a solution in search of a problem."[19] A month earlier, American Federation of Teachers leader William Scheuerman had denounced the Academic Bill of Rights in the identical words adding that it was "part of an extremist right-wing movement to promote a right-wing agenda."[20] Commenting on Brown's testimony, Democrat Dan Surra also repeated the union phrase: "I noticed at the end of your written remarks and your verbal remarks that you said that the Bill is a solution in search of a problem. I think I used those exact words during the floor debate [on the authorization bill]. In my view, and the more I listen to what we are doing in these hearings, and the more people testify, this is the educational equivalent of a hunt for Bigfoot."[21]

These dismissive words, which were not based on anything actually said at the hearings and did not reflect its announced purpose, were to become an unvarying theme of the Democrat and union opposition to the proceedings for their duration. To its opponents, no matter what was actually said in the sessions, the hearings remained a "witch-hunt" and a "waste of time." On the day Surra made his accusation, the Pennsylvania ACLU issued a press release with a headline that described the hearings as, "The 'Bigfoot' Committee" and compared Representative Armstrong to Senator McCarthy, while describing the proceedings as an attack on academic freedom. It also repeated the claim that there was in fact no campus problem that needed to be addressed.[22]

This was also the gist of the testimony by James V. Maher, Provost of the University of Pittsburgh, who failed to mention the fact that the University of Pittsburgh had no academic freedom policy for students, and consequently, that he had no way of knowing if there was a problem or not. Seeking to hide the lack of an academic freedom policy for students at

Pitt, Maher assured committee members that Pitt's existing "Policy on Academic Integrity" and a vague university statement about "respecting the academic rights of others" protected students sufficiently from abuses about which the committee might be concerned.[23]

Maher also cited the American Council on Education statement on academic freedom, without mentioning that the Pitt administration had failed to implement its recommendations. "The American Council on Education document," he said "... [is] entirely compatible with the University of Pittsburgh policies...." In fact the Pitt policies bore little relation to the American Council on Education statement. They did not provide students with academic freedom rights or provide them with grievance machinery for redressing academic freedom abuses.

Having deceptively insinuated that Pitt policies protected students' academic freedom rights, Maher dismissed the idea that there was any problem that needed to be addressed. "It happens that in the time that our policies have been in place and within the memory of the people that I've been able to consult who are responsible for the lower levels of the policy around the campus, I've not been able to find a case where the complaint involved the student feeling that they had been mistreated because of their political opinions."[24]

Representative Surra jumped on Maher's remarks, as confirmation that the committee's mission was a mythic quest. "So, we have 33,000 students, 4,000 faculty and numerous classes they have every week," he said, "and there's never been, never a case that's risen to formal review board?"[25] Dr. Maher responded, "That's correct; there have been a number of cases that have risen to review on issues of race and gender and such, but not on political orientation."[26] What Maher failed to mention was that Pitt actually had policies on race and gender discrimination and large apparatuses in place to deal with them, which was why there had been reviews of particular cases. There were no comparable policies or review boards bearing on academic freedom. No one on the Committee thought to point this out or to ask how students could be expected to complain about abuses to their academic freedom if there were no policies defining their academic freedom rights and no grievance procedures for complaints.

It was true, as Maher claimed, that Pitt policy included a faculty obligation to "encourage free inquiry and expression." But this policy was stated in the Faculty Handbook, which students would never see. The Faculty Handbook instructed teachers "not to consider, in academic evaluation race, color, religion, sex, sexual orientation, national origin, political or cultural affiliation." These words were *all* the University of Pittsburgh had to say on the subject. There was no statement addressing the problem of instruction and there was no grievance machinery provided to deal with the substantive issues that might arise from a political harangue by the instructor in class, or a one-sided curriculum designed to indoctrinate students in the professor's political prejudices.[27]

The only student right that the Faculty Handbook recognized in connection with political orientation was that students should be *graded* on academic merit, and not on other characteristics. Though laudable, that was an almost universally recognized right for students. But it didn't begin to address the issue of in-class proselytizing and indoctrination, which had been our concern from the beginning.

The specific Pitt policy to which Maher repeatedly referred to obscure the fact that Pitt had no academic freedom policy was called the "Policy on Academic Integrity." In fact, it had nothing to do with academic freedom but was about student ethics violations. The Policy had this to say about students: "A student has an obligation to exhibit honesty and to respect the ethical standards of the academy in carrying out his or her academic assignments."[28] And that was all. The rest of the policy listed fifteen ways in which students might violate it. Under questioning from Gib Armstrong, Maher conceded that in a recent year there had been sixty-one violations of the Academic Integrity Policy—"forty-eight of those involved plagiarism and thirteen involved cheating on quizzes or exams."[29]

Flaunting a policy about student ethics in front of ill-prepared legislators and pretending that it protected students' academic freedom rights, was hardly an elaborate form of deception, but it worked. Every administrator who subsequently testified before the committee followed Maher's example, misleading the legislators to conclude that existing policies might cover the problem, that in fact there was no problem, and that Surra was right—the hearings were just a hunt for Bigfoot.

While the hearings were in session, for example, Penn State University's administration supplied the *Centre Daily Times* with data showing that only thirteen complaints about political abuses by faculty could be located in their files over a five-year period.[30] Commenting on the article, a Democrat stated, "In Penn State, there were thirteen complaints filed. That's out of 80,000 students.... Excuse me, that doesn't seem to me like wide abuse."[31] To this Gib Armstrong responded, "If those few complaints had to do with diversity of gender or diversity of race, I think a dozen complaints would be a big deal. I think a dozen legitimate complaints on a college campus, where diversity of ideas is supposed to be at the core of what we do... deserves the full attention of the administration."[32]

It was an apt observation, but incomplete. How many gender and race complaints were actually made to justify the multi-million dollar diversity offices at institutions like Penn State? No one thought to ask during the hearings. But when we questioned officials at Penn State on this point after the hearings were over, we were told by Ken Lehrman, the Vice Provost for Affirmative Action,[33]

The following represents the number of administrative complaints of sexual harassment and race discrimination my office
has responded to over the past three academic years:

7/1/06–6/30/07
     Sexual Harassment: 1
     Race Discrimination: 2

7/1/07–6/30/08
     Sexual Harassment: 1
     Race Discrimination: 1

7/1/08–6/30/09
     Sexual Harassment: 1
     Race Discrimination: 6

So, an average of one sexual harassment complaint and three racial discrimination complaints per year over a three-year period among the same
80,000 students were sufficient to justify multi-million dollar diversity
bureaucracies, which included the salaries of diversity deans and the
expenses of administrative offices and millions of dollars in university
funds to make students aware of the problem. But an inquiry into political discrimination, violations of academic standards, and political harassment was a waste of time.

At the very moment Pennsylvania administrators were suggesting that
the rarity of academic freedom complaints indicated the lack of a problem, I happened to be reading a passage in a book by historian Lionel
Lewis on academic freedom, which described the actual number of professors persecuted in the McCarthy era.[34] The era is generally agreed to

span nine years—from 1947, when President Truman instituted a Loyalty Oath for government employees, to 1954, when Senator McCarthy was censured by his Senate colleagues and his agenda fell into disrepute. During these nine years, the number of cases where a professor's appointment was threatened because of his beliefs was 126 at 58 institutions nationally.[35] These cases led to 69 terminations of professors because of their political affiliations. Of the total, 31 were at a single institution, the University of California, which had instituted its own loyalty oath, independent of any congressional investigation and where professors who refused to sign the oath left voluntarily.

In sum, during the nine years of the McCarthy era, there were exactly 69 politically motivated terminations of professors, not counting the University of California, in all 48 states. The total number of professors at the time was several hundred thousand. There were one and a half cases per state of professors terminated because of their political beliefs. This was a far smaller number than the thirteen cases at a single university in five years considered negligible by the Penn State authorities and the Democrats on the Pennsylvania Committee. Yet, small as the number of victims in the McCarthy era was, the author concludes, "The chilling effect on the expression of all ideas by both faculty and students was significant, although in fact there is no way to measure adequately their full impact."[36]

Of course, those who complained about the infringement of their rights to free speech and association in the McCarthy era actually had such rights, and also had the knowledge that they existed. The students at Penn State had neither.

Unlike Pitt, Penn State actually had an admirable academic freedom policy (HR 64), which was taken verbatim from the AAUP Declaration, and which said among other things, "It is not the function of a faculty member in a democracy to indoctrinate his/her students with ready-made conclusions on controversial subjects."[37] But while this policy, unlike Pitt's, covered most of the issues we were concerned about, it was unavailable to students. The policy was part of the Employee Handbook, and its provisions and grievance procedures applied only to faculty. The policy for appeals stated, "Appeal: If a faculty member feels that his or her academic freedom rights have been violated, the procedure listed in the policy entitled 'Faculty Rights and Responsibilities' (HR 76) may be used."[38] Clearly, students were not authorized to avail themselves of these rights.

The same was true for the wider Pennsylvania State System of Higher Education (PASSHE), which included fourteen public universities.[39] It had no academic freedom provision except the one included in its contract with the faculty unions.[40] This, too was drawn from the AAUP documents, but did not apply to any of the 100,000 or more students in the system.

On November 11, the day after the Pitt hearings concluded, the unions organized a protest at the next scheduled site, which was Temple University in Philadelphia. The purpose of the protests was to denounce the committee and again falsely associate it with the McCarthy hearings of half a century before. To make the false connection, the organizers invited Ellen Schrecker, the left-wing academic who led the charge in the American Historical Association business meeting. Schrecker had written two books on McCarthyism, including one focused on the university called *No Ivory Tower*. In her remarks, Schrecker resurrected a McCarthy target named Barrows Dunham, who had been a Temple professor and Communist who had lost his job fifty years before because of his political associations. The keynote speaker at the protest who came to condemn his own committee as a witch-hunt was its minority co-chair Lawrence Curry.

The Temple Hearings

When the Temple hearings began on January 9, Schrecker did not attend but was allowed to have her written statement read aloud by Temple professor Rachel DuPlessis. It drew the familiar false parallels to the McCarthy era. "Just as in the 1950s," it said, "right-wing forces are threatening to impose political tests on the nation's faculties. This time, however, the threat may be even more serious, more like the McCarthy era when professors came under fire for their extracurricular political activities, their teaching and research that are at issue."[41]

There were no professors under fire at the Pennsylvania hearings—or even mentioned during the proceedings. Not one. There was not a sentence in the Academic Bill of Rights or anything else we had ever written or said in the course of our academic freedom campaign that could be construed as attempting to impose a political test on professors' teaching or research. On the contrary, the Academic Bill of Rights—and all our public statements—made clear that we were opposed to any political tests of teachers' opinions. What we were asking was that teachers would make clear to their students the line between their personal opinions and their scholarly judgments, and between opinions and what could be regarded as scientific facts.

Three weeks after Professor Schrecker's appearance, her views were presented to an academic audience of over 100,000 readers as the cover feature of the *Chronicle Review*, a weekly supplement of *The Chronicle of Higher Education*. The blazing headline read, "Worse Than McCarthy." The occasion for the charge was the Pennsylvania hearings. In an Internet advertising campaign for the issue, the *Chronicle* editors previewed the article's contents in the following terms:

> The conservative assault on higher education is worse than the anti-communist witch hunts of the late 1940s and 1950s, writes

Ellen Schrecker in this week's *Chronicle Review*. Rather than primarily attacking individual academics for their extracurricular activities, she says, critics today want the government involved in decisions about personnel, curricula, and teaching methods.[42]

The editors of *The Chronicle*, obviously sympathetic to the faculty leftists, did not think it pertinent to ask Schrecker what evidence she had to make such a statement, which was the opposite of the facts. For it was our campaign that was concerned about the way political criteria were being imposed on personnel, curricula, and instruction. We wanted to see an end to such practices through the institution of university academic freedom policies and grievance procedures—not government intervention. The purpose of the hearings was to inquire whether there were university policies in place to ensure that professional methods would be pursued and academic criteria would prevail, and to discover what university administrators were doing to rectify problems that occurred.

When we brought students before the committee to testify about abuses they had suffered, the Democratic members on the panel either ignored them or harassed them, invoking the disingenuous assurances of university administrators to the effect that students were already protected and abuses were rare. The academic freedom provision at Temple was itself taken verbatim from the 1940 academic freedom statement of the American Association of University Professors that controversial subject matter irrelevant to the course should not become part of the classroom instruction. As at Penn State, however, this regulation was part of the faculty contract, and students therefore were unaware of it.[43] The policy did not refer to student rights and did not provide a grievance procedure if professors violated the regulation. When Temple president David Adamany appeared before the Committee, he ignored these facts and, like Maher before him, testified that formal student complaints were rare.

> Mr. Chairman, we have reviewed our records and do not find any—and I want to emphasize that—any instances in which students have complained about inappropriate intrusion of political advocacy by teachers in their courses.... I've been here a good—more than five and a half years. I have not had a single complaint about inappropriate political or any political advocacy in the classroom.[44]

But why would there be complaints if students were not aware that political advocacy in the classroom was inappropriate, and there was no provision in Temple regulations for students to file such complaints? In order for students to know whether classroom conduct qualified as abusive, there would have had to be official guidelines defining appropriate faculty behavior available to them, along with a formal grievance machinery through which they could complain, and there was none.

Nonetheless, students had made informal complaints, of which President Adamany was apparently unaware. Representative Armstrong had received fifty of them from students at several Pennsylvania universities including Temple. All of the students who filed them asked Armstrong not to make their names public, because they feared reprisal from faculty. That in itself should have been alarming. Twelve of the complaints came from Temple students, who also wished to have their names withheld, including one from a student who had taken an English literature class.

> My professor used English class as a vehicle to spread his/her[45] view of Marxist/socialist ideology, often demonized President

Bush, called capitalism evil, blamed the administration for the Katrina response, oftentimes gave one side of an argument in readings, often disrespected President Bush and everyone else in favor of conservative views or the Republican Party, frequently criticized the war in Afghanistan. The day after the [2004 presidential] election said in class "I cannot believe it. I do not understand America, the American people. They vote that guy, President Bush, into office for four more years after they see what he has done. Why does the U.S. military study the languages cultures of other people? So they can kill them easier," referring to the defense language program of Monterey.[46]

When the student's letter was read to President Adamany, he prudently expressed concern about the situation, as any administrator testifying before a legislative committee would. But since he had already assured the Committee that policies were in place to take care of these matters, his concession had no real significance. Without an academic regulation specifying that an in-class performance like this was inappropriate, which Temple was lacking, and without a grievance machinery to protect students who spoke up, there would only be complaints when a legislator such as Armstrong actively sought them. Consequently, this kind of faculty behavior would continue.

Only one Temple student, Logan Fisher, was willing to testify in person. A Temple senior majoring in business law, Fisher was vice chairman of College Republicans and also our Students for Academic Freedom chapter president. Logan explained to me that he alone was willing to testify publicly, because he was enrolled in the business school, which was relatively free of these problems. In addition, he was a senior and consequently didn't feel as vulnerable as others might. These advantages notwithstanding, I admired students like Logan who were willing to stand up, particularly when I witnessed the way he was treated by Democrats on the committee.

There was really nothing to be gained by students voicing complaints. Most conservative students had learned to put their heads down and get by. They avoided conflict by tempering their views in accordance with their instructors' prejudices. Those who did not were often able to escape dramatically lowered grades, because there were grievance procedures in place for such practices. Radical professors understood that if, showed fairness in assigning grades, they could get away with saying almost anything they wished in the classroom, whether it was academically appropriate or not. What students principally suffered was in-class harassment and poor instruction, and this affected all students. There was no redress for that.

Logan Fisher appeared before the Committee at the end of the day on January 9. "I want to start off," he stated, "by saying that my testimony today will not only contain my personal experience but that of many students who are afraid to testify for fear of repercussion to their academic careers." Many students, he added, had expressed to him their concern about "retaliation by professors and fear of getting singled out in classes in the future." Another concern he said he was familiar with was about recommendations for jobs and graduate school. Sudents felt these would be withheld if they "made trouble."[47]

In his testimony, Logan said a matter of concern to him was the "partisan role" he thought Temple played in the 2004 election. He mentioned a Michael Moore rally to support John Kerry and then a "Vote or Die" rally and concert organized by rapper "P. Diddy" Combs with tickets distributed by the Student Center "free to anyone who had a student ID card." Ostensibly a rally to "get out the vote," the event proved anything but. "During the performance I was treated to entertainer-led chants of—

and excuse me, 'F— George Bush, F— George Bush, F— George Bush.' Throughout the performance, they lectured students on how important it was to 'Throw Bush out of the White House' and 'Send him the F— back to Texas.' It does not seem proper for a taxpayer-funded university to be institutionally partisan like this."[48] In fact, it was against the law, but it was a law no one was bothering to enforce.

Logan presented the legislators with several examples of instructors' behavior that troubled him. "I had a professor last semester ask if it is ever justified for the United States to break with the international community to protect our own interest [this was during the Iraq War when the Republican administration was being criticized for 'unilateralism']. When I answered 'Yes,' the professor told me 'Well you're going to have a rough semester in this class.'"[49] Logan then asked the panel, "Is it appropriate for a professor to threaten students like this just because they disagree with them on political issues? Many of my professors have pictures of Bush on their office doors with derogatory comments attached. This is not very reassuring to me when I show up to talk to them about non-political class related issues since they know I'm the vice chairman of the College Republicans."[50]

Overlooking the fact that there were no grievance procedures regarding students' academic freedom at Temple, Representative Armstrong asked Logan if, nonetheless, he had filed a formal complaint about the professor. Logan answered, "I have not lodged any formal complaint just for the fact that I don't think they would be handled at all. I've talked to several professors outside of class if I have disagreed with the way they've done one thing or another. And I'm usually dismissed by the professor. So I didn't feel that lodging a formal complaint would do much good."[51] Under questioning by another committee member, Logan conceded that he felt his grade had been lowered by the same professor because of his views.[52]

Finally, Armstrong asked him whether he felt he would "suffer any ill effects for having taken the time to appear before this committee today?" Logan replied, "I feel that if I was a freshman or a sophomore I might say— be inclined to say yes. I'm a graduating senior which is one of the things that convinced me that I need to step up and say something today."[53]

Instead of being alarmed by this testimony, the Democrats turned prosecutorial towards Logan, a distinct contrast to the soft questions they served up to administrators and union witnesses. Representative Surra attempted to brush off Logan's account of the Michael Moore rally for John Kerry on the Temple campus by comparing it to an appearance by President Bush at a football game where Penn State coach Joe Paterno gave the president a victory sign.[54] Lawrence Curry went a step further, seizing on an example Logan had provided of a student complaint, which the student herself had been too fearful to present.

The student had been required by her instructor to attend a dance concert "where the performers sang the national anthem, waved the white flag of surrender and hailed Hitler." The student complained that the instructor gave her a "C" for the paper she wrote on the event.[55] I knew the student in question, and she was an honor student on the Dean's list.

The questioning continued.

> Curry: We don't know whether that "C" was because of bad grammar or missing the point of the assignment.
> Fisher: No, we don't know.
> Curry: So we really can't use that as an example of bias....
> Fisher: No. I think the point that the student was trying to make was that she had done exceptionally well in the class up until then. And when she had a particular opposition to this one assignment, that's when she received a low grade.

As though Logan had not just provided his own example of a faculty retaliation, Curry asked, "Are you aware of any retaliation that a student experienced for disagreeing with a lecture and saying so?"

Logan was either too polite or too flustered from the browbeating Curry was administering to remind the legislator that he had just testified he felt his own grade had suffered, because he disagreed with his instructor. Instead, Logan answered, "No, just that students were made to feel that they were put down in class."

Logan's honesty earned him no slack from Curry, who proceeded with his interrogation, insinuating that it would only be appropriate for a student to challenge a professor's opinions if he himself had done research in their field.

> Curry: Is their disagreement with a professor in the class that would be substantive based on their research in the field or their reading in the field? What's the basis for their disagreement with the professor?
> Fisher: I don't understand the question.
> Curry: Well, they disagreed with the professor, something he says during the discussion or reading material. Is that based on the student's background or the student's research, or the student's reading?
> Fisher: I don't know what you're [saying] but I'm sure the students that would object, would be their personal opinions.
> Curry: It's their opinion?
> Fisher: I'm not sure I understand what you're asking?[56]

The reader should bear in mind that the examples of students' substantive disagreements with instructors in class that Curry was suggesting should be backed by research in their field were over professorial statements like this: "I cannot believe it. I do not understand America, the American people, they vote that guy, President Bush, into office for four more years after they see what he has done." And this: "Why does the US military study the languages and cultures of other people? So they can kill them easier."[57]

The exchange between Curry and Logan, which continued in the same vein at length, was as revealing as anything that had occurred during the hearing sessions. Twelve Temple students had submitted written complaints to Representative Armstrong and told him that they were afraid to have their names made public for fear of reprisal. Neither Curry nor any of his Democratic colleagues exhibited the slightest interest in these statements or concern about these students or about the situation their fears reflected. Instead, they essentially accused the students of lying. Curry's demeaning cross examination of Logan Fisher demonstrated exactly why students might think twice before voicing such complaints and exposing themselves to the wrath of adults who were in a position to embarrass them, damage their careers, and cast doubts on their credibility and intelligence.

An Important Victory

From my point of view, the hearings were going badly. This was not surprising since the Democrats had opposed them from the start, continuing their opposition as its sitting members, even joining its adversaries to denounce it as a "witch-hunt" and "waste of time." They had demonstrated no interest in finding out whether the complaints of students such as Logan Fisher reflected a campus reality, or whether the university actually had policies in place to deal with these problems as administrators who appeared before the Committee claimed. On the other hand, the Republicans involved, beginning with their chairman, were unwilling to confront the Democrats over their efforts to undermine the proceedings of their own committee and were both reluctant and ill-prepared to expose the bureaucratic subterfuge of the administrators who testified.

Gib Armstrong's questions were the only difficult ones Republicans asked administrators and the hostile witnesses supplied by the unions. In fact, Armstrong asked almost all the non pro forma questions on the Republican side, but Armstrong was only one of nine committee members with equal time constraints and was himself a freshman legislator with little experience on educational issues.

There were, however, positive aspects to the proceedings. We were able to put knowledgeable witnesses before the committee and provide valuable statements from experts unable to attend. There were important testimonies from Stephen Balch, president of the National Association of Scholars, and Anne Neal, head of the Association of College Trustees and Alumni, as well as professors such as Stephen Zelnick, who had been a vice provost at Temple.[58] We were also getting a lot of publicity across the state, and while most of it publicized the talking points of the teacher unions, it made people aware of the issues we were trying to raise.

The goal of our legislative strategy had always been to gain public attention and put pressure on administrators. The publicity generated by the hearings greatly magnified this pressure, not least because of the protests the radicals staged and the stories they planted whose hysterical tones sowed doubts about their credibility. In April, as the hearings headed for their final sessions, these pressures reached a critical mass and produced a victory for our cause. Because it gained so little publicity, however, I didn't learn of it until months later.

On April 25, 2006, the Penn State Faculty Senate passed a resolution to extend Penn State's academic freedom provision, which had been previously restricted to faculty members, to students. It was the first time academic freedom rights were being made available to Pennsylvania students, and it was through our efforts the result had been achieved.[59]

On July 19, the trustees of Temple met and adopted a new policy called "Student and Faculty Academic Rights and Responsibilities," which secured the same end. Marlene Kowal, who was head of our campus chapter of Students for Academic Freedom at Temple, had arranged for twenty of her peers to meet with Temple trustees. Many of these students had also submitted written testimonies to Gib Armstrong, who offered to share them with the Democrats on the Committee, including the names of the students. The Democrats were not interested, but the Temple trustees were. After meeting with the students, the trustees were disturbed enough by what they heard to write a new Temple policy on academic freedom.

The Temple policy declared that "freedom to teach and freedom to learn are inseparable facets of academic freedom."[60] They set up a grievance machinery for students who felt their rights had been infringed. The new policy was explicit that this was to be a different grievance machinery from existing university procedures, which dealt only with unfair grading practices. The new procedures would specifically address a student's right to learn free from political harassment and indoctrination. The policy further stipulated that all incoming freshmen would be made aware of their right to expect professional behavior from their professors.

This was a model of what could have been accomplished at every university in Pennsylvania if the faculty unions and their Democratic allies had not been so determined to block reform or even a serious inquiry into the problem. There would have been little difficulty in ascertaining whether there was a real problem of faculty abuse if university administrators had been determined to find out. Universities commonly submitted evaluation forms to students about their professors' performances in respect to racial and gender diversity issues. But there were no inquiries about instructors' professionalism or academic freedom issues. If there were, the entire controversy over whether there was a problem or whether there was only a "solution in search of a problem" would have been quickly settled.

Not a single story about these developments appeared in the press, including the education press. The creation of new academic freedom policies went entirely unnoted. The only significant notice of the hearings was one that ridiculed our efforts and cast doubt on our concerns. This was the result of an ambush that Lawrence Curry and the unions set for me when I appeared before the Committee.

I was the last witness of the day on the afternoon of January 10, 2006, and I spoke for forty-five minutes.[61] I began by observing that "contrary to the PR and advance work that has been done by the teacher unions, I am a friend of the universities of Pennsylvania both public and private. I want to see them strengthened and I want to see that students have a better education." I went on,[62]

> The most pressing matter before this committee is . . . to examine the failure of the administrators of Pennsylvania's institutions of higher learning to respect and observe federal and state law [regarding speech codes] and their own regulations pertaining to the academic freedom of their students.[63]

I then gave several examples of problems that had been addressed, drawing on the signed student complaints that had been submitted to Gib Armstrong. One was from a student at Penn State. It read, "I had a professor in a biology class go off on a twenty minute lecture about how Bush was a horrible president and had misled the people, and that if I supported the war in Iraq, I was a bad, ignorant person."[64] In my own campus visits, I had heard similar reports from other students about their physics teachers, Spanish teachers, French teachers, math teachers, chemistry professors, and even an accounting professor. Individuals will have strong opinions in wartime, which is one reason why professional restraints are necessary. As I frequently observed in the course of the speeches I gave on college campuses, "You don't go to your doctor expecting to get a lecture on the war in Iraq, so why should you get one from your English professor?"

It was on just such a point, however, that two of the Democrats were waiting to blind-side me. They had planned to raise an incident that had nothing to do with my actual testimony, regarding a claim that had not originated with me, which had proven inaccurate. It was originally made by someone in Gib Armstrong's office and concerned a report that Michael Moore's propaganda film against the Iraq War—*Fahrenheit 9/11*—had been shown in a biology class at Penn State. Since Armstrong was gathering student complaints, I assumed he knew and had confirmed the source, and therefore felt comfortable repeating the story. The example was never important in itself but was useful to illustrate a problem with which I was quite familiar. I referred to the general problem (without mentioning the film) in my testimony. "I have interviewed at least a hundred students in this state," I said, "and every one of them has been in a class or in several classes in which their professors have railed against George Bush, the war in Iraq, and the policies and attitudes of Republicans and conservatives."[65]

The Michael Moore film had been widely shown in university classes. When I spoke at Columbia University, for example, I was told by a student that *Fahrenheit 9/11* had been shown in his civil engineering class. Consequently, I had no reason to doubt the story about the biology class. But when a biology professor at one of the many Penn State campuses challenged the claim, I called Armstrong about it, and he said his office couldn't produce the source. As soon as I heard this, I dropped the story and told Armstrong that he should too.

Apparently no one told the committee chairman, Tom Stevenson, who brought it up during the Pitt hearings in a question put to Professor Burrell Brown. Brown was president of the faculty union at his university and maintained that existing university policies were sufficient to take care of the problems the hearings were attempting to address.

Stevenson: It has been said that in one of our universities in a biology class the professor showed the film *Fahrenheit 9/11*. Would that be inappropriate?

> Brown: What kind of class?
> Stevenson: Biology class.
> Brown: I cannot see a direct message [sic] between *Fahrenheit 9/11* and the subject.
> Stevenson: Thank you. So you just determined that it was probably inappropriate or irrelevant?
> Brown: Yes. That particular case.
> Stevenson: That's the point that is trying to be made.... Those extreme situations. But it does occur.
> Brown: Yes, I think it does, and I agree that where determination has been made and once that determination has been made that those actions should cease.[66]

In light of what took place during my testimony, this exchange is of more than passing interest. The two were actually interested in determining what might constitute an appropriate professional discourse in a classroom. Both the Republican legislator and the president of the faculty union agreed that there could be a discourse that was unprofessional and inappropriate, which violated academic freedom standards. They both agreed that if *Fahrenheit 9/11* were in fact shown in a biology class, it would constitute a case of inappropriate discourse. This was basically what we were asking universities to do—set up the machinery to decide such issues and deal with such cases. The exchange between Stevenson and Professor Brown showed that if we could get past the wall of distortions that our opponents had erected, we could find partners for reform on the other side.

Unfortunately, the opposition was determined to make sure this would not happen. As I finished my testimony and the question period began, Representative John Yudichak said he was concerned about the charge that *Fahrenheit 9/11* had been shown in a biology class, "which after further investigation was incorrect."[67] I immediately conceded the error.

> Yudichak: The charge against the Penn State biology class was incorrect?
> Horowitz: Yes. I think that was incorrect.
> Yudichak: Thank you. I'm finished.[68]

It was then Lawrence Curry's turn. Before returning to the Moore film, he questioned my veracity in reporting the case of a liberal student at a California college who claimed that his conservative, pro-life professor had given him a "D" because he was pro-choice. The student was also the leader of the anti-war movement on campus. In an article published on my website, he said, "I find most of David Horowitz's Right-wing views to be offensive," but he also supported my academic freedom activities.[69] I had asked him to write the article because of his support and not because I had investigated the merits of his case. I was interested in demonstrating that I would defend liberal students as well as conservatives. But Curry had no interest in this. His opening question was, "How do you know that the student in Foothills got a 'D' because of her point of view, as opposed to what she answered on—"

I interrupted Curry to point out that the student was male—he was also an honors student—and that my intention in publishing his article was merely to give him a platform, not to investigate his case. Curry then shifted his attack.

> Curry: In one of your essays . . . you recite about the showing of *Fahrenheit 9/11* before the election. Now we know that that didn't happen. . . . Are you prepared to retract that in a public setting? Horowitz: I did. I have already retracted it on my website . . . [70]

It didn't occur to me that these questions were part of a set up until the next day when I saw the lead story in InsideHigherEd.com and its title, "Retractions From David Horowitz."[71] The story was written by editor Scott Jaschik and began with these loaded sentences:

> Many faculty leaders have worried that this week's hearings by a Pennsylvania legislative committee would turn into just the kind of professorial inquisition that they have feared the "Academic Bill of Rights" might set off. But as hearings ended in Philadelphia Tuesday, critics of the Academic Bill of Rights were saying that they had scored key points. David Horowitz, the conservative activist who has led the push for the hearings in Pennsylvania and elsewhere, admitted that he had no evidence to back up two of the stories he has told multiple times to back up his charges that political bias is rampant in higher education.[72]

This was the *only* article on the hearings to appear in InsideHigherEd.com, and there was not a word in it about my testimony or the ten hours of testimony provided by others in the two days of the Temple Hearings. The author, Scott Jaschik, had called me as soon as I left the hearing to get my reaction, and he reported my response to Curry's question. "These are nit picking, irrelevant attacks," I said. But this quote from me was immediately followed in the article by the comments of a union official, who was the operative behind the Free Exchange coalition and had been the author of many ugly smears throughout the campaign. "'So much of what he has said previously," he wrote, "has been exposed to be lies or distortions that it makes any of his examples questionable,' said Jamie Horwitz, a spokesman for the American Federation of Teachers. The lack of evidence about the Penn State and other examples 'should give this committee and any committee anywhere in the country pause about considering an Academic Bill of Rights,' he added."[73]

Thanks to Jaschik's loaded report and the silence of the general media, the union slanders had become the story of the hearings, while the evidence we had amassed in five days of testimony and the case we had assembled (and eventually the reforms we achieved) went unreported.

The Final Committee Report

When the hearings drew to a close six months later, Gib Armstrong was assigned the task of writing the official committee report. The Republican caucus had a one vote majority which normally would have guaranteed its acceptance. Given the attitudes of several Republicans on the committee, particularly Lynn Herman who represented the Penn State district and was visibly hostile to the proceedings, I was not confident about the eventual result, but I was unprepared for what actually took place.

With Armstrong's support, I agreed to draft the report for the Republican majority, which would then be reviewed by Armstrong and the committee staff.[74] In writing it, I made an effort to be fair to the Democratic minority and report their skepticism and concerns. The report described the work of the committee and its proceedings and recommendations, which was the general purpose of such documents. When I was finished, two-thirds of the draft (or about 10,000 of its 15,000 words) were devoted to a "Summary of Testimony," reviewing the statements of witnesses and discussions between members of the Committee.

I regarded the centerpiece of this section to be the detailed review of the academic freedom regulations at Pitt, Penn State, Temple University, and the larger Penn State system, which included fourteen public universities. In each case, the review showed that, with the exceptions of Temple and Penn State, each of which had introduced new regulations in response to the committee's work, the existing academic freedom provisions at Pennsylvania's state universities did not apply to students, usually because they were part of the faculty contract or were included in regulations specific to employees. Furthermore, none of these schools had grievance machinery that specifically addressed the academic freedom of students. The draft underscored the fact that the two universities, Penn State and Temple, had adopted academic freedom provisions for students as a result of the committee's work, and included appendices which contained the new regulations.

The "Recommendations" section, which I also wrote, stressed the need for the other universities to create "student-specific" academic freedom rights, as Penn State and Temple had, and to accompany them with grievance procedures, and finally to notify students of their existence. The key recommendation was this:

> Public institutions of higher education within the Common-
> wealth should review their existing academic freedom policies
> and procedures to ensure that a student-specific academic free-
> dom policy, which includes student rights and a detailed griev-
> ance procedure is available.[75]

If this report had been adopted and published intact, we would have achieved what we sought in the Pennsylvania hearings. The legislature would have recommended that all Pennsylvania state institutions provide rights and procedures for students to protect their academic freedom. The universities would then be responsible for devising the actual policies and for enforcing them. There would have been no government control over curriculum or other university policies, and students in Pennsylvania public universities would finally have had the protections they needed.

Unfortunately, our opponents had other plans, and the political clout to implement them. It was an election year for the Pennsylvania legislature, and all the members of the committee were up for re-election and were out in their districts seeking support. The meeting of the Republican caucus at which the committee majority should have ratified the report never took place. Lynn Herman and another Republican committee member failed to appear at the scheduled time, depriving the group of a quorum. A week later, on November 21—the very eve of the deadline for filing the report—the Democrats showed up with a revised document and a new majority, which included the two Republican defectors.

There was no time left for the Democrats to write a new report, or perhaps they were so uninterested in the issues the committee had addressed they just didn't think it worth doing. They simply gutted the report that had been submitted, removing the entire "Summary of Testimony," including the analysis showing the lack of academic freedom protections for students at all but two of Pennsylvania's public universities. Summarizing their own unwavering view throughout the hearings, they inserted a sentence in the "Findings" of the report, which said, "The committee received testimony from each sector of public higher education and determined that academic freedom violations are rare."[76]

This was exactly the result our union opponents wanted (and no doubt had a hand in drafting). It gave the false impression that the committee had conducted a real inquiry into academic freedom violations, something the Democratic majority had done everything in its power to thwart. No such inquiry had taken place since students were intimidated from appearing in person, and the Democrats showed no interest in considering the complaints that had been submitted to Gib Armstrong in private.

The Democrats' report provided the unions with an additional argument to prevent students from getting academic freedom rights: there had been an inquiry, and no violations were found. The new version even removed the term "student-specific rights" from the recommendations. Consequently, no changes were made, and there were no new policies at the fifteen Pennsylvania public universities where students lacked academic freedom rights.

For me, the most dispiriting aspect of the episode was the fact that the Republicans did not protest this travesty, but actually validated it. Once the Democrats had the upper hand, the Republicans on the committee capitulated to the majority and voted to ratify the eviscerated report. It is true that they were demoralized by their defeat in the elections two weeks earlier, which was driven by a backlash against pay raises legislators had voted themselves that year. The Republicans lost fourteen seats, including those belonging to Gib Armstrong and Tom Stevenson. Armstrong explained to me afterwards that the Republican members were too embarrassed to vote against the report of a committee on which they were a paper majority, and just wanted to go home after their defeat in the elections. But I also was of the opinion that,with the exception of Gib Armstrong, the Republicans on the Committee—unlike their Democratic counterparts—never took the battle seriously, and were always just trying to get through the hearings with as little damage to their resumes as possible.

Naturally, the union coalition was thrilled by this turn of events. They issued a press release celebrating their victory, which summarized the final report as saying that Pennsylvania universities "should continue doing what they are doing."[77] This was followed by a post on the Free Exchange website titled, "The David Horowitz Fan Club Could Meet in a Phone Booth." It observed that not even conservatives had rallied to our cause.

> While we noted last week the crushing defeat David Horowitz and his so-called Academic Bill of Rights suffered, it is also worth pointing out his efforts were largely ignored by most conservative media, including PhiBetaCons [*National Review*] and *Human Events* Online. *Reason* magazine contributing editor Cathy Young branded Horowitz's Academic Bill of Rights efforts as "legislative interference." The obvious conclusion is that no matter how super-serious David Horowitz is about dictating what goes on in the college classroom, no one will listen to him.[78]

This flatly contradicted the claim otherwise trumpeted by the unions— that we were part of a vast right-wing conspiracy against left-wing academics. But consistency was not a consideration in their propaganda war. The obituary, on the other hand, was premature and pointedly omitted our success. We had suffered a setback, but we had also changed the academic policies at two major public universities, providing students with academic freedom rights and grievance procedures for the first time. This was no small achievement, especially with the cards stacked so heavily against us.

The lack of interest shown by conservatives was a frustrating fact but not a new one. Despite appeals I had made to the editors of the major conservative journals, all of whom I knew personally, and although we had been engaged in the campaign for more than three years, not a single story about our efforts in Pennsylvania had appeared in the conservative press. By now, I was used to the lonely battlefield on which we were forced to operate and the enormous odds we faced. There was not a single media outlet other than my websites that I could rely on to present the facts about the hearings or provide the public with an indication of the opportunity that had been missed. My requests to the *Chronicle of Higher Education* and InsideHigherEd.com to write an opinion column about the hearings were summarily turned down.

Yet, given what we had been able to accomplish with the odds we faced, I was not discouraged. There was another side of the story. We had inspired the first academic freedom hearings ever held in the state of Pennsylvania and probably in the nation. We had brought academic freedom rights to two major universities and had done so through the work of a handful of dedicated people. These included the Speaker of the Pennsylvania House, a freshman legislator, a silent but savvy financial backer, myself, and a two-person staff. Despite the opposition of teacher unions with massive budgets and agents in every college district in the state, and with powerful allies in the press, we had almost succeeded in changing the education policy of the Commonwealth of Pennsylvania. While we nursed our wounds, we took consolation from these facts and prepared for the battles ahead.

CHAPTER TEN

Two Attempts to Achieve a Result

A FTER THE PENNSYLVANIA HEARINGS, I DECIDED TO FOCUS OUR ENER-gies on the Penn State campus in the hope of testing whether the new academic freedom policy for students would actually work. At the beginning of the 2007 spring term, I published an ad in the Penn State newspaper, *The Nittany Lion*. It was headlined "Know Your Rights." It began, "As a result of the academic freedom hearings held by the Pennsylvania legislature between September 2005 and June 2006, students at Penn State now have academic freedom rights for the first time in history,"[1] and went on to explain the rights.

One major problem the Pennsylvania hearings had addressed was students' lack of awareness of academic freedom policies. It was the one issue that both parties agreed on. The committee recommended that, "public institutions of higher education should make students aware of the availability of academic freedom policies and grievance procedures. This should be accomplished by providing such information during student

orientation when other student rights policies and/or discrimination policies are discussed. Additionally, this information should be available in
the 'student' section of the institution's website."

The Penn State Administration had put the new policy in the *University Undergraduate Advising Handbook* which was posted online.[2] But this
alone was not sufficient to inform the very large student body at Penn
State of their rights under the Penn State regulations. Sexual and racial
discrimination policies were backed by an elaborate support apparatus,
which ensured that students would be aware of them. If students did not
know their rights, there was little likelihood they would avail themselves
of their provisions. The failure of Penn State to make these rights a prominent university concern, moreover, meant that students who did seek to
utilize them could not expect much institutional support. Since any complaint filed would be against their own professors, this was a daunting
obstacle for students who were anxious about possible retribution.

Penn State did not lack courses that violated the academic freedom
regulation HR 64. Jacob Laksin and I had written a report documenting
more than a dozen such courses whose posted syllabi were clearly
designed to indoctrinate students with one perspective on controversial
issues.[3] The catalogue description of an "Introduction to Women's Studies" course taught by Professor Michael Johnson began, "Men are privileged relative to women. That's not right. I'm going to do *something* about
it, even if it's only in my personal life." Johnson explains that he will
"spend most of the course on just a few of the ways that men are privileged
relative to women. We'll look at how and why women face more barriers
to happiness and fulfillment than do men, and how we might go about
helping our world to move in the direction of gender equity." These contentious propositions, Laksin and I observed in our report, "are not raised
as a potential object of disinterested academic inquiry, but as 'truths' stu-

dents are expected to embrace. The professor commends his course to those students who 'want a really full feminist experience.' This is an appropriate invitation to join a political party, not an academic class-room."[4]

I sent our report to Penn State President Graham Spanier and his board of trustees as well as to the head of the Faculty Senate, Dawn Blasko, with no result.[5] Without faculty and administration support for academic standards and the academic freedom rights of students, it was hardly surprising that I encountered difficulty in finding a student willing to file a formal complaint and face the wrath of his professors.

A regulation known as "R-6" established the guidelines for grievances. R-6 required the student to first file the complaint with the professor against whom the grievance was being made, and then with the depart-ment chair, before going to any other authorities. It also required com-plaints to be filed while the class was in progress and the professor still held the final grade over the students' head.[6] These were two good reasons not to file the complaint, especially if the infraction occurred in a course which was part of the student's major. A final consideration for a conser-vative student was that there were no visible conservatives on the Penn State faculty to provide counsel and support.[7]

Despite these obstacles, I was able to find a senior named A. J. Fluehr who was willing to file grievances over some of his courses once I explained the policy to him. Fluehr was hesitant at first, because he was not willing to file a complaint while the class was in session, as the R-6 regulation required. I encouraged him to do so after the semester was over, and to argue the point if it was subsequently raised by the faculty authority (as it was). Fluehr was quite skeptical of the chances of success, but I urged him to pursue the grievance in order to show others that it could be done. To encourage him, I informed him that I was already engaged in a correspondence with the Provost's office, and that Senator Gibson Armstrong, the chair of the Pennsylvania Senate Appropriations Committee (and father of Gib Armstrong) would be watching our progress. I assured him that the university would not be able to simply brush off his concerns.

Fluehr's first grievance concerned English 202A, a class devoted to "Effective Writing in the Social Sciences," taught by Professor Cynthia Mazzant. Fluehr had already talked to Mazzant about the concerns he had with her class with no effect, so he decided to submit his formal complaint directly to the Department chair, Robert L. Caserio. In his complaint, Fleuhr noted that the course focused on one social science issue—poverty—and that the instructor had presented only one perspective of poverty to her students. In Fleuhr's words:

> The course description says… "You will decide WHAT to write about and this course will focus on HOW to write about it." (Emphasis in original.) Despite this promise that students can make up their own minds as to the subject they want to write about and how they want to do it, the course is structured to give students a one-sided view of the problem of poverty in America and to promote that view lesson by lesson and day by day for the first half of the course. This is in direct violation of Penn State policy HR 64 which explicitly forbids the indoctrination of students to embrace one side of a controversial issue.[8]

Fluehr pointed out that the reading assignments for the course were also one-sided. "There are only two books assigned for mandatory reading by the course instructor," he wrote. "One is *Nickel and Dimed* by Barbara Ehrenreich and the other is *The Working Poor* by David K. Shipler. Ehrenreich is honorary co-chair of the Democratic Socialists of America with extreme left-wing views of America's market economy. At one point Mrs. Ehrenreich says she must refrain from 'going on a Marxist rant,' but her book is a frank argument for the Marxist point of view. David Shipler is a more moderate leftist who also has negative views of America's market system. Both books take a dim view of capitalism and large corporations such as Wal-Mart."[9]

Fluehr conceded that "students were allowed and encouraged to speak their minds," but observed that because "no alternative texts were provided... any student who wished to express a dissenting view [was put] at an extreme disadvantage, since the rest of the class was working off a text assigned by the instructor who clearly embraced the views it expressed." Fleuhr then observed,

> This class violates Penn State policy HR 64, which states that, "it is not the function of a faculty member in a democracy to indoctrinate his/her students with ready-made conclusions on controversial subjects. The faculty member is expected to train students to think for themselves, and to provide them access to those materials which they need if they are to think intelligently. Hence in giving instruction upon controversial matters the faculty member is expected to be of a fair and judicial mind, and to set forth justly, without supersession or innuendo, the divergent opinions of other investigators."[10]

Fluehr further complained that the instructor had shown Al Gore's environmental film *An Inconvenient Truth* to the class without any critical counters that would allow students to make up their own minds about global warming as the Penn State academic freedom regulation required.

Moreover, he pointed out that global warming was a matter for climatologists and not really a social science issue.

> The political agendas of the teacher in this class were made clear when, during a class session, the instructor used the last thirty minutes of class time to show Al Gore's *An Inconvenient Truth*, "a film unrelated to the subject of the course which was how to write a *social science* essay.... Global warming is a subject for *environmental* science, not for an English class designed to teach students to write papers on topics in the *social* sciences. Penn State Policy HR 64 could not be clearer in condemning this very practice: "No faculty member may claim as a right the privilege of discussing in the classroom controversial topics outside his/her own field of study. The faculty member is normally bound not to take advantage of his/her position by introducing into the classroom provocative discussions of irrelevant subjects not within the field of his/her study."

Fluehr continued,

> As with the main subject of the course, poverty, the left-wing view of global warming was inappropriately presented as though it were fact. No viewpoint opposing the one expressed in the Gore film was mentioned; no materials from opposing viewpoints were provided to allow students to make up their own minds or give them access to materials that would allow them to think for themselves. Again, this was a gross violation of Penn State's academic freedom provisions.

Fluehr concluded his complaint with these words:

> English 202A as taught by this instructor is clearly a course with
> an inappropriate agenda: indoctrinating students in a left-wing
> perspective on poverty in America. The teacher, who is creden-
> tialed in English literature, has no expertise for teaching about
> the American economy. More importantly, providing instruction
> on only one side of controversial issues and denying students
> access to dissenting materials violates Penn State's academic
> freedom regulations.[11]

Fluehr submitted his complaint on May 17, 2007, to the English Department chair, Robert Caserio, and to his instructor Cynthia Mazzant. A
reply was sent back to Fluehr from a third party, Stuart Selber, who said
he was acting at the chairman's request.

> Monday May 21, 2007
>
> Dear AJ Fluehr,
>
> Robert Caserio, head of the English department, passed along
> to me your concern about your section of 202A. I am director of
> the composition program. The composition office takes all com-
> plaints very seriously. In fact, we side with students as much as
> instructors. In this case, however, I couldn't find any real evi-
> dence to support your claims. The course assignments are con-
> ventional and follow program guidelines. And although the
> course texts may not have explored every side of an issue (what
> texts do?), your instructor tells me that students were asked to
> provide counter-arguments. Besides all that, you earned an A in

the class. This is terrific evidence that your views were seen as valid and that you were afforded academic freedom. I am in and out of town for the next month, but would be happy to meet with you in July (or the fall, if that is better) to discuss this matter. Let me know.

Stuart[12]

This peremptory dismissal of Fluehr's complaint without a hearing, which the regulation required, was indicative of the kind of response a student was likely to get, in the absence of support from university officials and a strong institutional endorsement of academic freedom rights for students.

When Fluehr filed his complaint, I wrote to the Penn State provost Rodney Erickson and called the head of the faculty senate, Dawn Blasko, to inform them about his case and provide copies of his filing.[13] I made it clear to both of them that my own intentions were to work within the system they had devised. I praised the faculty senate resolution applying the academic freedom provisions to students and told them I regarded it as a model for other schools. "My sole concern," I said, "is whether the policy will be observed and, in those cases where it has not been observed, whether steps will be taken to enforce it."[14] I expressed my hope that Penn State was going to enforce its policy. I also instructed Fluehr to copy his e-mails to Caserio and Selber to the provost's office and Dawn Blasko.

In responding to Selber's casual dismissal of his claim, Fluehr began by reviewing the text of the Penn State regulation. Selber had brushed aside Fluehr's observation that Mazzant had required texts arguing only one side of a controversial issue claiming that students were "asked to provide counter-arguments" to the texts. In fact, according to Fluehr, Mazzant had *not* asked students for counter-arguments; Fluehr had volunteered them. But this was beside the point, since HR 64 clearly stipulated that the instructor herself was *obligated* to present students with "the divergent opinions of other investigators" and to do so in a fair-minded manner. In other words, the academic freedom concern—dating back to the AAUP Declaration—was how an instructor presented controversial issues to students, not how students reacted to them.

Flue's second point addressed Selber's contention that since he received an "A" in the class, there was no real problem.

> The fact that I received an "A" in this class is irrelevant to the question of whether the class was taught according to the university's academic freedom guidelines. These guidelines refer to the way the course is taught, not to the methods the instructor uses to grade the course. Fair grades are important but they are covered by other regulations. It would be possible to get an "A" in a course where an instructor insists on students agreeing with his or her opinions by simply parroting them. This would not be an education but an indoctrination, and would violate Penn State regulation HR 64. The fact that I received an "A" in this class is thus not evidence that I was afforded academic freedom as you suggest. Academic freedom requires the instructor to behave professionally in the classroom, and to provide students with the materials they need to think for themselves. As I see it, English 202A as taught by Cynthia Mazzant was indisputably violating Penn State Policy. Please let me know how HR 64 does not apply to these situations.[15]

Fluehr then added, "I am troubled that the Department Chair who is identified in the academic freedom policy as the official responsible for these matters would not have responded to my complaint himself."

Two days later, Fluehr received a dismissive e-mail from the Department Chair:

> Dear A. J. Fluehr:
>
> Professor Selber, who directs all Composition classes, has written to you with my approval, and after consultation with me. I too have consulted with your instructor. In looking into your complaint, and in speaking with your instructor, Professor Selber and I find that your section of English 202A fulfills HR 64.
>
> Sincerely yours,
>
> Robert L. Caserio Professor and Head English
>
> Penn State University Park, PA.[16]

Fluehr was extremely frustrated by these responses, which dismissed his complaint in a peremptory manner. The Penn State regulation R-6 clearly stipulated that when a student filed a complaint, he was to be given an opportunity to present his case in person before a decision was made as to its merits. This had been circumvented in Fluehr's case, which was after all the first case filed under the new regulations.

> Dear Dr. Caserio,
>
> ... My reading of the regulations is that you should have met with me and/or discussed my complaint with me before reaching any conclusion as to the merits of my complaint. This is the procedure clearly indicated in Faculty Senate Policy 20-00 as set forth in Policy R-6. I don't regard a process which consults only one of the parties—in this case my instructor—and not the other as fair. In effect you have taken the instructor's word about what happened and dismissed mine without a hearing. I also note that

neither you nor the instructor has responded to the very specific examples of violations of HR 64 that I brought to your attention. I don't see how this response is in keeping either with the letter or the spirit of the Penn State regulations and am therefore taking my complaint to the next administrative level.

Sincerely,

AJ Fluehr[17]

At this point in their exchanges, Caserio evidently became aware that he was not dealing with a lone student but with the forces we had set in motion with the academic freedom hearings, and in which the Office of the Provost was involved. On June 12, Fluehr received another e-mail from Selber in which he provided what he referred to as "a more significant response" to Fluehr's complaint, and also offered to meet with him. "I would also encourage you to meet with your instructor in person and to meet with the Head of English, Dr. Caserio. We take all complaints of this nature very seriously. You have access to us if you want it."[18]

In this response Selber once again attempted to dismiss the problem of one-sided texts by contending that students rather than instructors were responsible for providing multiple viewpoints. "Part of training students to think for themselves," he wrote, "is not handing them everything. Rather, teachers set a context that encourages students to become expansive thinkers and people who can research a topic and form an argument or opinion. The policy says that teachers must provide 'access' to materials that help students think intelligently. That access was provided . . . the acceptance of multiple student views by the teacher."[19]

In regard to the Al Gore film, Selber side-stepped the same issue and instead focused on whether the propaganda film was pertinent to a course about writing social science papers.

Actually, issues of global warming have everything to do with the social sciences. My quick search of the social science citation index (through PSU LIAS) turned up nearly 5,000 hits for global warming. Go to the social sciences library and work with a reference librarian. You'll quickly see that many different disciplines are working on this problem, from scientists to social scientists and more.

This was a transparent evasion. The issue was not whether there were aspects of the global warming controversy that came under the heading of social science. Of course there were. But the Gore film was not about social science issues. It was very specifically an argument that global warming was a scientifically established fact, that the degree of warming was a product of human activity of such magnitude to make it a matter of extreme urgency. These were claims that only climatologists or scientists in related fields could assess, not a professor of English literature. Nor were they pertinent to a class devoted to teaching students how to write papers in social science.

Responding to Fluehr's contention that his "A" grade was irrelevant to whether the class was indoctrinating, Selber implausibly maintained that "the ways a course is taught and graded are highly related. These cannot be so easily separated. One must have grading criteria for all that they ask students to do. Approaches and assessment go hand in hand. Your 'A' is evidence that your viewpoints were not discriminated against—that opposing viewpoints were tolerated (even rewarded)."

Fluehr's instructor Cynthia Mazzant, who had previously ignored his e-mails, now offered to have a phone conference with Fluehr. (Fluehr had since taken an internship in Washington and was unable to meet with her in person.) Their conversation focused on the central point made in Selber's e-mails, which were summarized in a memo Fluehr prepared. "I asked her if this statement was a fair assessment of both our positions: 'I feel that HR 64 was violated because the teacher only provided one-sided Leftist texts and materials on class subjects and conversely she felt that it was not violated because students provided the differing viewpoints and that constituted access to the necessary materials required under HR 64.' She said it was."[20]

We had reached an impasse, but had succeeded in isolating the crucial principle since there was no disagreement about the facts. According to Mazzant and Selber, HR 64 did not obligate an instructor to present students with the "divergent opinions of others," but was satisfied if students themselves provided dissenting views and were allowed to do so without reprisal.

After I read Fluehr's memo, I sent an e-mail to Robert Pangborn, Vice President and Dean for Undergraduate Education who was representing the provost's office, and asked him for an administrative ruling. "Mr. Fluehr has had a phone conference with Dr. Mazzant," I told him, "which was very useful in clarifying matters. There is no significant dispute between them about the facts concerning what took place in English class 202A. Instead, Mr. Fluehr and Dr. Mazzant are divided over a difference of interpretation of policy HR 64. This creates an opportunity to resolve the matter through a legislative ruling by the administration."[21]

But there was not going to be any such ruling or resolution. On July 25, Pangborn replied to my e-mail with a formal letter in which the Provost basically washed his hands of the matter saying that under "shared governance," the administration had no authority to interpret its own rules. "With respect to the procedure governing resolution of classroom problems," he wrote, "I believe you are aware that I do not have a prescribed role in making a 'ruling' on a specific case, as you have urged me to do. As with other curricular matters, such as teaching assignments and insuring course content is consistent with Faculty Senate approved outlines, the college dean and campus chancellors are charged with insuring that conduct in the classroom meets standards that are consistent with both the pedagogical approaches and expectations of the discipline and campus environment, as well as University policy." [22]

In September I made a trip to Penn State to meet with Pangborn and Vice Provost Blannie Bowen, whose position remained immovable. In their view, it was a matter for faculty to decide. In January, Fluehr had a meeting with Pangborn. "When I pressed him about Mazzant's reinterpretation of HR 64," Fleuhr wrote to me, "he said it was up to the department to decide that issue." [23]

This was only the first of Fluehr's complaints that led to a deadlock with the Penn State faculty. Fluehr also filed a second complaint which he regarded as more important in terms of what actually went on in his classes. The complaint was about a course in the Department of Communications Arts and Sciences which was designed to teach students "effective speech." For one class assignment, Fluehr gave a speech on the Mohammed cartoons whose publication in a Danish newspaper had sparked violent Muslim demonstrations throughout the world, resulting in the killing of several people. During the talk, the subject of which was free speech, Fluehr displayed one of the cartoons and a photo of the artwork *Piss Christ* in which a crucifix had been submerged in urine, and which had led to a more peaceful protest by Christians. Fluehr defended both artists.

In his formal complaint, Fluehr described what happened next.

When I was handed my grade later that week, a note was attached. The teacher said that three students had approached her and felt offended by my speech. She told me that if I did not respect my audience, she would lower my grade on subsequent presentations. Her point seemed to be that if I did not consider the audience's feelings, I could not make an effective speech. In other words, I was to submit my ideas to the censorship of the other students. As a conservative in a class that was composed predominantly of liberal students, mine was the only speech deemed "offensive." In other words, my opinions were the only ideas which were judged to be "wrong" by the instructor on the basis of the liberal prejudices of the students in the class. This is a violation of the Penn State academic freedom provisions which forbid the establishment of a classroom orthodoxy on controversial matters.[24]

Intimidated by the professor's warning, Fluehr tailored the rest of his classroom presentations to her prescription.

I am embarrassed to say that out of concern for my grade, I bowed to the instructor's wishes and watered down my next speech, although I did point out to the instructor the irony in the fact that she had censored a speech about the censorship of free speech. The students who had complained earlier were not satisfied by my attempts at self-censorship and called me a "racist" in class. The instructor did not defend me or my right to express myself; nor did she reprimand these students for failing to respect my views. I am not asking for special treatment and I can take criticism and defend myself however harsh it might be. But applying a double standard in regard to what is offensive and what is permissible speech in a classroom not only handicaps the student, but is wrong and violates Penn State's academic freedom regulations.[25]

Fluehr's instructor, Amber Walker, rejected his complaint. Fluehr then arranged a phone conference with the chairman of the Department of Communications Arts and Sciences, Professor James Dillard. In a memo Fluehr prepared for me, he recounted the conversation. "The summary of [the Chairman's] response is: Amber Walker's actions violate no existing policy; she only told you to make a more effective speech; you were not told to alter your ideas, just the way you presented them. That's her job. . . . He said 'Your life is ok; your grade is good; and the teacher thought you were satisfied.' I responded that I'm not ok, because I felt that my free speech rights were violated."

Dillard advised Fluehr that the issue was not his point of view but his respect for others. According to Dillard, effective communication and good public speaking didn't offend. Fluehr responded that only three students out of the entire class claimed to be offended, while others thought his speech was informative and made them think. Dillard maintained his position. "I don't see this as any different than her telling you that you need to talk louder during a speech or you will lose points. She told you that if you didn't speak more effectively to your audience you would also lose points." Then Dillard added, "So you're not a fan of civil discourse?" a remark Fluehr found particularly upsetting.[26]

In my view the most depressing part of the memo Fluehr wrote to me was a paragraph near the end.

David, to be honest, I think we know that all the complaints will be rejected, even by the deans of the colleges. These people live on a different level and have completely different values. They devalue individual freedom and the flow of information to make room for inclusiveness and emotional security. I honestly don't think that some of these bureaucrats see the big deal about all of this. To them, they're not censoring ideas, just making them less offensive.

I didn't like to see a student feeling this way about his teachers. I had to acknowledge, though, that the kind of run-around and evasions to which Fluehr had been subjected were likely to discourage any student who attempted to complain. Nonetheless, there was an optimistic note at the conclusion of Fluehr's memo. "Regardless, I plan to finish all of these complaints to the end, until we get what we want or they are forced to admit they agree with the actions of the teachers."

Since the Penn State administration was not going to take responsibility for interpreting its own rule, we had reached an impasse. To overcome this obstacle, I advised Fluehr to take his complaints to the highest ranking faculty member who also occupied an administrative position.[27] This was Professor Susan Welch, who was dean of the College of the Liberal Arts, a division of Penn State with 13,000 students. I had already had an encounter with Welch, a feminist professor of political science, when I sent her my analysis of Penn State courses. She dismissed my concerns peremptorily, but also affably.[28] This wasn't very encouraging, but I thought she might respond differently to a student complaint. I also knew it would help that the Provost's office was looking on.

Accordingly, I advised Fluehr to send his file to her. The result was better than I expected. In mid-February, nine months after Fleuhr had filed his original complaint, Welch issued a judicious six-page ruling on the issue of Fleuhr's speech on the Mohammed cartoons.

First, Welch noted that there was agreement on many of the facts. The one disputed claim was whether Fluehr had been called a racist in class by other students without eliciting a comment in his defense from the instructor, Amber Walker. Walker maintained that she had not heard the attack. In these circumstances, Welch's response was a cautious but also significant support for Fluehr's position. "In terms of your second complaint," she wrote, "that Professor Walker stood by while other students called you a racist, I agree that this would be unprofessional and not in keeping with Penn State's policies of classroom behavior. However, Professor Walker claims that she did not hear any students call you a racist, so she could not have responded. I am not in a position to judge whether she could have heard what you did. If she did, as you allege, she should have responded. If she didn't, as she alleges, she couldn't have responded."[29]

Having indicated the limits of her ability to determine the facts, Welch went a step further and wrote, "You were understandably disgusted when other students called you a racist." This was the first time in the nine months since Fluehr had filed his complaints that a Penn State official had validated Fluehr's sense that he might have suffered a wrong, was innocent of the slander against him, and was responding in a reasonable manner in seeking redress.

On the central issue of the warning that his instructor had given to him—not to offend anyone lest his grade be lowered—Welch's ruling provided Fluehr the vindication we were looking for. "I would not argue with speech professionals that reaching the audience is a crucial element of good speech," Welch wrote. "How could it not be? But how many people in the audience need to disagree before it can be judged not a good speech?" Then she delivered a direct rebuke to the department chair. "And what does 'disrespect' mean anyway? I imagine that thousands of slaveholders felt disrespected by Abraham Lincoln's second inaugural address, when he pointed out that it may be that the Civil War was God's punishment of our nation for slavery. But that speech is one of the greatest speeches in American history. Obviously, then, even great speeches can be offensive to some."

As for the academic freedom implications of Professor Walker's action, Dean Welch had this to say:

> One of the components of HR 64 states that "The faculty member is expected to train students to think for themselves...." The lack of clarity and specifics of her comments in asking you to remove some material from your speech allegedly led you to the conclusion that you should censor yourself to be less controversial. In my view this does not comport with the words and intent of that sentence in HR 64.[30]

Dean Welch then made three recommendations. First, she noted that there was an elaborate training program for instructors of Communication Arts and Sciences courses, including a five-day workshop at the beginning of the year. "I am recommending that the training program give additional attention to HR 64 and the potential of the 'audience reaction,' criterion for inhibiting the free flow of ideas." The "audience reaction criterion" referred to sensitivity issues which had been invoked in Fluehr's case to limit his free speech.

Free speech was also the focus of Welch's second recommendation. This was to engage a "First Amendment expert" to examine these issues and discuss them with instructors. The third was to recommend that a statement Fluehr's instructor had actually included on her syllabus that different viewpoints should be respected "be on every syllabus in CAS100."[31]

This was the result I had sought from the outset of our campaign: institutional support for principles which were generally shared in the academic community but often neglected. It had come, moreover, from a faculty member well to the political Left, showing that it was possible within the existing system to get these issues addressed. It was a very positive result.

The problem that remained, however, was that eliciting even this modest response had required so much outside pressure on the university. Without the Pennsylvania hearings, the presence of Gibson Armstrong on the Senate Appropriations Committee, and my personal role in providing encouragement and advice to Fluehr, these rulings would not have taken place.

There was another factor in play that helped to shape Welch's welcome decision. The issue in this class was primarily one of free speech—a clearly understood and well-established right. Regarding academic issues, and particularly the newly acknowledged academic freedom rights of students, the ground was less familiar and the result less satisfactory.

Welch's next ruling, issued two months later, made that clear. It dealt with the English composition course, the battle I considered more important, because its central issues related to academic freedom and the nature of instruction. Welch's ruling was disappointing. She did not find "substantive merit" in either of Fluehr's complaints. She agreed that the course's required texts did not represent the full spectrum of opinion on poverty, but said that no two books could. As Welch interpreted HR 64, the instructor had not formally required students to embrace a single point of view and therefore had not violated their academic freedom rights. "The key issue from my perspective in deciding whether this was a violation of HR 64," she wrote, "is whether the instructor encouraged diverse views and helped the students to obtain material that would allow them to critique whatever reading was assigned."[32]

Welch's opinion came close to confirming those of the teacher, Mazzant, and her chairman—that if an instructor allowed a student to dissent from her views and from those presented in the texts she assigned, she had fulfilled the academic freedom requirement. But there was no indication that the instructor had in fact "encouraged" or helped students to obtain materials critical of the assigned texts, as Welch claimed. According to Fluehr,

> She did encourage students to research and present their points of view on the chapters. However, to my recollection she never said "Ehrenreich is kind of a Marxist, here's a point of view that balances that out." As I recall, she always started any discussion from the left side of the debate meaning it was up to students to bring it back to the center. However, that was assuming the students knew enough about the subject material to do that. As the AAUP 1915 statement said, she was using her position of influence to advance these positions on the class by assigning these texts. The presentation of course material never satisfied HR 64's requirement to present divergent views on controversial topics.

In fairness to Welch, the facts themselves were in dispute, and there was no way for her to adjudicate the disagreements. Mazzant made the reasonable claim that Shipler's text presented different viewpoints on poverty, although Shipler was himself a liberal. However, Welch accepted Mazzant's more dubious claim that her interest in assigning two texts by left-wing authors was to introduce students to "rhetorical arguments," not to influence their social philosophy. The Ehrenreich text assigned alongside Shipler's was an extreme polemic by a radical activist that made no attempt to present other views fairly. Welch could have asked Mazzant why, if her intention was to compare rhetorical strategies, she would not have assigned a similar polemic from a pro-capitalist author.

In her ruling, Welch hardly mentioned the Al Gore film *An Incon-venient Truth*, but assimilated it under her general conclusion that Maz-zant's purpose was to explore rhetorical strategies rather than persuade students of the correctness of Gore's views about climate change. Since several films critical of Gore's argument were publicly available (e.g., *The Global Warming Swindle* produced by Britain's ITV), it was diffi-cult to understand why Mazzant would pass up a similar opportunity to compare their rhetorical strategies if that had been her intention. It is also Fluehr's contention that the clear purpose of showing the film, and of the discussions Mazzant led, was not to examine rhetorical strategies but to impress her students with the wisdom of Gore's claims about global warming.[33]

Missing from Welch's ruling was a discussion of the academic freedom principle articulated in HR 64 as it related to Gore's controversial film. The instructor's purpose should have been to examine its controversial thesis analytically, not to advance its partisan agendas. Welch could have made this general point in her ruling in the same way she had asserted the free speech principle in her previous statement. Unfortunately, she did not. Consequently, unlike the principle of free speech which Welch forth-rightly supported, the principle of academic freedom—specifically a stu-dent's right not to be subjected to indoctrination in the classroom—went undefended.

The importance of defending the principles embodied in Penn State's academic freedom regulation HR 64 was subsequently underscored by the publication of Cary Nelson's *No University Is an Island*. This was a book by the president of the American Association of University Profes-sors attacking our campaign, which bore the subtitle "Saving Academic Freedom." As though to prove that any measure remotely associated with David Horowitz would become a target of condemnation by the opposi-tion, Nelson attacked Penn State's academic provision HR 64, and did so even though HR 64 is taken verbatim from the AAUP's own *Declaration*. Nelson describes HR 64 as an example of "McCarthyism."

Nelson also attacks the original Temple academic freedom policy which was *verbatim* the AAUP's own 1940 statement on academic freedom. He writes,

> Where Horowitz has had some direct success is in getting universities to institute procedures for students to complain about political speech in the classrooms and trigger investigations. Temple University and Penn State University both already had on the books overly restrictive policies limiting classroom speech. Penn State's policy (HR 64), on the books for some years, is especially bad.... Although [its] non-sexist language was added in the 1980s, the policy itself dates from the 1950s. It is thus McCarthy era rhetoric, taking passages from the 1915 AAUP Declaration out of context and ignoring subsequent clarifications.[34]

But the opposite is true. The Penn State policy was instituted in the 1950s to *protect* faculty from the McCarthy inquisition, while the passage from the Declaration is quite clear and is independent of context, which in any case Nelson fails to analyze or explain. The modification Nelson refers to is the introduction of a single adjective, "persistently," into the sentence barring professors from introducing controversial material that has no relation to the subject of the class. The "sexist language" refers to the use of the pronoun "his" instead of the "his/her."

The explanation Nelson provides for his strange views about HR 64 is this:

> Like Horowitz, Penn State failed at the time to conceptualize the sense in which all teaching and research is fundamentally and

deeply political.... Both Horowitz and Penn State argue, in
effect, that overt political remarks (and for Penn State covert
ones) can be strictly separated from the intricate web of connec-
tions between the academy and the politics of culture. I disagree.... What Penn State ended up with is nothing less than
thought control.[35]

Nelson seems to think that the Penn State policy bars the discussion of
political issues from the classroom, which is not the case. It does not say
anything about the nature of the issues discussed, but merely that the
instructor should not present students "with ready-made conclusions on
controversial subjects."[36] Yet this is regarded by the president of the American Association of University Professors as "thought-control."

At the conclusion of the Fluehr grievance, we had reached another
impasse. In an effort stretching over eleven months, we had shown that it
was possible for universities to set up a workable grievance process to
specifically address students' academic freedom claims. But the Fluehr
experiment also demonstrated that even with the procedure in place, it
would *not* be possible to get a satisfactory result without faculty support.
This support was necessary, 1) to explain to the student his or her rights;
2) to get the necessary attention of the central administration so that the
case would not be peremptorily dismissed; 3) and to advise the student
during the process in order to surmount the obstacles his instructors
would put in his or her way.[37]

Fluehr himself wrote a critique of the process as stipulated in regulation R-6, which he sent to the administration, calling it "a hindrance to the
effective implementation of HR 64."

The foremost problem with R-6 is the biased process the student
must follow. First, the student has to talk to the teacher about

whom he or she is filing the complaint, then the student has to talk to the department head, and then the student's final recourse is to appeal to the dean of the college. Because it forces the student to appeal to authorities who are colleagues and share a common interest in supporting the viewpoint of the instruction, this process is inherently biased against the student and favors the teacher's version of events and interpretation of HR 64. My personal experience has confirmed this point of view.... The department chairs backed my instructors 100%. No concern was shown for my concerns.[38]

When the dust had cleared, we found ourselves facing the same problem with which we had started—how to implement policies in an academic community that was either indifferent or actively hostile to these concerns. There were no faculty members at Penn State to whom students with grievances could appeal, and there were no administrators willing to take up the cause of such students if there was any prospect of a conflict with faculty.

A College Try Fails

Six months after Dean Welch handed down her rulings in the Fluehr matter, an article appeared on InsideHigherEd.com with the headline "Power Grab at DuPage." It reported a decision by the trustees of a community college in Illinois with a student body of 24,000 to adopt the Academic Bill of Rights.

Periodically, colleges debate such questions as the future of the curriculum, the role of the student newspaper, how outside speakers should be selected, and so forth. At the College of DuPage, a community college outside of Chicago, the board recently proposed major overhauls on all these issues with a common theme—power that currently rests elsewhere would be moved to the trustees. Not only did the board set out to change the power structure at the college, but it moved to adopt as official college policy a version of David Horowitz's controversial "Academic Bill of Rights."[39]

The InsideHigherEd.com story was the first inkling I had that the trustees at DuPage were contemplating such a move. It would be a significant step if the DuPage trustees were able to succeed in their plans, but I was pretty confident that they wouldn't. They had displayed a political naïveté in plunging into a battle over so contested a measure as the Academic Bill of Rights without contacting me to ask what they could expect from their opponents. Typically, the DuPage trustees were businessmen who had little first-hand knowledge of the daily activities in the institution they presided over other than the memories they retained from their own years in school. Under the "shared governance" principle, which guides the administration of most collegiate institutions, they were kept at arm's length from curricular concerns.

While the DuPage trustees proceeded with their normal tasks of fundraising and support, and in relative ignorance of what was taking place inside their institution, an event occurred that was similar to the surfacing of Ward Churchill at Hamilton, which caused them to react—and overreact. DuPage faculty had extended an invitation to the unrepentant terrorist Bill Ayers to speak in the school's Living Leadership series for a $10,000 fee. Ayers had only recently achieved notoriety as a result of the recently concluded presidential campaign of Barack Obama, with whom he was on close terms. When Ayers' terrorist past was dredged up by the press, he became an instant *cause célèbre*.

When a DuPage trustee named Kory Atkinson finally contacted me and asked me to look into the speakers program, I discovered that Ayers' invitation was merely incidental to a larger agenda. I had Sara Dogan prepare a report on the speakers invited over the previous five years.

> Out of a total of 117 speakers, we found that 64 speakers or presentations (55% of the total) leaned to the left politically—often far to the left. 20 speakers or presentations (17%) were judged to have been neutral. In 33 cases (28% of the total), we were unable to identify the political leanings of the speaker or presentation.... Not one of the 117 speakers or presentations at DuPage was found to represent conservative views or views to the right of center even though roughly half the nation holds such views.[40]

Specific examples provided in the report showed that the political loading of the programs was hardly accidental.

> Several political forums involving more than one speaker were found to be entirely one-sided. A forum entitled "Jerusalem Women Speak: 3 Women, 3 Faiths, One Shared Vision" featured Dr. Nina Mayorek, Aitemad Mater Muhanna, and Diana Kattan. Though these three women belong to different faiths—Judaism, Islam, and Christianity respectively—they each hold the view that Israel is the aggressor in the Israeli-Palestinian conflict. Partners for Peace, the sponsor of the forum, is an organization which claims to be raising awareness of "peace and justice in Palestine/Israel" but which vilifies the Israeli military and "has researched cases of human rights abuse by Israel against American citizens of Arab origin" but does not appear to research

Palestinian terrorism, human rights abuses or attacks on Israeli and American citizens.[41]

The program was hardly in keeping with the intellectual pluralism that the American Council of Education had declared to be a central principle of an American higher education, but that was not untypical.[42] The fact that DuPage was a publicly funded college in a Republican congressional district had brought the problem to the surface. But the academic forces that created it had been at work for a long time, and the trustees' hastily implemented plan was unlikely to succeed.

In the first place, without exactly intending it, they took an approach that was imprudently confrontational. Although they had not identified the Academic Bill of Rights as such, they had included its language in their proposed reforms, a fact that their opponents would not miss. It was the most hotly contested reform proposal in the academic world, and they had included it among 230 other proposed changes. The decision to construct such an omnibus plan was made under the mistaken assumption that such a large package would diminish the significance of any of its contents. Instead, it had the opposite effect. It made their plans seem even more threatening and provided adversaries with a very fat target.

As the opposition began to mount, Kory Atkinson expressed concern to the local paper, observing that there was "a lot of unjustified paranoia and suspicion regarding the board and its policies," and cautioning, "There's not much to be concerned about," because "90 percent of the proposed manual is noncontroversial." InsideHigherEd.com conceded as much, but then pointed to the elephant in the room. "Many of the 230 planned changes in policy are indeed noncontroversial," they wrote.[43] "But amid all the routine updates are changes that stunned faculty members. Indeed, DuPage is probably not the only college where professors would object if what was billed as a routine updating of board rules ended up including the Academic Bill of Rights."

The article continued, describing the Academic Bill of Rights as a "document, framed as a measure to protect academic freedom [that] is widely viewed by professors as an attack on their autonomy and as a measure that would lead to professors constantly looking over their shoulders, make it impossible for them to express strong views, and force them to include conservative interpretations of everything or face criticism for not doing so."[44] The InsideHigherEd.com article noted the trustees' subterfuge as well. "In the board's list of policy changes, the section that mirrors the Academic Bill of Rights is not labeled as such; it is simply called 'Educational Philosophy,' and faculty members say that they were not told that the board wanted to include this measure. But the section ... largely mirrors the language drafted by Horowitz."[45]

If the DuPage trustees had sought my advice before undertaking their reforms, I would have told them *not* to wave the red flag of the Academic Bill of Rights. Instead, I would have advised them to draw on the language of the American Council on Education statement and its recommendation to set up grievance machinery to protect student rights. Because it was the speakers programs they were concerned about, they could employ the language of the Council to require that DuPage programs support intellectual pluralism. I would then have suggested they incorporate Penn State's academic freedom provision instead of the parallel points set forth in our bill. This might have given their proposals a fighting chance against the academic Left whose power (and unscrupulous methods) the DuPage trustees were about to test.

On December 19, 2008, following the announcement of the new policy, a public meeting of the board of trustees took place. I did not attend the proceedings but viewed them on video. InsideHigherEd.com's reporter captured the atmosphere. "Last week, faculty members and students—the latter with tape over their mouths to symbolize what they say the trustees are doing to their freedoms—flocked to a board meeting to protest the plans that appear to be dividing the college.... Not only do the critics say that academic freedom is in danger, but they charge that the board's policies in some instances would violate state law."[46] The president of the DuPage College Faculty Association (a branch of the powerful National Education Association) declared, "This is really an attempt by the board to gain complete control over everything."[47]

In a letter it made public the Faculty Association claimed—without evidence—that the Academic Bill of Rights would require the teaching of Intelligent Design Theory, and that the College already had an academic freedom policy in place, allowing students to complain if they believed their instructors were treating them unfairly.[48] This was also false. As at other schools, the existing DuPage academic freedom policy did not apply to students. The DuPage policy was part of the Faculty Association contract and consequently referred only to faculty.[49] The DuPage College Catalogue did contain a section on "Student Rights and Responsibilities," but this was only a statement that students could expect the college to exercise its power to regulate student behavior with restraint. The policy said nothing about intellectual diversity, intellectual pluralism, or students' academic freedom. DuPage's student grievance and harassment procedures also failed to mention academic freedom or disputes related to a student's political beliefs.[50]

Joining the Faculty Association in opposition was the American Association of University Professors. Its Illinois chapter objected to the fact that the proposed policy change would "prohibit discrimination based on an individual's viewpoint or opinion." They explained, "The danger of adding 'viewpoint or opinion' to the list of prohibited acts is that quite obviously there are correct and incorrect opinions about reality. Certainly the professor's job is to discriminate between them. Students are in school to learn how to discriminate between them. If they fail to do so, of course they will be 'discriminated' against—questioned in class; or get a poor grade, for instance."[51]

In the AAUP's view, apparently, a student failing to grasp the "correct opinion" about "reality" should *expect* to receive a failing grade. This was as succinct a definition of indoctrination as one could ask for—imposing a matter of opinion as though it were a statement of fact. But leaving aside the question of whether there is a "correct opinion" about "reality," the anti-discrimination strictures in the Academic Bill of Rights referred specifically to opinions about matters that were controversial and not to matters of fact.

On April 16, 2009, the DuPage trustees adopted the new policy in a unanimous 6 to 0 vote with one member of the board absent. But it was already only a symbolic victory. A week earlier an election had taken place which nullified the result.

Because they had reacted precipitously to Ayers' invitation, and had not appreciated the power of the forces ranged against them, the DuPage trustees had no serious plan for the war they had invited. In addition to all their other tactical missteps, they had announced their reform proposal on the eve of a trustee election. The unions immediately went into action, creating a slate of four candidates supported by a political action committee called "Friends for Education." The incumbent trustees who had proposed and then passed the new policy ran as individuals. Through their political PAC, the unions spent $50,000 to unseat the board majority. By contrast, the four incumbent trustees ran as individuals and spent only $12,000, or less than a quarter of their opponents' total.[52]

On April 8—a week before the new trustee policies were adopted—the elections were won by the union slate, creating a new majority. Four weeks later the new trustees rescinded the board's policies, including the Academic Bill of Rights.[53]

CONCLUSION

IN THE SIX YEARS I'D BEEN WORKING ON UNIVERSITY REFORM, OUR academic freedom movement had succeeded in mobilizing thousands of students and making the Academic Bill of Rights a national cause. There was not a faculty organization or university administration that was not familiar with the bill, or at least some distorted version of it, and thus with the issues we had raised. Through articles, studies, books, and reports we had documented the situation on university campuses so that only our most determined opponents, or those who were unfamiliar with what we had actually written, could deny the existence of the problems we described. We had prompted the American Council on Education to artic-ulate a policy identifying academic freedom and intellectual pluralism as "central principles of American higher education" and applying the pol-icy specifically to students. Our efforts had inspired changes at major institutions of higher education in Ohio and Pennsylvania, providing students with academic freedom rights and grievance machinery to enforce them for the first time.

Yet, we were forced to pay heavily for our efforts. We had been stigmatized and ridiculed by the unions and their allies who had conducted an unprincipled war against us. We had been demonized time and time again as "McCarthyites" and "thought-police," though these accusations were more applicable to our adversaries themselves. As a result, the very modest proposal we had made to restore basic educational principles—that students should be provided with two sides to controversial issues, and a clear guide as to what was a professorial opinion and what an established scientific fact—was still a long way from being realized.

Prior to the DuPage incident, the editor of the journal *Illinois Academe* published a book that came along with an endorsement from AAUP president Cary Nelson. It described our efforts in these words: "The Academic Bill of Rights is the story of how David Horowitz, pretending to stand up for 'student rights' and moral conduct by professors, led a crusade to have every college in the country adopt the most coercive system of grievance procedures and investigations of liberal professors ever proposed in America."[1]

False representations like this had made our campaign so noxious in academic circles that no faculty member could support us without expecting retribution. Consequently, no academic body or professional association had extended an invitation to us to present our views or discuss our proposed reforms, although there was no lack of appropriate venues. This was a particularly revealing test of our opponents' good faith, because their entire campaign against the Academic Bill of Rights was based on the false premise that our policy statements and documents didn't mean what they said, but were instead written to enable us to advance hidden agendas. It would have been simple to test that assumption by inquiring whether we were willing to alter the wording of the Academic Bill of Rights. But they had no interest in such an engagement, and despite my best efforts, they offered us no opportunity to show our good faith.

Even more important than the failure to test our intentions was their unwillingness to concede the obvious—that the problems that concerned us were real and were prevalent enough to warrant attention. Since the entire effort of the opposition campaign was to deny the facts, its spokesmen failed to present reasonable arguments for rejecting our reforms. Nor did our academic critics take a single practical step to provide faculty support for students like Ruth Malhotra, A. J. Fluehr, and others whose academic rights were being infringed. And while the faculty senate at Penn State did make an admirable advance by extending academic freedom rights to Penn State students, no Penn State faculty or faculty committees showed any interest in providing the kind of support system they did to students who suffered racial or sexual discrimination.

The venom of the opposition campaign prevented other, independent and well-intentioned voices within the university from stepping forward to address these problems. Fear of association with anything I may have proposed or supported was sufficient to block such intentions. I never claimed to have a monopoly on a workable solution, and therefore made extensive attempts with AAUP officials such as Cary Nelson and Robert Post, and AFT president William Scheuerman to move the discussion away from destructive confrontation in favor of private meetings to explore the possibility of closing the gap between our positions—all to no avail.

Why was this so? Why was the opposition to our campaign so ferocious and uncompromising? Why had the AAUP and the faculty unions eschewed a path of negotiation and compromise and decided to conduct a political war instead? When I reflected on these questions, I could come up with only one answer. The scorched earth campaign against us could be understood only if our opponents felt it necessary to defend the practices—indoctrination and political proselytizing in the classroom—that the Academic Bill of Rights and our campaign were designed to prevent.

As if to confirm this, in October 2007 the AAUP issued a new statement on academic freedom—its first in almost fifty years. Called "Freedom in the Classroom," it was an explicit attempt to answer critics who raised the issue of classroom indoctrination.

Six months before the AAUP report, I had published *Indoctrination U: The Left's War Against Academic Freedom*, which provided a sustained argument against current practices of indoctrination, providing examples of many courses in which only one side of controversial issues was presented, and which required students to absorb a sectarian doctrine as though it were scientific fact. I had also authored or co-authored a series of lengthy articles that had been posted on our websites, examining more than 150 courses at a dozen major universities. These were the most extensive studies of their kind that had yet been conducted, and they showed conclusively that courses were being designed with the sole purpose of teaching students doctrine rather than subjecting that doctrine to academic scrutiny and analysis. Reading lists for the courses were absurdly one-sided, and no familiarity with critical materials was required of students. I eventually assembled these studies in a book co-written with Jacob Laksin, titled *One-Party Classroom*.[2]

It was clear that the AAUP's new report was intended, in part, as an answer to the arguments I had raised both in that text and in the campaign for an Academic Bill of Rights. Yet, in keeping with its strategy of denying legitimacy to our concerns, the AAUP report ignored what we had written. Instead, it framed its arguments in terms of a complaint that had been lodged by the obscure "Committee for a Better North Carolina," which it evidently considered an easier target. The Committee for a Better North

Carolina had lodged a complaint against UNC-Chapel Hill about the assignment of a single book to incoming freshman, which it regarded as indoctrination. Obviously, no single assignment of a text could be regarded as indoctrination, because although this book had been assigned by the university to all incoming freshman, it did raise other problems ignored by the AAUP report.[3]

The heart of the AAUP's new policy was its defense of the indoctrination practices prevalent in new inter-disciplinary fields such as Women's Studies. This had been a principal concern of the curricular studies we had conducted. In three books—*The Professors, Indoctrination U.*, and *One-Party Classroom*—and numerous articles, I had singled out the academic doctrine of "social construction," which held that gender differences between men and women are socially rather than biologically determined. I had argued that this was a prime example of an ideological claim that was being taught—often in extreme versions—as though it were a scientific fact. Among the examples I gave was a political science class at the University of Arizona, the catalogue description of which began, "Because gender is socially constructed..." and went on to say that the course would explore the impact of socially constructed gender roles as an instrument of exploiting classes, races, and patriarchies. In other words, the course presented the claim that gender was a product of social forces as though it were an uncontested truth, whereas it is a claim disputed by modern neuroscience and biology, both of which have demonstrated empirically that while gender characteristics may be influenced by society, they have a firm biological basis.[4]

These were the arguments to which the AAUP's report "Freedom in the Classroom" was an intended response. It said:

> It is not indoctrination for professors to expect students to comprehend ideas and apply knowledge that is accepted as true within a relevant discipline.[5]

In other words, if ideological doctrines such as the social construction of gender are widely accepted concepts in Women's Studies, then even though this claim is contested by biologists and thus controversial, Women's Studies professors are free to teach this doctrine as though it were true. The same logic would allow the teaching of racist doctrines as scientifically true if racists formed an academic department and were able to establish an academic field of study based on them. If the academic community as a whole were to accept this approach, it would set back the academic clock a hundred years, transforming the liberal arts divisions of the modern research university into versions of their nineteenth century counterparts, the mission of which was to transmit received religious doctrines rather than to subject all ideas to critical examination.

In the debates I have had with AAUP president Cary Nelson, he has taken issue with my comments on gender theory. In his book, *No University Is an Island*, he writes,

In a debate with me—broadcast on C-SPAN on March 17 and 18, 2007—Horowitz complained about a University of Arizona syllabus that assumes as an uncontroversial fact that gender is "socially constructed." Horowitz insists students be informed that there is disagreement about this matter. My guess is that most instructors do mention the opposing argument, the traditional claim that maleness and femaleness are fundamental, immutable categories. But I doubt that many contemporary humanities or social science faculty give equal time to the earlier view; they would not consider it professionally responsible to do so.[6]

Nelson is undoubtedly right about most contemporary humanities and social science faculty. But most biologists, neuroscientists, and evolutionary psychologists would subscribe to the "earlier view" that gender characteristics are hard-wired or biologically determined, and would be able to produce empirical studies to show that this is so. Nelson seems unaware of these scientific facts. "Horowitz," he writes, "... believes anatomical differences between the male and female brains mandate greater facility for men in such fields as math and music, a view, as he seems unable to understand, that is itself socially constructed."[7] But these differences are in fact not socially constructed; they are scientifically proven, and there is a large body of empirical evidence to back them up. Nelson's comment reflects the triumph of ideology over reason and scientific fact.[8]

At the end of 2008, I was invited to appear on a panel at the annual meeting of the Modern Languages Association. The invitation was extended by Brian Kennelly, a professor at Cal State Poly in San Luis Obispo, who was on the panel along with Cary Nelson, Mark Bauerlein, and Norma Cantu, the former Education Department official in the Clinton Administration.

My appearance at the MLA conference was greeted by a protest from the Association's "Radical Caucus" led by Grover Furr, a professor of English at Montclair State College, who was profiled in *The Professors*, and who had earned notoriety on academic Internet threads as a passionate and determined defender of Joseph Stalin, the Moscow show trials, and the Communist state. Professor Furr appeared in a Lenin cap, denim jacket, and red t-shirt, along with thirty of his followers who handed out a leaflet warning that "[Horowitz] is not a scholar, but a liar of the Goebbels school."[9]

In my presentation, I said, "The theory that gender is socially constructed has every right to a place in a university curriculum. But if instructors are to observe academic standards and respect students' academic freedom they cannot teach the social construction of gender as a scientific fact, rather than as an opinion held by radical feminists, which is what it is."[10] Cary Nelson responded to this comment by saying that, in his own classes, he taught the social construction of gender as a fact. He added, "When I teach the social construction of gender, we have an open discussion about the idea. I make it clear where I stand, and the students are free to agree or disagree. . . . If that's indoctrination, higher education should come to an end."[11]

I agreed that giving students the right to dissent was not indoctrination. But Nelson did not seem to realize that if he taught the doctrine as a scientific fact, allowing students to disagree with a "fact" was a charity, not a gesture of respect for an opinion that differed from his own. It was tantamount to saying that he permitted his students to assert that the earth is flat.

Among those attending the MLA session were two prominent liberal academics, Gerald Graff and Stanley Fish, both of whom provided moral support for my appearance and also gave some grounds for hope that the academic horizon was not as dark as it otherwise seemed. Stanley Fish was the nation's leading Milton scholar and had headed the Duke English Department in the 1980s when it promoted such left-wing academic fashions as "deconstructionism" and came under attack from conservatives. Fish had recently published a book based on his earlier article called *Save the World on Your Own Time*, the argument of which he summed up by stating, "I return in the end to my one-note song: if academics did only the job they are paid and trained to do—introduce students to disciplinary materials and equip them with the necessary analytic skills . . . [their opponents'] criticism would have no object, and the various watch-dog groups headed by David Horowitz, Daniel Pipes, and others would have to close shop."[12]

This was tantamount to saying that if professors behaved professionally in the classroom and followed the guidelines laid down in the

1915 Declaration to "carry on their work in the temperate manner of the scientific inquirer," and never use the classroom "for uncritical and intemperate partisanship," there would be no problem that required an Academic Bill of Rights.[13]

Gerald Graff was the outgoing president of the Modern Language Association, and a contributor to *Radical Teacher*. His left-wing credentials were even more solid than Fish's, yet his presidential address at the MLA convention was an even more comprehensive endorsement of the concerns we had raised. Referring to the criticisms of higher education made by organizations such as ours, Graff commented, "Unfortunately, in responding to the conservative charges we too often deny or minimize the possibility that abuse of classroom authority is a genuine problem, evading the issue by accusing the accusers of being the ones who are motivated only by ideology." Graff then referred to the union website Free Exchange On Campus, which, he said, "dismisses David Horowitz's Academic Bill of Rights as 'a solution in search of a problem.' The statement goes on to suggest that the alleged problem is a fabrication of right-wing ideologues."[14]

Graff disagreed. "Since the 1960s," he observed, "'transforming' the political consciousness of students has been widely defended in print as a legitimate goal of teaching, as is seen in such self-described trends as 'the pedagogy of the oppressed,' 'critical pedagogy,' 'teaching for social justice,' 'radical pedagogy,' and 'anti-oppressive education.'" Graff could also have pointed to the remarks Norma Cantu had made earlier on our panel, saying that she hoped students were "radicalized" by her courses and trusted that other faculty shared the same aim.[15]

Earlier in his presidential speech, Graff had complained that he and his peers knew "shockingly little about what our colleagues do in their classrooms." But now he added, "I do know, however, that what the advocates of these [radical] pedagogies say in print is often disturbing."[16] To be more specific about what they said, Graff cited an article by two professors, Jackie Brady and Richard Ohmann, which was published in 2008 in *Radical Teacher*. "What are the conditions for teaching radically in 2008?" the two wrote. "For opening students' minds to Left, feminist, anti-racist, and queer ideas? For stimulating them to work for egalitarian change?...What pedagogies have the best chance of helping students become radicals?"[17]

In this article, as in the field of radical pedagogy generally, Graff noted, "Questions about whether the project of radicalizing students should be attempted at all have been replaced by instrumental ones about how to achieve this goal." This was a reflection of how accepted such proselytizing conceptions of the educational mission had become. "I'm all for teachers' 'opening students' minds to Left, feminist, anti-racist, and queer ideas' (which are often underrepresented in the major media)," Graff said, "but again only if students are free to disagree with those ideas and are presented with strong models of how to do so, whether through the course reading list or through dissenting colleagues invited in to debate or teaching a paired course."[18]

Graff's idea of an appropriate way to deal with controversial issues in the classroom—by "teaching the conflicts" instead of prosecuting one side of them—was pretty much what our academic freedom campaign was about. But, as he observed, "this condition seems unlikely to be met when the course has the expressed aims of 'stimulating' students to work for egalitarian change and 'helping' them become radicals, the latter euphemism suggesting that our students, if only in some inchoate and as yet inarticulate way, are yearning to become radicals and lack only a little 'help' from a friendly radical teacher to show them the way."

In our panel discussion, Cary Nelson assured the academic audience that attempts to use the classroom to promote radical political agendas was not a problem at all. "On a typical campus, said Mr. Nelson, one or two professors proselytize, and their effect is nil. 'That does not require a new mechanism for surveillance of faculty members.'"[19] Graff's presidential speech exposed the willful deception behind Nelson's statement. In the first place, he didn't know what went on in his colleagues' classrooms, anymore than anyone other than their students did. In the second, his statement was implausible given the fact of an established and entrenched pedagogical movement among academic radicals, whose objectives had been made clear in print, and whose goal was to turn classrooms into political training and recruitment programs for radical agendas. In the third place, Nelson had admitted that he did just that in his own classroom by promoting the ideology of social construction as though it were a scientific fact.

Although Graff gave Nelson an overly generous benefit of the doubt, he was quite familiar with the bad faith of academic radicals in explaining away what they did.

> When I've voiced such criticisms elsewhere, radical-pedagogy advocates have indignantly retorted that they regularly assign views strongly opposed to their own and do not bully their students but invite them to make up their own minds. I don't doubt the sincerity of these disclaimers, but I can sympathize with conservative critics who aren't satisfied to simply take the radical teacher's word for it.... If it's true that radical teaching in practice consists of little more than asking students to choose from a spectrum of political positions, I have to wonder why its advocates don't call it "teaching political debate" instead of "the pedagogy of the oppressed," "teaching for social justice," "radical pedagogy," and other labels that inevitably suggest an effort to

convert, if not to brainwash. If you want to issue manifestos to
teachers that urge "helping students become radicals" and "stimulating them to work for egalitarian change," so be it, but then
don't get angry and defensive if someone says that sounds like
coercion.[20]

Graff then described his own recommendation for avoiding classroom
indoctrination in dealing with issues that were volatile and controversial.
"In my view… teaching politics as *debate*—teaching the conflicts about
politics if you will—is the surest way to protect students from being bul-
lied by teachers."[21] I couldn't agree more.

The views of a left-wing academic such as Gerald Graff are encouraging. They reflect the educational philosophy that created the modern
research university and that still prevails in most of its divisions. It was still
alive, if not all together well, even within the liberal arts schools, where
academic activists were concentrated. I was hopeful that as we continued
to make our case for an Academic Bill of Rights, professors and administrators holding views like Graff's would increasingly step forward with
their own proposals to address the problem. The radicals themselves
would not go away. Nor would the problems caused by their determination to use the university as platform for their political goals. But the university was a very large institution and the vast majority of its schools,
both professional and scientific, operated on principles that were non-
political and non-partisan, and the members of those schools—faculty and
administrators alike—had a powerful vested interest in keeping them that
way.

The American public, moreover, was not ready to give up its traditions
of intellectual pluralism and democratic fairness. The liberal university
as an institution dedicated to the pluralism of ideas and values, and sci-

entific methods of inquiry, was a cornerstone of the democratic system. It was hard to conceive of an American future without it. With our academic freedom campaign, we had laid the grounds for its defense, and we were not about to give up the fight.

ACKNOWLEDGMENTS

F IRST OF ALL, I WANT TO THANK MY PUBLISHER MARJI ROSS, WHO ALSO published *The Professors*, for making this book possible. The environment for books like this is difficult and having a dedicated and understanding publisher like Marji is a blessing to authors, and a service to the country. In this regard, I also want to thank Jeff Carneal, the president of Eagle Publishing for taking the risks associated with my books and for being a support to my work, and a friend.

I am grateful to Sara Dogan, the campus director of Students for Academic Freedom, and editor of www.studentsforacademicfreedom.org for her work in the campaign and for her indispensable assistance in fact checking, researching, and copy-editing this text. Also assisting me in all my efforts and in the preparation of this text was my redoubtable executive assistant, Elizabeth Ruiz, who has provided support for my work in ways too numerous to mention. My Regnery editor Farahn Morgan provided a meticulous review of the text for which I thank her.

My friend and longest collaborator Peter Collier edited the original manuscript and as always made it better than it would otherwise have been.

I could not have conducted this campaign or any other without the extraordinary efforts of Mike Finch, president of the David Horowitz Freedom Center, who has contributed to my efforts in more ways than even I can imagine for nearly a decade.

Nor could I have accomplished the tasks that went into the making of this book, and the campaign it chronicles, without the loving support of my wife April, who has stood by me through thick and thin, and shouldered these burdens with me.

ACADEMIC BILL OF RIGHTS

1. All faculty shall be hired, fired, promoted and granted tenure on the basis of their competence and appropriate knowledge in the field of their expertise and, in the humanities, the social sciences, and the arts, with a view toward fostering a plurality of methodologies and perspectives. No faculty shall be hired or fired or denied promotion or tenure on the basis of his or her political or religious beliefs.
2. No faculty member will be excluded from tenure, search and hiring committees on the basis of their political or religious beliefs.
3. Students will be graded solely on the basis of their reasoned answers and appropriate knowledge of the subjects and disciplines they study, not on the basis of their political or religious beliefs.

4. Curricula and reading lists in the humanities and social sciences should reflect the uncertainty and unsettled character of all human knowledge in these areas by providing students with dissenting sources and viewpoints where appropriate. While teachers are and should be free to pursue their own findings and perspectives in presenting their views, they should consider and make their students aware of other viewpoints. Academic disciplines should welcome a diversity of approaches to unsettled questions.

5. Exposing students to the spectrum of significant scholarly viewpoints on the subjects examined in their courses is a major responsibility of faculty. Faculty will not use their courses for the purpose of political, ideological, religious or anti-religious indoctrination.

6. Selection of speakers, allocation of funds for speakers programs and other student activities will observe the principles of academic freedom and promote intellectual pluralism.

7. An environment conducive to the civil exchange of ideas being an essential component of a free university, the obstruction of invited campus speakers, destruction of campus literature or other effort to obstruct this exchange will not be tolerated.

8. Knowledge advances when individual scholars are left free to reach their own conclusions about which methods, facts, and theories have been validated by research. Academic institutions and professional societies formed to advance knowledge within an area of research, maintain the integrity of the research process, and organize the professional lives of related researchers serve as indispensable venues within which scholars circulate research findings and debate their interpretation.

To perform these functions adequately, academic institutions and professional societies should maintain a posture of organizational neutrality with respect to the substantive disagreements that divide researchers on questions within, or outside, their fields of inquiry.

NOTES

INTRODUCTION

1. The other member of my staff, Brad Shipp, accepted an administrative post at large state university close to three years ago. In the last year, I have hired a replacement, Craig Snider. My campus coordinator Jeffrey Wienir has devoted his efforts mainly to issues not directly related to academic freedom.

2. The organized opposition to our campaign, operating under the umbrella "Free Exchange Coalition" is described here: "Indoctrination Lobby," DiscoverTheNetwork.org, February 14, 2005; available at: http://www.discoverthenetworks.org/groupProfile.asp?grpid=7484 [accessed June 23, 2010].

3. Stephen H. Aby, ed. *The Academic Bill of Rights Debate: A Handbook*, (Praeger 2007), 1.

4. James J. Duderstadt, "Intellectual Transformation," academic paper; available at: http://milproj.ummu.umich.edu/publications/transformation/index.html [accessed June 23, 2010].

5. John Sexton, president of New York University, November 9, 2004; available at: http://www.nyu.edu/about/leadership-university-administration/office-of-the-president/redirect/speeches-statements/graduate-and-professional-education-in-the-research-university.html [accessed June 25, 2010].

6. These include, among others, African American Studies, Peace Studies, American Studies, Cultural Studies, Post-Colonial Studies and Gay and Lesbian Studies. For a detailed critique of the Women's Studies curriculum by two of its founders who later had second thoughts; see Daphne Patai and Noretta Koertge, *Professing Feminism: Education and Indoctrination in Women's Studies* (Lanham, MD: Lexington Books, 2003).

7. "Preamble to the Constitution of the National Women's Studies Association," *NWSA Journal*, March 22, 2002; available at: http://www.accessmylibrary.com/coms2/summary_0286-25351356_ITM [accessed June 23, 2010].

8. "A Tail of Two Testimonies: Testimony from Steven Zelnick and Logan Fisher," FrontPageMag.com, January 10, 2006; available at: http://www.studentsforacademicfreedom.org/news/1326/StephenZelnickLoganFisherPaTestimony.htm [accessed June 23, 2010].

9. Ibid.

10. I have documented these changes in a book written with Jacob Laksin in which we analyzed more than 150 contemporary courses at 12 major universities that are designed to inculcate such orthodoxies; David Horowitz and Jacob Laksin, *One-Party Classroom: How Radical Professors at America's Top Colleges Indoctrinate Students and Undermine Our Democracy*, (New York: Crown Forum, 2009).

11. Horowitz and Laksin, *One Party Classroom*, 1–2.

12. Ibid., 141.

13. Gerald Graff, "Presidential Address 2008: Courseocentrism," *PMLA*, May 2009, Vol. 124, No. 3 p. 739; Graff is critical of this development.

14. "Our History," Intercollegiate Studies Institute; available at: http://www.isi.org/about/our_history/our_history.html [accessed June 23, 2010].

15. The Leadership Institute now sponsors campus groups but does not direct or attempt to organize them. Young America's Foundation has one campus chapter at George Washington University.

16. Robert C. Post and Matthew W. Finkin, *For the Common Good, Principles of American Academic Freedom* (New Haven: 2009), 8. Post is Dean of the Yale Law School and Finkin is the Edward W. Cleary Chair in Law at the University of Illinois.

17. Ibid., 60.

18. "1915 Declaration on Academic Freedom and Academic Tenure," American Association of University Professors; available at: http://www.aaup.org/AAUP/pubsres/policydocs/contents/1915.htm [accessed June 23, 2010]; see also, Stanley Fish, *Save the World on your own Time* (New York: Oxford University Press, 2008).

19. Horowitz and Laksin, op. cit. 98–100; courses in "empire" taught by equally unqualified professors also abound, op. cit., 223–4

20. Spring 2007 Course Listings for the Duke University Program in Education; available at: http://educationprogram.duke.edu/under graduate/courses?semester=spring&year=2007 [accessed June 23, 2010]. The Department of Literature has an entire "certificate" program with the same title "Perspectives on Marxism and Society," headed by a professor of film studies. Information available at: http://literature.aas.duke.edu/undergrad/MarxismandSociety.php [accessed June 23, 2010].

21. Slavoj Zizek, "Have Michael Hardt and Antonio Negri Re-written the Communist Manifesto for the Twenty-First Century?," Rethinking Marxism, Volume 13, Number 3, p.190–98 (2001); available at: http://www.rethinkingmarxism.org/cms/node/884 [accessed June 23, 2010].

22. Sociology Courses Synopsis for Undergraduate Courses, Duke University; available at: http://www.soc.duke.edu/courses/synopses.html [accessed June 23, 2010].

23. Faculty profile of Michael Hardt, Duke University; available at: https://fds.duke.edu/db/aas/Literature/hardt [accessed June 23, 2010].

24. For an example of how the prejudices of the left have resulted in a blacklist of "politically incorrect" candidates for faculty positions, cf. Cary Nelson, *No University Is An Island* (New York: NYU Press, 2010), Chapter 4, "Barefoot In New Zealand," 119 et. seq. In this account Nelson describes how a candidate for a position in the English department at the University of Illinois was not hired because they had written a letter to a New Zealand newspaper about a local ordinance requiring the wearing of shoes on city streets which leftists in the department deemed "racist" and "imperialist." Their presumption was that the targets of the ordinance were Maoris and "people of color" when in fact the offenders were local hippies, who were white.

25. Ibid.

26. Robert Maranto, Richard E. Redding and Frederick M. Hesst, ed., *The Politically Correct University: Problems, Scope, and Reforms* (Washington, D.C.: AEI Press, 2009).

27. The books were *Uncivil Wars: The Controversy Over Reparations for Slavery* (New York: Encounter Books, 2002), *The Professors: The 101*

Most Dangerous Academics in America (Washington, D.C.: Regnery, 2006), *Indoctrination U: The Left's War Against Academic Freedom* (New York: Encounter Books, 2007), and *One-Party Classroom: How Radical Professors at America's Top Colleges Indoctrinate Students and Undermine Our Democracy* (New York: Crown Publishers, 2009).

28. James Piereson, "The Left University," *The Weekly Standard*, October 3, 2005; available at: http://www.weeklystandard.com/Content/Public/Articles/000/000/006/120xbklj.asp [accessed June 25, 2010].

CHAPTER ONE

1. C. de Russy, M. Langbert, and P. Orenstein, "New York Academia vs. the Academic Bill of Rights," Students for Academic Freedom, January 2006; available at: http://www.studentsforacademicfree dom.org/news/1301/CdeRussyNYaborarticle012306.htm [accessed June 25, 2010].

2. Cary Nelson, *No University Is an Island*, 4.

3. Nathaniel Nelson, "My Name is Michael Vocino and I Like Dick," (This was Professor Vocino's self-introduction on the first day of class), FrontPageMag.com, August 1, 2005; available at: http://frontpagemag.com/readArticle.aspx?ARTID=7757 [accessed June 23, 2010].

4. David Horowitz, "Attack of an Academic Zero," Students for Academic Freedom, March 21, 2006; available at: http://www.students foracademicfreedom.org/news/1351/DHVocinoAttackofAcadZero0 32106.htm [accessed June 23, 2010].

5. Ernest van den Haag, *Is Capital Punishment Just?* (Washington: 1978).

6. [Various] Studies on Faculty and Campus Diversity, Students for Academic Freedom, July 4, 2006; available at: http://www.students foracademicfreedom.org/news/1893/FacultyStudies.htm [accessed June 23, 2010].

7. Dan Knecht, "The Monolith on the Hill." FrontPageMag.com, January 28, 2005; available at: http://frontpagemag.com/Articles/ ReadArticle.asp?ID=16811 [accessed June 23, 2010].

8. Richard A. Posner, *Public Intellectuals: A Study of Decline* (Cambridge: Harvard University Press), 2001.

9. For my account of my reception at the time, see http://online.front pagemag.com/readArticle.aspx?ARTID=8826 LINK NOT ACTIVE

10. I have described this event in greater detail in *Left Illusions: An Intellectual Odyssey* (Spence Publishing Company, 2003), 230–4.

11. "My Visit to Vanderbilt" in *Left Illusions: An Intellectual Odyssey* (Spence Publishing Company, 2003).

12. David Horowitz, "The Campus Blacklist," FrontPageMag.com, April 18, 2003; available at: http://www.frontpagemag.com/readArticle. aspx?ARTID=18634 [accessed June 23, 2010]. When I visited Gonzaga University in Spokane a philosophy professor circulated an e-mail describing me as a "racist." He later apologized when I confronted him with my actual writings on the subject of race and brought the matter to the attention of the Vice President of the University. But the damage he inflicted on the students who invited me who were now associated with a "racist" in their own community could not really be undone.

13. Ibid., The one exception was an invitation from Professor Maurice Isserman, a Left-wing professor at Hamilton College who taught a seminar in the Sixties. I had called Isserman and remarked on this boycott and then asked him to invite me, and he did. Isserman subsequently made a public incident out of this calling me a "liar" when I

failed to acknowledge his gesture on a TV show because of the ambiguity of the invitation, which was not unsolicited.

14. Author's e-mail to Professor Arthur Eckstein.

15. The water buffalo incident (along with others like it) is recounted in detail in, Harvey Silverglate and Alan Kors, *The Shadow University: The Betrayal of Liberty on America's Campuses* (New York: Harpers Paperback, 1999).

16. "Second Thoughts," January 6, 1993; tape available through the Center for the Study of Popular Culture, Los Angeles.

17. Alan Dershowitz, conversation with the author, "When I teach rape [law] ... these days I will not teach the subject without having a recording."

18. Alan Kors, "Thought Reform 101," *Reason Magazine*, March 2000.

19. For ample documentation of this, see David Horowitz and Jacob Laksin, *One-Party Classroom: How Radical Professors at America's Top Colleges Indoctrinate Students and Undermine Our Democracy,* (New York: Crown Forum, 2009).

20. Kors, "Thought Reform 101," *Reason Magazine.*

21. Larry Elder, "Campus Gulag," FrontPageMag.com, , October 2, 2000.

22. Ibid.

23. This is really the analog of the charge made by Stalinist prosecutors in the 1930s that any dissent from the party line was "anti-Soviet"— i.e., tantamount to joining the class enemy.

24. Larry Elder, "Campus Gulag," FrontPageMag.com, October 2, 2000.

25. Ibid; see also Harvey Silverglate and Alan Kors, *The Shadow University: The Betrayal of Liberty on America's Campuses* (New York: Harpers Paperback, 1999).

26. David Horowitz, *Uncivil Wars: The Controversy Over Reparations for Slavery* (Encounter Books, 2002). In the ad for this book that was published in college papers, I dropped the phrase "for blacks," so as not

to invite the reaction that I was being racially presumptive. My view was that the reparations claim would isolate the black community and put a claim on immigrant groups like Mexican Americans and many others which had no responsibility for slavery, and thus would be racially divisive and detrimental to the claimants themselves.

27. Fred Dickey, "An Uncivil Discourse," *Los Angeles Times Magazine*, May 6, 2001; Hernandez was articulating the radical doctrine of "repressive tolerance," which holds that the repression of those who dissent is justified if it is done in the name of social retribution and "liberation."

28. Ibid.; see also, David Horowitz, "Horowitz's Notepad: A Challenge to the Chancellor of UC Berkeley," FrontPageMag.com, March 9, 2001; available at: http://www.frontpagemag.com/readArticle.aspx?ARTID=19931.

29. David Horowitz, *Uncivil Wars: The Controversy Over Reparations for Slavery*.

30. *Brown Daily Herald*, April 4, 200.

31. Marion Davis, "Anger At Brown Still Simmers Over Divisive Ad," *Providence Journal-Bulletin*, April 8, 2001.

32. Political Science professor Donald Downs took a similar courageous (and lonely) stand at the University of Wisconsin.

CHAPTER TWO

1. David Horowitz, "Horowitz's Notepad: Behind the Iron Curtain in Michigan," FrontPageMag.com, March 21, 2002; available at: http://www.frontpagemag.com/Articles/ReadArticle.asp?ID=4395 [accessed June 25, 2010]; see also, http://www.michigandaily.com/vnews/display.v/ART/2002/03/20/3c98423ad27c9.

2. Center for the Study of Popular Culture, "One Party State," FrontPageMag.com, September 3, 2003; available at: http://www.front

pagemag.com/Articles/ReadArticle.asp?ID=9647 [accessed June 24, 2010].

3. Letter dated September 7, 2001.

4. In 2006, the Center's board changed its name to The David Horowitz Freedom Center.

5. "The Problem with America's Colleges and the Solution," Front-PageMag.com, September 3, 2002; available at: www.frontpage mag.com/Articles/Printable.asp?ID=2637 [accessed June 24, 2010].

6. "1915 Declaration on Academic Freedom and Academic Tenure," American Association of University Professors; available at: http://www.aaup.org/AAUP/pubsres/policydocs/contents/1915.ht m [accessed June 23, 2010].

7. "Academic Bill of Rights," posted by Students for Academic Freedom; available at: http://www.studentsforacademicfreedom.org/docu ments/1925/abor.html [accessed June 24, 2010].

8. "1915 Declaration on Academic Freedom and Academic Tenure," American Association of University Professors; available at: http://www.aaup.org/AAUP/pubsres/policydocs/contents/1915.ht m [accessed June 23, 2010].

9. The letter I sent to each of the three Left-wing academics introduced its subject in these words (with slight variations in each letter tailored to the individual):

"Dear Professor ___

I have drawn up an Academic Bill of Rights (which is attached). I'd like to know what you think of it, and if you have any reservations. I'm trying to put together a University Committee to Support the Bill. It's really just a codification of the academic freedom tradition, but I think it's needed now because the campus has become so politicized. My position in designing this is pretty much that of Fish in

Professional Correctness. There's a place for politics and a place for scholarship and education and they aren't particularly the same place. In any case even if you couldn't see your way to supporting this, I'd like to know what you think."

10. Stanley Fish, "Save the World on Your Own Time," *Chronicle of Higher Education*, January 23, 2003. The article was subsequently expanded into a book with the same title. The principle in the Academic Bill of Rights reads: "8. Knowledge advances when individual scholars are left free to reach their own conclusions about which methods, facts, and theories have been validated by research. Academic institutions and professional societies formed to advance knowledge within an area of research, maintain the integrity of the research process, and organize the professional lives of related researchers serve as indispensable venues within which scholars circulate research findings and debate their interpretation. To perform these functions adequately, academic institutions and professional societies should maintain a posture of organizational neutrality with respect to the substantive disagreements that divide researchers on questions within, or outside, their fields of inquiry."

11. This is the original text of the clause: "All tenure, search and hiring committee deliberations will be recorded and made available to appropriately constituted authorities empowered to inquire into the integrity of the process. (The names of committee members may be redacted). No faculty member will be excluded from tenure, search and hiring committees on the basis of their political or religious beliefs." As a result of the criticisms made by Todd Gitlin and seconded by Michael Bérubé and Stanley Fish, the first three sentences were struck from the text, and only the final sentence remained.

12. Mike Adams, "How the Academic Blacklist Works," Front-PageMag.com, June 4, 2004; available at: http://www.frontpage

mag.com/readArticle.aspx?ARTID=12800 [accessed June 24, 2010].

13. Bérubé's e-mail was sent September 17, 2003. He was the last of the three Left-wing academics I consulted. I had already posted the draft of the Academic Bill of Rights on our website, which contained the clause on tenure and hiring committees, and now removed it.

14. E-mail to the author from Candace de Russy, December 6, 2005.

15. Commentary by William Scheuerman, "Academic Bill of Rights: A Stealth Attack on the Truth," American Federation of Teachers archives, March 2005; available at: http://archive.aft.org/topics/aca demic-freedom/billofrights.htm [accessed June 25, 2010].

16. E.g., Alan Bloom, *The Closing of the American Mind* (New York: Simon & Schuster, 1988); Dinesh D'Souza, *Illiberal Education: The Politics of Race and Sex on Campus* (New York: Free Press, 1998); Roger Kimball, *Tenured Radicals: How Politics Has Corrupted Our Higher Education* (New York: Harper Collins, 1990); Neil Hamilton, *Zealotry and Academic Freedom* (Piscataway, NJ: Transaction Publishers, 1995); Richard Bernstein, *Dictatorship of Virtue: How the Battle over Multiculturalism Is Reshaping Our Schools, Our Country, and Our Lives* (New York: Vintage Books, 1995); and Daphne Patai and Noretta Koertge *Professing Feminism: Education and Indoctrination in Women's Studies* (Lanham, MD: Lexington Books, 2003). Organizations such as the National Association of Scholars, the American Council of Trustees and Alumni, and Students for Academic Freedom along with websites such as Noindoctrination.org documented the abuses.

CHAPTER THREE

1. These comments were reported to me by my student hosts.

2. My student hosts provided me with a copy of the flyer.

3. I have reconstructed my remarks drawing on an article I wrote at the time.

4. Publication of the Center for the Study of Popular Culture, Los Angeles (June) 2003. The cover line reads: "Without diversity of viewpoint, there is no academic freedom."

5. Students For Academic Freedom, Mission and Strategy, http://www.studentsforacademicfreedom.org/documents/1917/pamphlet.html [accessed June 25, 2010].

6. David Horowitz and Eli Lehrer, Executive Summary, "Political Bias in Administrations and Faculties of 32 Elite Colleges and Universities," Students for Academic Freedom, August 28, 2003; available at: http://www.studentsforacademicfreedom.org/reports/lackdiversity.html [accessed June 24, 2010].

7. Ibid.

8. Ibid.

9. "Studies on Faculty and Campus Diversity," Students for Academic Freedom, July 4, 2006; available at: http://www.studentsforacademicfreedom.org/news/1893/FacultyStudies.htm [accessed June 24, 2010].

10. Cindy Yee, "DCU Sparks Various Reactions," *The Chronicle* Online, February 10, 2004.

11. Peggy Lowe, "GOP Takes on 'Leftist" Education," *Rocky Mountain News*, September 6, 2003; available at: http://www.studentsforacademicfreedom.org/archive/2003/RMN090603.htm [accessed June 24, 2010].

CHAPTER FOUR

1. "Curricula and reading lists in the humanities and social sciences should reflect the uncertainty and unsettled character of all human knowledge in these areas by providing students with dissenting sources and viewpoints where appropriate...." Excerpted from the "Academic Bill of Rights," posted by Students for Academic Freedom; available at: http://www.studentsforacademicfreedom.org/docu

ments/1925/abor.html [accessed June 24, 2010].

2. Peggy Lowe, "Campus Ideology Under Fire," *Rocky Mountain News*, September 6, 2003; available at: http://www.studentsforacade micfreedom.org/archive/2005/March2005/OldCORMNpeggylowe campusideolunderfire090603.htm [accessed June 24, 2010].

3. Petty Low, "School Plan Blasted," *Rocky Mountain News*, September 9, 2003; available at: http://www.studentsforacademicfreedom.org/archive/2005/March2005/OldCoRMNGOPproposalmccarthyism 090903.htm [accessed June 24, 2010].

4. Dave Curtin, "David Horowitz Says No Quotas," *Denver Post*, September 10, 2003; available at: http://www.studentsforacademicfree dom.org/archive/2003/DenverPost091003.htm [accessed June 24, 2010].

5. "Absurdity in Higher Ed," *Denver Post*, September 13, 2003; available at: http://www.studentsforacademicfreedom.org/news/124/DenverPost091303.htm [accessed June 24, 2010].

6. I say "deliberately" because I attempted to contact the editor of the *Denver Post* directly to no avail.

7. Gail Schoettler, "Mind Police Are At It Again," *Denver Post*, September 14, 2005.

8. For press coverage on the academic freedom campaign, see "Press Coverage," Students for Academic Freedom; available at: http://www.studentsforacademicfreedom.org/reports/PressCoverage.html [accessed June 24, 2010].

9. Mike Rosen "Hysteria Over Academia," *Rocky Mountain News*, January 30, 2004; available at: http://www.studentsforacademicfree dom.org/news/395/hysteriaoveracademia020204.htm [accessed June 24, 2010].

10. For a sampling of news commentaries see "Colorado News Links: September 12," Students for Academic Freedom; available at:

http://www.studentsforacademicfreedom.org/news/60/COnewsli
nks091203.html [accessed June 24, 2010].

11. Cary Nelson, *No University Is An Island*, 188.

12. Peggy Lowe, "Horowitz Decries 'Hate Campaign,'" *Denver Rocky
Mountain News*, October 2, 2003; available at: http://www.students
foracademicfreedom.org/news/212/RMN100203.html [accessed
June 24, 2010].

13. I have reconstructed my remarks from articles I wrote at the time and
reports that appeared in the press.

14. Peggy Lowe, "Metro President Says No To Inquiry," *Denver Rocky
Mountain News*, October 8, 2003.

15. *Handbook for Professional Personnel*, Revised June 2006,
http://www.mscd.edu/trustees/policies/docs/prof_per_hndb-
k_june_2006c_1_AM.pdf [accessed June 25, 2010].

16. John Ensslin, "Students Say Views Ridiculed," *Rocky Mountain
News*, December 19, 2003; available at: http://www.studentsforaca
demicfreedom.org/news/377/DPJimSpencerProfsmouthmaysilenc
e022604.htm [accessed June 24, 2010].

17. Dave Curtain, "Tempers Boil at Hearing on Academic Bill of Rights,"
Denver Post, February 26, 2004; available at: http://www.students
foracademicfreedom.org/news/379/DPtempersboilathearing02270
4.htm [accessed June 24, 2010].

18. Jim Spencer, "Prof's Mouth May Silence All Educators," *Denver Post*,
February 26, 2004.

19. Colorado House Bill 04–1315.

20. While the Churchill scandal was the precipitating factor, there were
other major problems, including the expenditure of half a million dollars in university funds on alcohol and a sexual harassment scandal
involving the football team. The university costs of the Churchill fiasco

were revealed to me in a discussion with university regent Tom Lucero.

21. When our conversation was concluded without her agreeing to take up the Academic Bill of Rights, she did agree to support the Kopff project, but without connecting it to the larger problem.

22. The Memorandum of Understanding was signed in March 2004. State Representative Shawn Mitchell, "Memorandum of Understanding,"Students for Academic Freedom," May 25, 2004; available at: http://www.studentsforacademicfreedom.org/reports/COmemo randumofunderstanding.htm [accessed June 24, 2010]; see also, S.J. Res. 04-033, 64th Gen. Assem., Reg. Sess. (Colo. 2004); available at: http://www.leg.state.co.us/clics2004a/csl.nsf/fsbillcont3/B68E085 ABB9BD50C87256E6300037C2F?Open&file=SJR033_enr.pdf [accessed June 24, 2010].

23. Office of the President, Colordao State University; available at: http://www.president.colostate.edu/index.asp?page=academic_free dom [accessed June 24, 2010].

CHAPTER FIVE

1. "Academic Bill of Rights," AAUP, 2003; available at: http://www.aaup.org/AAUP/comm/rep/A/abor.htm [accessed June 25, 2010].

2. Transcript, *Public Hearing of Select Committee On Academic Freedom In Higher Education*, Thursday November 9, 2005, 187. Reprinted in Stephen H. Aby, ed., *The Academic Bill of Rights Debate* (Praeger, 2007), 192, et seq. On Joan Wallach Scott, see *Indoctrination U.*, 39–45 and below. Scott also described her Communist father as a Jeffersonian democrat in the same testimony.

3. "The proposed Academic Bill of Rights directs universities to enact guidelines implementing the principle of neutrality, in particular by requiring that colleges and universities appoint faculty 'with a view

toward fostering a plurality of methodologies and perspectives.' The danger of such guidelines is that they invite diversity to be measured by political standards that diverge from the academic criteria of the scholarly profession. Measured in this way, diversity can easily become contradictory to academic ends. So, for example, no department of political theory ought to be obligated to establish 'a plurality of methodologies and perspectives' by appointing a professor of Nazi political philosophy, if that philosophy is not deemed a reasonable scholarly option within the discipline of political theory." See also: "Academic Bill of Rights," AAUP, 2003; available at: http://www. aaup.org/AAUP/comm/rep/A/abor.htm [accessed June 25, 2010].

4.   See Bérubé's e-mail quoted above.

5.   Academic Bill of Rights, 2003, http://www.aaup.org/AAUP/comm/ rep/A/abor.htm [accessed June 25, 2010].

6.   See footnote 70 for the text of this clause.

7.   My reply to the AAUP statement, "The Professors' Orwellian case," Students for Academic Freedom, December 5, 2003; available at: http://www.studentsforacademicfree-dom.org/news/96/HorowitzAAUPResponse120503.htm [accessed June 25, 2010]. It is reprinted in Aby, *The Academic Bill of Rights* Debates, 57 et seq.

8.   Marcus Harvey, "An Introduction to the [Graham Larkin-David Horowitz] Debate," in Stephen H. Aby, *The Academic Bill of Rights Debate* (Praeger, 2007), 67. At the time of writing, Harvey was the AAUP's West Coast Field Representative. He is now a secretary of the organization.

9.   Cary Nelson, *No University is an Island,* 191.

10. Harvey in Aby, *The Academic Bill of Rights Debate,* 68.

11. Frank Luntz, "Inside the Mind of An Ivy League Professor," Front-

PageMag.com, August 30, 2002; available at: http://www.frontpage
mag.com/articles/Read.aspx?GUID=08DE7057-EA18-4775-B58
A-D7A361431936 [accessed June 24, 2010].

12. Graham Larkin, "What's Not To Like About The Academic Bill of
Rights," in Stephen Aby, op. *The Academic Rights Debate*, 70 et seq. Aby
reprints my reply and then an additional exchange between Larkin
and me. The exchange can also be found here: http://www.front
pagemag.com/Content/read.aspx?Area=Replies%20to%20Critics
%20of%20AF [accessed June 24, 2010].

13. To say that knowledge is unsettled is hardly the same as saying that
there is no truth.

14. Larkin in Aby, *The Academic Bill of Rights Debate,* 75.

15. Graham Larkin, "David Horowitz's War on Rational Discourse,"
InsideHigherEd.com, April 25, 2005; available at: http://www.inside
highered.com/layout/set/print/views/2005/04/25/larkin [accessed
June 24, 2010].

16. Larkin also accused me of falsely claiming the AAUP was silent when
speech codes were instituted. I have no access to the original transcripts, I am unable respond to his other charges. However, while a
1992 AAUP statement on speech codes forthrightly condemns them,
it is a fair comment that the AAUP has not been in the forefront of the
battles to repeal them. Thus in his 2005 book *Restoring Liberty and
Free Speech on Campus*, libertarian author Donald Downs describes
the AAUP as "a group that has retreated from prominence during the
battles discussed in this book." Its ambivalent attitude is on display in
a review of F.I.R.E's 2005 *Guide to Free Speech on Campus* by Joan
Wallach Scott, recently retired head of AAUP's Committee on Academic Freedom which begins: "In the last two decades, in the name
of individual rights, conservatives have attacked and often succeeded

in weakening, if not dismantling, the anti-discrimination programs of the 1960s and '70s." Scott clearly regards FIRE as a conservative organization, although it was founded by a liberal and a conservative, and has conducted itself in a non-partisan manner.

17. John J. Sanko, "Colorado Academic Showdown," *Rocky Mountain News*, September 2, 2004.

18. David Horowitz, "Colorado: The Student Speaks," Front-PageMag.com, March 18, 2005; available at: http://97.74. 65.51/readArticle.aspx?ARTID=9207 [accessed June 25, 2010].

19. Erin Bergstrom, "Statement on University of Colorado Case," Students for Academic Freedom, March 15, 2005; available at: http://www.studentsforacademicfree-dom.org/news/1006/ErinBergstromStatement031505.htm [accessed June 24, 2010].

20. David Horowitz, "Why an Academic Bill of Rights Is Necessary," FrontPageMag.com, March 15, 2005; available at: http://www.front pagemag.com/Articles/Printable.aspx?GUID=AD857325-5138-47BA-A3E8-FA847EA219D7 [accessed June 24, 2010].

21. Reginald Fields, "Legislator Wants Law to Restrict Professors," *Plain Dealer* Bureau, February 20, 2005; available at: http://www.students foracademicfreedom.org/news/1060/PlainDealerBureauOHarticle 030305.htm [accessed June 24, 2010].

22. "AAUP Plan Protest of Academic Bill of Rights at Ohio Statehouse," Students For Academic Freedom, March 3, 2005; available at: http://www.studentsforacademicfreedom.org/news/970/AAUP plansOhioProtest030305.htm [accessed June 25, 2010]. The statement was amended in 1970 by the AAUP to include the word "persistently"—"The passage [i.e., from the 1940 AAUP] statement serves to underscore the need for teachers to avoid persistently intruding material which has no relation to their subject." "1940 Statement of

Principles on Academic Freedom and Tenure," AAUP, http://www.aaup.org/AAUP/pubsres/policydocs/contents/1940statement.htm [accessed June 25, 2010].

23. The Board of Trustees, "Academic freedom and responsibility," The Ohio State University; available at: http://trustees.osu.edu/rules5/ru5-01.php [accessed June 24, 2010].

24. Mano Singham, "The Liberal Fiend Can't be Found," *The Plain Dealer*, March 3, 2005; available at: http://www.studentsforacademicfreedom.org/news/1062/PlainDealerliberalfiendcantbefound030305.htm [accessed June 24, 2010].

25. Ibid.

26. "The Poster Child Who Can't Be Found," InsideHigherEd.com, March 14, 2005; available at: http://www.insidehighered.com/news/2005/03/14/horowitz3_14 [accessed June 24, 2010].

27. The question of whether he actually was a Republican is itself a question, however, since all attempts we made to identify his party affiliation through the election lists and Republican rolls in his district failed.

28. U. Northern Colorado Exam Timeline, Students for Academic Freedom; available at: http://www.studentsforacademicfreedom.org/news/2672/u-northern-colorado-exam-timeline [accessed June 24, 2010].

29. Doyle Murphy, "Professor calmly refutes test tales," *Greely Daily Tribune,* March 22, 2005; available at: http://www.studentsforacademicfreedom.org/news/1020/GreeleytribuneProfCalmlyRefutesTest032205.htm [accessed June 24, 2010].

30. Critics have also claimed that the question could have been requiring students to be devil's advocates, and pointed out that there were two questions to choose from. But as I have pointed out elsewhere, the other question was similarly framed to require the student to take a

left-wing point of view. I have printed all four questions from Dunkley's reconstructed exam and analyzed them to show their common
political bias in *The Professors,* 128–131.

31. David Horowitz, "The Case of the Colorado Exam," Students for
Academic Freedom, April 21, 2005; available at: http://www.students
foracademicfreedom.org/news/690/DHCaseofColoradoExam0421
05.htm [accessed June 24, 2010]. This was also reprinted in a pamphlet we published called The Campaign For Academic Freedom

32. Statement by Erin Bergstrom, Students for Academic Freedom,
March 15, 2005; available at: http://www.studentsforacademicfree
dom.org/news/1006/ErinBergstromStatement031505.htm
[accessed June 24, 2010].

33. Michael Bérubé, *What's So Liberal About the Liberal Arts?: Classroom Politics and "Bias" in Higher Education* (New York: W. W. Norton, 2006), 29.

CHAPTER SIX

1. Among them were Missouri, Georgia, Florida, Ohio, Arizona, Maine,
Tennessee and New York.

2. A list of Ohio faculty senates that condemned the legislation is provided in Aby, *The Bill of Academic Rights Debates,* 127.

3. David Horowitz, "Why an Academic Bill of Rights is Necessary,"
FrontPageMag.com, March 15, 2005; available at: http://www.stu
dentsforacademicfreedom.org/news/997/DHohiotesti-
mony031505.htm [accessed June 25, 2010].

4. "Indoctrination Lobby," DiscoverTheNetwork.org, February 14,
2005; available at: http://www.discoverthenetworks.org/groupPro
file.asp?grpid=7484 [accessed June 23, 2010].

5. Scott Jaschik, "August Heat," InsideHigherEd.com, August 16, 2005;

available at: http://www.insidehighered.com/news/2005/08/16/ teaching [accessed June 25, 2010].

6. "Office of Civil Rights Director Norma Cantu ordered an investigation of Ohio's high school proficiency exam when she learned that a third of the 2.6 percent of graduating seniors who had failed the exam were black. Notwithstanding an earlier federal court ruling that the exam was free of racial bias, Cantu was determined to use her authority to rid Ohio—and presumably other states—of achievement tests that yield disparate outcomes among racial groups." Robert Detlefsen, "Affirmative Agony," *Reason Magazine*, July, 1996; available at: http://www.reason.com/news/show/29965.html [accessed June 25, 2010].

7. Resume, Norma V. Cantu; available at: http://www.utexas.edu/ law/faculty/cvs/ncantu_cv.pdf [accessed June 25, 2010]. In one calendar year, 1800 universities resolved the cases brought against them without challenging the government's opinion. A search of the AAUP and AFT websites failed to turn up a single critical comment on Cantu's regency. Her only appearance was a notice that she was an AFT guest speaker.

8. Joshua Cuneo, "Prof Causes Student to File Grievance," The Technique, April 21, 2004; available at: http://www.studentsforacade micfreedom.org/news/270/gatechprofcausesstudent042104.htm [accessed June 25, 2010]; see also, "Timeline of Ruth Mahorta Case at George Tech," Students for Academic Freedom, May 28, 2009; available at: http://www.studentsforacademicfreedom.org/news /2700/timeline-of-ruth-malhotra-case-at-georgia-tech [accessed June 25, 2010].

9. Ibid.

10. Ibid.

11. The hearings were held on February 23, 2004.

12. "Timeline of Ruth Mahorta Case," Students for Academic Freedom.

13. Kelly Simmons, "Students Fight Alleged Political Prejudice," Students For Academic Freedom, March 24, 2004; available at: http://www.studentsforacademicfree-dom.org/news/495/AJCstudentsfightpolprejudice032404.htm [accessed June 25, 2010]. Article originally published in Atlanta Journal Constitution. See also, "Timeline of Ruth Mahorta Case," Students for Academic Freedom."

14. Ibid.

15. Letter from Georgia Tech Vice-Provost McCath, Students for Academic Freedom, July 9, 2004; available at: http://www.studentsfor academicfreedom.org/news/1013/GAtechletterfromMcmath070804.htm [accessed June 25, 2010]. For the complete correspondence with McCath, see: http://www.studentsforacademicfreedom.org/news/?c=Georgia-Institute-of-Technology&pg=2 [accessed June 25, 2010].

16. "Response from SAF to GA Tech Vice-Provost McGrath," Students for Academic Freedom, July 20, 2004; available at: http://www.stu dentsforacademicfreedom.org/news/1016/GATechSAFfirstrespons etoMcMath071904.htm [accessed June 25, 2010].

17. "Response from Georgia Tech Provost McCath," Students for Academic Freedom, July 29, 2009; available at: http://www.students foracademicfreedom.org/news/1014/GAtechletterfromMcmath072 904.htm [accessed June 25, 2010].

18. "Response from Georgia Tech Provost McCath to SAF," Students for Academic Freedom, September 23, 2004; available at: http://www.studentsforacademicfreedom.org/news/1433/GAtech McMathresponsetoSAF.htm [accessed June 25, 2010].

19. "Timeline of Ruth Mahorta Case," Students for Academic Freedom.

20. Ibid.

21. This was a guide to academic freedom issues that we provided to students in our campaign.

22. "Timeline of Ruth Mahorta Case," Students for Academic Freedom.

CHAPTER SEVEN

1. Sara Dogan, "Letters from the National Campus Director: Brown Students Pass Academic Freedom Resolution," Students for Academic Freedom, April 30, 2004; available at: http://www.students foracademicfreedom.org/letters/2012/letter-brownresolupas [accessed June 24, 2010].

2. "Victory for Academic Freedom at Brooklyn College," FIRE, November 23, 2004; available at: http://www.thefire.org/ index.php/article/5054.html/print [accessed June 24, 2010].

3. Alisha Wyman, "U. Montana Student Government Fails Academic Bill of Rights by One Vote," Students for Academic Freedom, November 13, 2003; available at: http://www.studentsforacademic freedom.org/find/Montana111703.htm [accessed June 24, 2010].

4. Susan Russo, "Letters from National Campus Director: Introducing The Student Bill of Rights," Students for Academic Freedom, November 19, 2003; available at: http://www.studentsforacademic freedom.org/letters/1999/letter-studentbill111 [accessed June 24, 2010]; see also, Alisha Wyman, "U. Montana Student Government Fails Academic Bill of Rights by One Vote," Students for Academic Freedom, November 13, 2003; available at: http://www.studentsfor academicfreedom.org/news/184/Montana111703.htm [accessed June 24, 2010].

5. Maine College Republicans, "Maine Republican Party Unani-

mously Approvse Inclusion of Academic Freedom Language in 2006 Maine Rep.," Students for Academic Freedom, May 10, 2006: available at: http://www.studentsforacademicfreedom.org/news /1401/MaineRepubPartyApprovesAFplatform051006.htm [accessed June 24, 2010]. Schuberth, who managed to get the Academic Bill of Rights adopted by the Bowdoin student government was then made the youngest Vice President of the Maine Republican Party in its history.

6. Ibid.

7. I have described this committee and the events surrounding the Churchill invitation in greater detail in The Professors, pp. viii–xx.

8. Jacob Laksin, "Terrorist Teacher," FrontPageMag.com, December 2, 2004.

9. "Ward Churchill September 11 attacks essay controversy," Wikipedia.org, September 12, 2001; available at: http://en.wikipedia. org/wiki/Ward_Churchill_9/11_essay_controversy [accessed June 24, 2010].

10. "Faculty Action In the Ward Churchill Case," American Association of University Professors, (Updated) March 2005; available at: http://www.aaup.org/newsroom/Newsitems/Faculty&churchill- .htm [accessed June 24, 2010].

11. David Horowitz, "Ward Churchill Is Just The Beginning," Denver Rocky Mountain News, February 9, 2005; availabl at: http://www. frontpagemag.com/readArticle.aspx?ARTID=9637 [accessed June 24, 2010].

12. Doug Lederman, "A Rising Star Takes a Fall," Inside Higher ED, March 8, 2005; available at: http://www.insidehighered.com/ news/2005/03/08/hoffman3_8 [accessed June 24, 2010].

13. Data available at: http://thomas.loc.gov/cgi-in/query/F?c109:3:./

temp/~c109NC0ToD:e32394 [accessed July 12, 2010].

14. Bruce L.R. Smith, Jeremy D. Mayer and A. Lee Fritschler, *Closed Minds? Politics and Ideology in American Universities*, Brookings Institution, 2008, 95.

15. Ibid.

16. Ibid. These are the words of the Brookings authors but they were written to reflect the sentiments of the university presidents who pressed the compromise. I confirmed these attitudes with Terry Hartle, senior vice president of the American Council on Education.

17. Brookings, op. cit., 96.

18. Ibid., 97.

19. Ibid., 98.

20. Ibid., Appendix D, 236.

21. Ibid., 99.

22. ACE statement

CHAPTER EIGHT

1. Ibid.

2. Kathy Lynn Gray, "Bill could limit open debate at colleges," The Columbus Dispatch, January 27, 2005; available at: http://www.dispatch.com/live/contentbe/dispatch/2005/01/27/20050127-C1-04.html [accessed June 25, 2010].

3. Stephen H. Aby, *The Academic Bill of Rights Debate: A Handbook* (Westport, CT: Praeger Publishers, 2007), 131.

4. Ibid., 132

5. "Academic Policies," Online Student Handbook, Ohio State University; available at: http://www.ohio.edu/students/handbook/policies/index.cfm [accessed June 24, 2010].

6. Office of Academic Affairs, "The Ohio State University's Reaffirma-

tion of Academic Rights and Responsibilities for Addressing Concerns," The Ohio State University, April 2006; available at: http://oaa.edu/acad_rts_respons.php.

7. Jon B. Gould, *Speak No Evil: The Triumph of Hate Speech Regulation* (Chicago: University of Chicago Press, 2005), 175.

8. In the book I gave an estimate of about half that in an effort to deflect criticism that I was overstating the problem. However, having written a second book—*One-Party Classroom: How Radical Professors at America's Top Colleges Indoctrinate Students and Undermine Our Democracy*, (New York: Crown Forum, 2009)—about indoctrination curricula, I am more than ever persuaded that the higher figure is reasonable.

9. Bruce L. R. Smith, Jeremy D. Mayer, and A. Lee Frischler, *Closed Minds? Politics and Ideology in American Universities* (Washington, D.C.: The Brookings Institution, 2008), 110. See also, "Spotlight on Speech Codes Reports," FIRE, Update, December 7, 2006; available at: http://www.thefire.org/code/speechcodereport/ [accessed June 24, 2010].

10. Jon B. Gould, *Speak No Evil*, 149 et seq.

11. David Horowitz, *The Professors*, 2006, xlvi.

12. Ibid., xlvii.

13. Ibid., 29 et. seq.

14. Ibid., 224

15. Ibid., lii–liii.

16. I have discussed the attacks on the book at greater length in *Indoctrination U.* (New York: Encounter Books, 2007), 81–85, 89–90, 102. See also, Preface to the paperback edition of *The Professors*.

17. "Indoctrination Lobby (IL)," discoverthenetworks.org; available at: http://www.discoverthenetworks.org/groupProfile.asp?grpid=7484 [accessed June 24, 2010].

18. Press Release, American Federation of Teachers, "Free Exchange on Campus," previously available at: http://www.aft.org/higher_ed/news/2006/free_exchange.htm.

19. Horowitz, *The Professors*, xxvi.

20. Jacob Laksin, "Discounting the Facts," FrontPageMag.com, June 15, 2006; available at: http://97.74.65.51/readArticle.aspx?ARTID=4039 [accessed June 24, 2010].

21. Scott, Jaschik, "David Horowitz Has A List," InsideHigherEd.com, February 13, 2006; available at: http://www.insidehighered.com/news/2006/02/13/list [accessed June 24, 2010].

22. Ibid.

23. Horowitz, *The Professors*, 215.

24. Caroline Higgins, Syllabus for "Methods for Peacemaking," Spring 2004; available at: http://www.earlham.edu/~pags/syllabus/pags_374_ch/PAGS_374_1_CH.pdf [accessed June 24, 2010].

25. Horowitz, *The Professors*, 215.

26. "Theory and Practice Revisited," course syllabus; available at: http://www.earlham.edu/%7Epags/syllabus/pags_80_ch/pags_80_2_ch.pdf [accessed June 25, 2010].

27. A student commenting on Professor Higgins on RateMyProfessor.com, writes: "This woman is horribly disorganized and I agree with the other comments that she absolutely does not allow for critical discussion or analysis. I am an extreme liberal but even I found her way to presenting information to be very akin to propaganda." Comment available at: http://www.ratemyprofessors.com/ShowRatings.jsp?tid=462407 [accessed June 24, 2010].

28. Ibid.

29. Ibid.

30. Horowitz, *The Professors*, 216.

31. Cited in Daniel Won-gu Kim, "In the Tradition: Amiri Baraka, black

Liberation, and Avant-garde Praxis in the U.S—Critical Essay,"
African American Review, Summer-Fall, 2003. Diana Russell, The
Politics of Rape: The Victim's Perspective (Lincoln, NE: iUniverse,
1984).

32. Amiri Baraka, "Somebody Blew Up America," View From The Right,
October 5, 2002; available at: http://www.amnation.com/vfr/
archives/000834.html [accessed June 24, 2010].

33. Herb Denenberg, "Find Out About The Candidate Before The Vote,"
Campus   Watch,   November   16,   2008;   available   at:
http://www.campus-watch.org/article/id/6301 [June 24, 2010].

34. Margaret Hunt Gram, "Professors Condemn War in Iraq At Teach-
In," *Columbia Spectator*, March 27, 2003; see also Douglas Feiden,
"Poisin Ivy," New York Daily News, November 5, 2006; available at:
http://www.campus-watch.org/article/id/2898 [accessed June 24,
2010].

35. Horowitz, *The Professors*, 35, 123, 304 et seq.

36. Michael Bérubé, "Discipline and puzzle," Crooked Timber, March
29, 2007; available at: http://crookedtimber.org/2007/03/29/dis
cipline-and-puzzle/ [accessed June 24, 2010].

37. In particular, he hadn't read the 17,000-word argument of the book,
contained in the introduction and the two concluding chapters.

38. First National Academic Freedom Conference, "LUNCH PANEL: Is
Legislation Necessary or Advisable?" Students For Academic Free-
dom, July 24, 2006; transcripts available at: http://www.students
foracademicfreedom.org/news/?c=First-National-Academic-Free-
dom-Conference [accessed June 24, 2010]. I put AFT vice president
William Scheuerman on the panel to discuss "Academic Freedom: Is
Legislation Necessary or Advisable," alongside Terry Hartle of the
American Council on Education. I invited Scott Jaschik, editor-in-

chief of InsiderHigherEd.com to moderate. A transcript of the panel can be found here: http://www.studentsforacademicfreedom.org/news/2095/AFconferenceLegislationNecessaryPanel072406.htm [accessed June 24, 2010].

39. Second National Academic Freedom Conference, Students for Academic Freedom, March 12, 2007; available at: http://www.students foracademicfreedom.org/news/?c=Second-National-Academic-Freedom-Conference [accessed June 24, 2010]; I invited Cary Nelson to debate me over the question "Political Indoctrination and Harassment on Campus: Is There A Problem?" Scott Smallwood of the Chronicle of Higher Education moderated and the event was televised on C-SPAN, Students For Academic Freedom, March 4, 2007; transcript available at: http://www.studentsforacademicfreedom.org/news/2420/political-indoctrination-and-harassment-on-campus-is-there-a-problem [accessed June 24, 2010].

40. Transcript from Student Panel, Students for Academic Freedom, July 24, 2006; available at: http://www.studentsforacademicfree dom.org/news/2097/AFconferenceStudentPanel072406.htm [accessed June 24, 2010].

41. Cary Nelson, *No University Is an Island: Saving Academic Freedom* (New York: NYU Press, 2010), 186.

42. The UUP Voice, April 2005. My encounters with Scheuerman are reviewed in David Horowitz, *Indoctrination U.* (New York: Encounter Books, 2007), 97–104.

43. Cary Nelson, "Ignore This Book," *Academe*, November-December 2006.

44. Ibid.

45. "Political Indoctrination and Harassment on Campus: Is there a Problem?," FrontPageMag.com, March 23, 2007; available at:

http://www.frontpagemag.com/Articles/ReadArticle.asp?ID=27446 [accessed June 24, 2010].

46. Stanley Fish has drawn the distinction between academic discussion of political issues and political proselytizing and with admirable clarity: "Academic freedom is the freedom of academics to study anything they like; the freedom, that is, to subject any body of material, however unpromising it might seem, to academic interrogation and analysis.... Any idea can be brought into the classroom if the point is to inquire into its structure, history, influence and so forth. But no idea belongs in the classroom if the point of introducing it is to recruit your students for the political agenda it may be thought to imply."Kevin Barrett, "Conspiracy Theories 101," *New York Times*, July 23, 2006; available at: http://www.nytimes.com/2006/07/23/opinion/23 fish.html?_r=1&ex=1154318400&en=ed83a53b32783208&ei=507 0 [accessed June 24, 2010].

47. Cary Nelson, *Repression and Recovery: Modern American Poetry and the Politics of Cultural Memory (1910-1945)* (Madison: University of Wisconsin Press, October 1992).

48. Ibid.

49. Michael Rothberg and Peter K. Garrett, *Cary Nelson and the Struggle for the University,* (Albany: SUNY Press, January 2009), 223.

CHAPTER NINE

1. Studies on Faculty and Campus Diversity, Students for Academic Freedom, July 4, 2006; available at: http://www.studentsforaca demicfreedom.org/news/1893/FacultyStudies.htm [accessed June 24, 2010].

2. Press Coverage, Students for Academic Freedom; available at: http://www.studentsforacademicfreedom.org/news/?c=Press-Coverage [accessed June 24, 2010].

3. "More Criticism of the Academic Bill of Rights," InsideHigh-erEd.com, January 9, 2006; available at: http://www.insidehigh ered.com/news/2006/01/09/resolutions [accessed June 24, 2010].

4. Ibid.

5. Ibid.

6. "Who Are We," American Historical Association; available at; http://www.historians.org/info/WhoAre.cfm [accessed June 24, 2010].

7. David Horowitz, "An Academic Freedom Bill I Will Oppose, Front-PageMag.com, February 13, 2006; see also, Report to the SSSP Board of Directors, Standards of Freedom in Research, Publication, and Teaching Committie, Society for the Study of Social Problems; available at: http://www.sssp1.org/extras/2005%20Standards %20and%20Freedom%20Committee%20Report%20with%20atta chments.pdf [accessed June 24, 2010].

8. Data available at: http://www.mla.org/governance/mla_resolutions/ 05resolution_delassembly [accessed July 12, 2010].

9. AAC&U Board of Director's Statement, "Academic Freedom and Educational Responsibility," AAC&U, January 6, 2006; available at: http://www.aacu.org/about/statements/academic_freedom.cfm [accessed June 24, 2010].

10. S.B. 1331, 47th Leg., 2nd Reg. Sess. (Ariz. 2006).

11. David Horowitz, "An Academic Freedom Bill I Won't Support," FrontPageMag.com; available at: http://www.frontpagemag.com/ readArticle.aspx?ARTID=5574 [accessed June 24, 2010].

12. Ibid.

13. Ibid.

14. David Horowitz, "Ideologues at the Lectern," *Los Angeles Times*, January 23, 2006; available at: http://www.frontpagemag.com/Arti cles/Read.aspx?GUID=906B5004-A8A5-4B7A-8927-35F806E5B E41 [accessed June 24, 2010]; see also, Michael Janofsky, "Profes-

sor's Politics Draw Lawmakers Into The Fray," *New York Times*, December 25, 2005; available at: http://www.nytimes.com/2005/ 12/25/national/25bias.html?_r=1&scp=2&sq=gibson%20armstrong &st=cse&oref=slogin [accessed June 24, 2010].

15. Author's conversation with Representative Gib Armstrong.

16. H.R. Res. 177, Gen Assem., Reg. Sess. (Pa. 2005); available at: http://www.legis.state.pa.us/CFDOCS/Legis/PN/Public/btCheck.c fm?txtType=PDF&sessYr=2005&sessInd=0&billBody=H&billTyp =R&billNbr=0177&pn=2553 [accessed June 24, 2010].

17. Veon's post has since been removed from the website.

18. Transcript, Public Hearing of Select Committee On Academic Freedom In Higher Education, November 10, 2005, 141.

19. Transcript, 118.

20. Cara Matthews, "Conservative Group Seeks College 'Bill of Rights,'" Gannett News Service; available at: http://www.studentsforacademic freedom.org/news/1184/GannettNewsConserv-GroupSeeks101305.htm [accessed June 24, 2010].

21. Transcript, 141.

22. "The 'Bigfoot' Committee," ACLU blog; available at: http://aclupa.blogspot.com/2005/11/bigfoot-committee.html [accessed June 24, 2010].

23. Transcript, 7–15.

24. Transcript, 17.

25. Transcript, 37.

26. Transcript, 37–38.

27. *Faculty Handbook*, University of Pittsburgh, July 2002 (updated January 2009; available at: http://www.provost.pitt.edu/info/Facul tyHandbook.pdf [accessed June 24, 2010].

28. "Faculty Conduct" in "Academic Integrity," University of Pittsburght;

available at: http://www.as.pitt.edu/faculty/policy/integrity.html #faculty [accessed June 24, 2010].

29. Transcript, 48.

30. Adam Smeltz, "Penn State University Fields 13 Bias Claims," *Center Daily Times*, January 25, 2006.

31. Transcript, 20–22.

32. Ibid.

33. E-mail correspondence of Ken Lehrman to Sara Dogan, August 18, 2009.

34. The book was Neil Hamilton, *Zealotry and Academic Freedom* (New Jersey: Transaction Publishers, 1995).

35. Lionel Lewis, *Cold War On Campus* (New Jersey: Transaction Publishers, 1988), supra note 122 at p. 12; cited in Neil Hamilton, *Zealotry and Academic Freedom*, (New Jersey: Transaction Publishers,1995), 27. Hamliton is Trustee Professor of Legal Studies at William Mitchell College of Law.

36. Lewis, 279.

37. "The faculty member is entitled to freedom in the classroom in discussing his/her subject. The faculty member is, however, responsible for the maintenance of appropriate standards of scholarship and teaching ability. It is not the function of a faculty member in a democracy to indoctrinate his/her students with ready-made conclusions on controversial subjects. The faculty member is expected to train students to think for themselves, and to provide them access to those materials which they need if they are to think intelligently. Hence in giving instruction upon controversial matters the faculty member is expected to be of a fair and judicial mind, and to set forth justly, without supersession or innuendo, the divergent opinions of other investigators. No faculty member may claim as a right the privilege of

discussing in the classroom controversial topics outside his/her own field of study. The faculty member is normally bound not to take advantage of his/her position by introducing into the classroom provocative discussions of irrelevant subjects not within the field of his/her study." See, Policy HR64, Penn State University; available at: http://guru.psu.edu/POLICIES/OHR/HR64.html#A"http://guru.psu.edu/POLICIES/OHR/HR64.html#A [accessed June 24, 2010].

38. Ibid.

39. Penn State University is separate from the Pennsylvania State System of Higher Education (PASSHE) which includes Bloomsburg U., Kutztown U, Indiana U. Millersville U., Shippensburg U., etc.

40. "Agreement Between Association of Pennsylvania State College and University Faculties (APSCUF) and The Pennsylvania State System of Higher Education (State System)," APSCUF, July 1, 2007–June 30, 2001; available at: http://www.passhe.edu/executive/HR/labor/unions/Pages/APSCUF.aspx.

41. Transcript, Temple Hearings, 113.

42. Editorial staff, Review of Ellen Schrecker, "Worse than McCarthy," *Chronicle of Higher Education*, February 10, 2006.

43. Faculty Handbook, Temple University; available at: http://policies.temple.edu/getdoc.asp?policy_no=02.78.02 (link no longer active).

44. Transcript, Temple Hearings, 12.

45. The gender of the professor was concealed as an extra precaution to protect his/her identity.

46. Transcript, Temple Hearings, 31–32.

47. Ibid., 140–1.

48. Ibid., 142.

49. Ibid., 143.

50. Ibid., 144. Logan Fisher's testimony is also available at: http://www.studentsforacademicfreedom.org/news/1326/Stephen ZelnickLoganFisherPaTestimony.htm.

51. Ibid., 155.

52. Ibid., 164–5.

53. Ibid., 159.

54. Ibid., 170.

55. Ibid., 145.

56. Ibid., 175–6.

57. See student complaint above, p. 163-64.

58. Testimonies available at: http://www.studentsforacademicfreedom.org/news/?c=Pennsylvania-Academic-Freedom-Hearings.

59. "Students having concerns about situations that arise within the classroom, or concerns with instructor behavior in a course that violates University standards of classroom conduct as defined in Policy HR64 'Academic Freedom,' may seek resolution according to the recommended procedures established under Policy 20–00, Resolution of Classroom Problems.

"In every case, student concerns arising from questions about classroom situations or behavior shall be resolved in a manner that provides for equity and due process for students and for instructors. Students may attempt to resolve classroom problems with assurance that confidentiality will be maintained as appropriate." "20-00 Resolution of Student Classroom Problems," http://www.senate.psu.edu/policies/20-00.html. The associated grievance policy R-6 can be found here: http://www.psu.edu/dept/oue/aappm/R-6.html New Policy; Passed April 25, 2006.

60. The Temple policy is available at: http://policies.temple.edu/get doc.asp?policy_no=03.70.02; see also Letter from the National Cam-

pus Director, "Temple University Trustees Adopt Policy on Students' Academic Rights," Students for Academic Freedom, July 21, 2006; available at: http://www.studentsforacademicfreedom.org/archive /2006/July2006/TempleTrusteesAdoptPolicyPressRelease072106. htm [accessed June 24, 2010].

61. David Horowitz, "What I Told Pennsylvania's Academic Freedom Hearings," Students for Academic Freedom, January 11, 2006; available at: http://www.studentsforacademicfreedom.org/news/1307/ DHPaTestimony011106.htm [accessed June 24, 2010].

62. Transcript, Temple Hearings, 139.

63. Ibid., 141.

64. Ibid., 159.

65. Ibid., 148.

66. Ibid., 120–1.

67. Ibid., 185.

68. Ibid., 186.

69. Michael Weisner, "Collegiate Intimidation," FrontPageMag.com; available at: http://www.frontpagemag.com/readArticle.aspx?AR TID=10231 [accessed June 24, 2010].

70. Transcript, Temple Hearings, 207–8.

71. Scott Jaschik, "Retractions from David Horowitz," InsideHigh- erEd.com, January 11, 2006; available at: http://www.insidehigher ead.com/news/2006/01/11/retract [accessed June 24, 2010].

72. Ibid. The second story was apparently the Foothills case.

73. Ibid.

74. For a copy of this Report in its original form, see: http://www.studentsforacademicfreedom.org/news/2324/pennsyl vanias-academic-freedom-reforms [accessed June 24, 2010].

75. Ibid.

76. Final Report of the Select Committee on Academic Freedom in Higher Education Pursuant to House Resolution 177, November 21, 2006; available at: http://www.studentsforacademicfreedom. org/news/2656/final-report-of-the-select-committee-on-academic-freedom-in-higher-education [accessed June 24, 2010].

77. "Victory in Pennsylvania," Free Exchange on Campus, November 21, 2006; available at: http://www.freeexchangeoncampus.org/index. php?option=com_content&task=view&id=374 [accessed June 24, 2010].

78. "The David Horowitz Fan Club Could Meet in a Phone Booth," Free Exchange on Campus, November 27, 2006; available at: http://www.freeexchangeoncampus.org/index.php?option=com_content&task=view&id=377&Itemid=51 [accessed June 24, 2010].

CHAPTER TEN

1. Insert: "Know Your Rights," Students for Academic Freedom; Available at: http://www.studentsforacademicfreedom.org/file_download/39 [accessec July 12, 2010].

2. "Discrimination Complaints" in University Undergraduate Advising, Penn State University; available at: Handbook,http://www.psu.edu/dus/handbook/afirmact.html [accessed June 25, 2010].

3. David Horowitz and Jacob Laksin, "Breaking the Rules at Penn State," FrontPageMag.com, January 22, 2007; available at: http://www.frontpagemag.com/readArticle.aspx?ARTID=518 [accessed June 25, 2010].

4. David Horowitz and Jacob Laksin, One-Party Classroom, 94.

5. Later, I sent the report to Susan Welch, Dean of the College of Liberal Arts. Our correspondence is reprinted in One-Party Classroom, 108–11.

6. "R-6: CLASSROOM ACADEMIC FREEDOM CONFERENCE

AND MEDIATION," AAPPM; available at: http://www.psu.edu/ dept/oue/aappm/R-6.html [accessed June 25, 2010].

7. Inquiries to find one led us to only one assistant professor who lacked tenure and was afraid to come forward.

8. E-mail provided to the author by A.J. Fluehr. Hereinto referred to as "Fluehr File." For the full correspondence, see "English 202A Academic Freedom Complaint Department Communications," discoverthenetworks.org; available at: http://www.discoverthenet works.org/Articles/acadfreepsubuehler.html [accessed June 25, 2010].

9. Ibid.

10. Ibid.

11. Ibid.

12. Fluehr file, May 21, 2007.

13. E-mail to Erickson, May 29, 2007. I followed up my call to Blasko with an e-mail on May 27.

14. E-mail to Blasko, May 27, 2007.

15. Fluehr file, May 23, 2007.

16. Fluehr file, May 25. 2007.

17. Fluehr file, June 6, 2007.

18. Fluehr file, June 12, 2007.

19. Selber also maintained that the access was provided "through assignment activities." But as Fluehr pointed out the assignments were based on the required texts.

20. Fluehr File, July 6, 2007.

21. Fluehr File, July 17, 2007.

22. Fluehr File, letter from Pangborn, July 25, 2007. Pangborn's letter continued: "As with other personnel matters, if issues or matters are

raised that need to be addressed in connection with a particular class or instructor, I am confident that the college and department administrators will provide timely counsel on modifications that should be made. I assure you that the Provost and I are in regular communication with the academic leadership at all levels, and especially with the deans and chancellors, to carry out these responsibilities faithfully."

23. Fluehr File, January 25, 2008.

24. Fluehr File, formal complaint in re CAS100A.

25. Ibid.

26. Memo sent to the author.

27. There was actually a third complaint which I have omitted for simplicity's sake.

28. The entire e-mail exchange is published at the end of the chapter on Penn State, "Breaking the Rules," in *One-Party Classroom*, 108–113. The chapter itself consists of an edited version of the report I sent her.

29. Fleuhr File, February 19, 2008. I spoke to a classmate of Fluehr's who confirmed that a Muslim student in the class had called him a racist over the speech. The student who reported this was shocked because prior to that the two had played on the same soccer team and it was obvious to him that Fluehr had no animus against the Muslim student.

30. Ibid.

31. Ibid.

32. Fluehr file, April 28, 2008.

33. Fluehr himself maintains, "there was no discussion of Gore's film in the class which makes Mazzant's claim she showed it to discuss rhetorical strategies laughable. It's depressing that Welch took this assertion at face value, especially when Mazzant admitted and confirmed in our phone conversation that no discussion of the film

occurred and that the only reason she showed the film was because kids in class were doing projects on it. All of this is further undercut because Mazzant fast forwarded to all the 'best' parts of the film she thought most effectively made the anthropomorphic global warming argument. Additionally, in at least two other presentations she referred to global warming and presented as fact that it was man-made." Fluehr e-mail to author, July 31, 2009

34. Nelson, *No University Is An Island*, 189.

35. Ibid.

36. "It is not the function of a faculty member in a democracy to indoc-trinate his/her students with ready-made conclusions on controver-sial subjects. The faculty member is expected to train students to think for themselves, and to provide them access to those materials which they need if they are to think intelligently. Hence in giving instruction upon controversial matters the faculty member is expected to be of a fair and judicial mind, and to set forth justly, with-out supersession or innuendo, the divergent opinions of other inves-tigators." Excerpted from HR64.

37. Time and again, for example, he was told that he had not followed the procedures required by R-6 because he had waited until his grade was in to file his complaint. See Fluehr file, Pangborn correspondence.

38. Fluehr file, "An Analysis of R-6."

39. Scott Jaschik, "Power Grab at DuPage," InsideHigherEd.com, November 24, 2008; available at: http://www.insidehighered.com/news/2008/11/24/dupage [accessed June 25, 2010].

40. Sara Dogan, "A Public College Funds the Left," Students for Aca-demic Freedom, February 20, 2009; available at: http://www.students foracademicfreedom.org/news/2673/a-public-college-funds-the-left-report-on-dupage [accessed June 25, 2010].

41. Ibid.

42. Ibid.

43. "Policy Manual of the Board of Trustees," College of DuPage; available at: http://www.cod.edu/adminstr/misc/New%20Board%20 Policy%20Manual%202008%2010%2013.pdf [accessed June 25, 2010].

44. Scott Jaschik, "Power Grab at DuPage," InsideHigherEd.com.

45. Ibid.

46. Tyler Stoffel, Sun-Times Media; photo and caption available at: http://www.suburbanchicagonews.com/napervillesun/news/12920 80,NA21_PROTEST_P1.fullimage [accessed June 25, 2010].

47. Ibid.

48. Letter from Glenn Hansen and Lisa Higgins to the DuPage Board of Trustees, November 13, 2008; available at: http://www.codfa culty.org/documents/current/Letter_to_Board_on_Policies_111308. doc [accessed June 25, 2010].

49. CONTRACTUAL AGREEMENT BETWEEN THE BOARD OF TRUSTEES OF COLLEGE OF DuPAGE and COLLEGE OF DuPAGE FACULTY ASSOCIATION IEA/NEA 2007–2011; available at: http://www.codfaculty.org/documents/Agreement/Fac ulty%20Contract%2005-13-08.doc [accessed June 25, 2010].

50. Sara Dogan, "The Smear Campaign Against the Academic Bill of Rights: A Response to the Dupage Faculty Association," Front-PageMag.com, January 27, 2009; available at: http://www.front pagemag.com/Printable.aspx?ArtId=33810 [accessed June 25, 2010].

51. Illinois AAUP statement.

52. Illinois Board of Elections reports sent to the author by Kory Atkinson; see also, Jake Griffin, "Both Incumbent lose in College of Dupage," *Daily Herald*; available at: http://www.dailyherald.com/

story/?id=284861 [accessed June 25, 2010].

53. Chronicle of Higher Education, May 4, 2009

CONCLUSION

1. John K. Wilson, *Patriotic Correctness: Academic Freedom and Its Enemies* (Paradigm Publishers, 2008), 70.

2. The articles were published on FrontPageMag.com and posted on the web as "Indoctrination Studies"; available at: http://www.discover thenetworks.org/viewSubCategory.asp?id=522 [accessed June 24, 2010].

3. I have analyzed the report at length in Horowitz and Laksin, One-Party Classroom, 278 et. seq.

4. Daniel D. Federman, "The Biology of Human Sex Differences," *New England Journal of Medicine*, Volume 354 (2006): 1507–1514.

5. Report, "Freedom in the Classroom," AAUP, 2007; available at: http://www.aaup.org/AAUP/comm/rep/A/class.htm [accessed June 24, 2010].

6. Cary Nelson, *No University Is An Island* (New York: NYU Press, 2010), 168.

7. Ibid.

8. Cf., e.g, Stephen Pinker, *The Blank Slate: The Modern Denial of Human Nature* (New York: Penguin Books, 2002) for a summary of the evidence.

9. Liz McMillen, "David Horowitz Meets His Critics," *Chronicle of Higher Education* (online), December 29, 2008; available at: http://chronicle.com/article/MLA-2008-David-Horowitz-Me/42170/ [accessed June 24, 2010].

10. Ibid.

11. Ibid.

12. Stanley Fish, *Save the World on your own Time* (New York: Oxford University Press, 2008), 153.

13. "1915 Declaration on Academic Freedom and Academic Tenure," American Association of University Professors; available at: http://www.aaup.org/AAUP/pubsres/policydocs/contents/1915.ht m [accessed June 23, 2010]; see also, Stanley Fish, *Save the World on your own Time* (New York: Oxford University Press, 2008).

14. Gerald Graff, "Presidential Address 2008: Courseocentrism," *PMLA*, May 2009, Vol. 124, No. 3, p. 739

15. Cf. Cary Nelson's account in Nelson, op. cit., p.13

16. Graff, "Presidential Address 2008: Courseocentrism," *PMLA*, p. 738.

17. Ibid., 739-40.

18. Ibid.

19. McMillen, "David Horowitz Meets His Critics, *Chronicle of Higher Education*.

20. Graff, "Presidential Address 2008: Courseocentrims," *PMLA*, p. 740.

21. Ibid., 737.

INDEX

If you enjoyed *Reforming Our Universities*, look for these other great titles by David Horowitz...

The Professors: The 101 Most Dangerous Academics in America

Coming to a campus near you: terrorists, racists, and communists—you know them as *The Professors*.

Revealing a shocking culture of academics who are poisoning the minds of today's college students, Horowitz's blockbuster book reveals your childrens' professors for who they really are: alleged ex-terrorists, racists, murderers, sexual deviants, anti-Semites, and al-Qaeda supporters.

Frightening because it's true, *The Professors* is an intellectual call to arms from a courageous author who knows the radicals all too well.

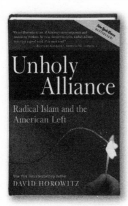

Unholy Alliance: Radical Islam and the American Left

In his *New York Times* bestseller, Horowitz blows the lid off the dangerous liaison between U.S. liberals and Islamic radicals. Taking you behind the curtain of this *Unholy Alliance* Horowitz confronts the paradox of why so many Americans—including the leadership of the Democratic Party—turned against the War on Terror. An eye-opening book that unsettles conventional assumptions, *Unholy Alliance* is a must-read.

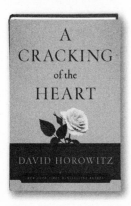

A Cracking of the Heart

Unlike anything he has ever written, *A Cracking of the Heart* is Horowitz's personal and poignant story about the death of his beloved daughter, Sarah.

As a conservative, Horowitz struggled with Sarah's liberal world-view. Yet he came to realize that there was much to learn from her and the empathetic way she lived.

A Cracking of the Heart offers consolation to those grieving a sudden death, reconciles what could have been with what is, and takes the reader through a father's frustration, grief, admiration, and ultimately love.

Available at Regnery.com

Since 1947
REGNERY PUBLISHING, INC.
An Eagle Publishing Company • Washington, DC